QUESTIONING BACK

QUESTIONING BACK

The Overcoming of Metaphysics in Christian Tradition

Joseph Stephen O'Leary

A Seabury Book
Winston Press
Minneapolis • Chicago • New York

Cover design: Art Direction, Inc.

Library of Congress Catalog Card Number: 85-50251

ISBN: 0-86683-988-7

Printed in the United States of America

5 4 3 2 1

Winston Press, Inc.
430 Oak Grove
Minneapolis, Minnesota 55403

*In memory of my father and his questions—
in gratitude to my mother and her faith.*

My thanks to Justus G. Lawler who commissioned this work and offered invaluable critical advice, to Tina Whitehead who typed the manuscript, to the staff of Winston Press, and, for their unfailing encouragement, to Paul Surlis, James Mackey, Enda McDonagh, Philippe and Kathleen Bernard, Richard and Anne Kearney, Martin and Margaret Murphy, Maria Villela-Petit, Jean Greisch, Stanislas Breton, John P. Keenan, Andre Schuwer, Paul Bove, the late Jean Beaufret, and the late Bernhard Welte.

CONTENTS

I: IS IT POSSIBLE TO OVERCOME METAPHYSICS? 1
    Delimiting Metaphysics 6
    God and Being 13
    Uncertain Margins 23
    The Path of Overcoming 29
    Inauthentic Overcoming 36
    Notes 48

II: FAITH IN CRISIS, THEOLOGY IN BONDS 57
    The Contemporary Mutation of Faith 60
    God as Concept 67
    The Christ of Metaphysics 73
    Rahner's Foundations 87
    Barth's Partial Overcoming 99
    Notes 109

III: THE HISTORIC FLAW 113
    The Tradition of the Question 117
    Faith as Deconstructive Principle 129
    Conditions of a Hermeneutic "from Faith to Faith" . . . 136
    Hellenization 145
    The Origin of Dogma 152
    Negative Theology 156
    Notes 162

IV: OVERCOMING AUGUSTINE 165
    Suffering the Text 172
    Ontotheology or Theologal Ontology? 178
    A Christic Ontology? 191
    Augustine the Believer 196
    Notes 201

V: THE ESSENCE OF CHRISTIANITY 203
    The Imperative of Simplicity 204
    The Nicene Creed 212
    The Fourth Gospel 221

I: IS IT POSSIBLE
TO OVERCOME METAPHYSICS?

Metaphysics has been normative for Western thinking for two and a half millennia, the governing Logos of our culture, identical with the force of reason itself. Yet it has increasingly become a fact that we are no longer at home in metaphysics, that it no longer chimes with reality as it used to. Metaphysics has become questionable in a radical sense and the adequacy of its procedures and categoreal oppositions (sc. spirit/matter, rational/irrational) can no longer be taken for granted. In the past, one metaphysics has been pitted against another and every "anti-metaphysics" has been shown to its place within the discourse of metaphysics. But in the present shift in the foundations of thinking the limits or the "closure" of metaphysics as a whole are coming into view. This, of course, does not spell the abolition of the metaphysical tradition, but it does prescribe a new, critical relationship to it. The struggle to articulate that relationship, in opposition to the tendency to fall back uncritically into the language of metaphysics, may be called "the overcoming of metaphysics."

Clearly this situation has implications for Christian theology, implications which may be far more extensive than is commonly understood. However, the overcoming of metaphysics is not a totally unfamiliar project for theology. In light of the present crisis of metaphysics we can see that Christian theology has always been inhabited by a restlessness in regard to metaphysics, a sense of its inadequacy to the truth of revelation. We can retrospectively retrieve this counter-metaphysical current in Christian thinking and allow it to deploy its critical force in a way it never could within the limits of the metaphysical regime of thinking. Thus, the quest undertaken in this book can appear as profoundly traditional, as it attempts to articulate the "unthought" counter-metaphysical element to be detected in all the great Christian theologies.

1

Consciousness of the "closure" of metaphysics is reflected in the flurry of recent theological controversies about the "death of God," the "dehellenization of dogma," the "deobjectification" of religious language, controversies originating in the nineteenth century for the most part, but sharpened by the advances of human sciences, secularism, and philosophical reflection. Despite the general awareness to which these controversies testify, however, it does not seem to me that theologians have mastered and clarified the problematic of metaphysics in theology in any sufficient degree. The subject is full of temptations, to which most theological critics of metaphysics appear to have succumbed. These theologians who most confidently declare the demise of metaphysics usually propose as an alternative only another variant of metaphysics. Underestimating the scope and power of metaphysics, and imagining that it is possible to "leave metaphysics behind," these theologians remain bound to the most traditional paths of metaphysical thinking without knowing it. For instance, if one opposes the speculative, impersonal character of metaphysics to the intuitive, engaged character of faith, or if one plays off the concrete, narrational texture of Scripture against the abstract, timeless character of dogma, in both cases one's thought is still firmly structured by metaphysical oppositions which have eluded critique and analysis, the oppositions of concept and intuition, personal and impersonal, temporal and eternal, concrete and abstract. Through these schemata the biblical revelation is still being "put in its place" by metaphysics. A "narrative theology" capable of resisting the powerful sway of metaphysics, one which will not be reduced to a merely illustrative or edifying status within an overarching metaphysical structure which absorbs it, cannot be established without explicit vigilance against metaphysical language. The same is true for every other effort to shape a language of faith more adequate to the truth of revelation. Metaphysics has shaped the language of faith for so long that this language can now be renewed only in a conscious struggle with metaphysics. The struggle is an unending one, because our language is metaphysical through and through, so much has it been fashioned by Greek reason over twenty-five centuries.

To think through the crisis of metaphysics is a task of great methodological complexity, as one can see from the most determined efforts in this direction: Kant's dialectic of pure reason, Wittgenstein's linguistic therapy of metaphysical language, Heidegger's de-struction of the history of metaphysics and Derrida's deconstructive reading of metaphysical texts (including several would-be anti-metaphysical ones). An adequate theological equivalent of these efforts is still lacking, perhaps because the leading theological critics of metaphysics, such as Schleiermacher, Ritschl, Harnack and Barth, have had an inadequate historical and systematic grasp of what metaphysics is. Theologians have often taken a divinatory approach to the overcoming of metaphysics, orchestrating a certain Lutheran or Pascalian, or more recently Nietzschean, pathos. But prophetic gestures, which in any case are rarely free of Oedipal resentment and messianic pretentions, cannot provide the basis for a rethinking of the metaphysical heritage of Christian theology. Instead a method of patient historical questioning is required, which begins from the awareness of how difficult it is to decipher the ultimate sense of two thousand years of metaphysically shaped theology, and to bring to light the "unthought" hidden in this history.

All the great texts of this tradition come before us as riddles, in that we can neither wholeheartedly subscribe to them nor dismiss them as belonging to a stage we have surpassed. This is as true of a text as apparently non-metaphysical as the Nicene Creed as it is of such confidently metaphysical utterances as the following:

> The impression of an agent does not remain in an effect, when the action of the agent has ceased, unless it becomes part of the nature of the effect. . . . But what belongs to the nature of a higher genus in no way remains after the action of the agent, as light does not remain in a diaphanous medium when the source of light is withdrawn. Being, however, is not the nature or essence of any created thing, but of God alone. Therefore no thing can remain in being when the divine operation has ceased.[1]

Few theologians would be comfortable with this language today. But why not? Where exactly does such language fail to connect with ours? What are we to make of Thomas's vivid contemplative sense of the dependence of the being of beings on the will of the Creator? Is it merely an illusion generated by language? Or can it be translated into our language, freed from the causal frameworks of scholasticism and even from the terminology of "being" and "essence"? What hermeneutical strategies are possible in regard to such a discourse? The question is even more urgent in regard to the Nicene Creed, which presumably cannot simply be allowed to follow St. Thomas into his present state of relative eclipse. To what extent does the word "consubstantial" symptomatize or generate a metaphysical ordering of the truths of revelation in this creed? How and why would our present apprehension of these truths be incompatible with such an ordering or in critical tension with it?[2] It is with the articulation of such questions that the present work is concerned. Perhaps at the end the questions will remain, and even the question mark in the title of this chapter may not let itself be erased. But it seems more worthwhile to attain some clarity about a question affecting the whole range of theological hermeneutics and indeed the very roots of Christian identity (which has been metaphysical at least since Justin) than to provide premature answers to it. Indeed, if I do venture any answers in this book, I would ask the reader to take them as no more than suggestions, hints for further lines of questioning. My effort is to provide signposts for an ongoing questioning dialogue with the tradition of metaphysical theology (and with the scriptural tradition as it comes to us indelibly marked by two millennia of metaphysical interpretation) at a time when there has occurred a fundamental shift, a tilting of the plane, in our hermeneutical relationship to tradition. It is not possible to step above this hermeneutical situation and view it objectively. Such critical strategies as "the overcoming of metaphysics" represent not authoritative maps of our situation but paths to be tried in exploring the situation from within. The value of any such path is warranted only by the contemporary readability it confers on tradition. That restorationist strategies like biblicism or the speculative bolstering of metaphysical theology are hermeneutically unfruitful can also be shown.

Of course there is a formidable phalanx of theologians and scholars who will not agree that there is any real crisis of metaphysical language or thought, or that if such a crisis exists it has any bearing on Christian theology. For some Nicea and Chalcedon are the indestructible rocks on which Christian metaphysics is built; for others it is a Harnackian slur to speak of the "metaphysics" of Nicea or Chalcedon. In either case the language of faith remains inviolable to critiques coming from philosophy, which at most are seen as affecting the external shell of that language, not its inner core. Against such positions I hold that there is no irenic translation of classical Christian language into contemporary terms. Whatever is metaphysical in that language must pass through the crucible of the critique of metaphysics. The dogmatic formulae of the past, the great theologies of Augustine and Aquinas, are accessible to us today only in a critical struggle with their metaphysical content. To shy away from this struggle is to prevent that past from communicating with us any longer. Unless we allow tradition to become questionable it cannot question us in return. Without the circulation of questioning between text and interpreter the tradition freezes in the hands of its guardians, whether in the name of scholarship or of orthodoxy. If the rewriting of tradition is vetoed we become unable to read it. So throughout the following discussions I shall be fighting on a double front, both against those who imagine they have left metaphysics behind by some hermeneutical shortcut and against those who shut out awareness of the questionability of metaphysics. My two sets of opponents have much in common; they usually provide the two sides of those struggles between "orthodoxy" and "heresy" which have provided some slightly archaic spectacles in contemporary church life. Perhaps if we follow our line of questioning patiently we may reach an attitude beyond these oppositions, a higher heterodoxy (the art of thinking otherwise) which may turn out to be a higher orthodoxy (the art of landing on one's feet), a questioning of tradition which links up with the inner dynamic of tradition as neither rejection nor repetition can.

In attempting to clarify the complex issue of the "overcoming of metaphysics" insofar as it is a theological project, I shall make use of only two philosophers, Heidegger and Derrida, and even the latter will figure here principally only as an acolyte to Heidegger. Other possible critical approaches to the metaphysical tradition in theology, notably the Wittgensteinian one, have been left aside, not only to avoid overburdening the argument and falling into eclecticism, but also because the Heideggerian critique, oriented towards historical hermeneutics and a phenomenological apprehension of the fundamental matter-for-thinking *(die Sache selbst),* has a certain affinity with the concerns of Christian theology and provides the most essential philosophical equipment needed to focus the contours of the problem of metaphysics in theology. In this first chapter I shall attempt, in opposition to the radical interpretation of Heidegger and Derrida proposed by some theological deconstructionists, to discern what these thinkers really mean by the "overcoming of metaphysics" and how theology should go about appropriating their insights and methods. Next I shall study the texture of contemporary theological discourse and show that its ability to do justice to the Word of God is still greatly hampered by the metaphysical presuppositions embedded in it (Chapter Two). Then I shall argue that the overcoming of metaphysics in theology cannot be adequately achieved except in the form of a full-scale historical hermeneutic: the struggle to purify our language of faith is a struggle with the weight of a complex bimillennial tradition of metaphysical theology (Chapter Three). Derrida provides the weapons for the struggle, in a deconstructive method of reading the Christian classics, which takes its cue from the tension between faith and metaphysics inscribed in the texts of all the major Christian theologians. St. Augustine's *Confessions* will provide a practical example (Chapter Four). Finally I shall deal with the problematic of the goal of this deconstructive hermeneutic—the contemporary equivalent of what an older generation of theologians used to call "the essence of Christianity."

Delimiting Metaphysics

"Metaphysics" is a slippery term, commonly used in a vast variety of senses, and people who talk of "overcoming metaphysics" are likely to find that the phrase assumes different connotations from context to context, connotations which have a way of changing places quickly and unnoticed unless subject to vigilant reflexive control. I shall try, as a matter of semantic convenience, and also because, as a theologian, I cannot pretend to find better definitions than those worked out by the philosophical masters of our time, to stick closely to the Heideggerian understanding of metaphysics and its overcoming, taking into account as well the correction or radicalization of this understanding made necessary by subsequent reflection, especially that of Derrida. Since my concern is with the influence of metaphysics only within the relatively narrow sphere of Christian theology, and since I am seeking to overcome this influence in view of the "truth of revelation" (let this phrase stand as an abstract, merely schematic, designation of our goal) and not in view of what Heidegger first called the "truth of being" and later the "clearing" (the primordial opening in which all phenomena come to presence), I may be excused from taking up positions in regard to every dimension of the Heideggerian problematic. To discern the original questions buried in the metaphysical tradition as such is not the theologian's business.

Theology has no special competence to interpret the various modalities of the interplay between "being" and "beings" in Western metaphysics, but seeks instead to uncover the animating intention of faith buried in the tradition of metaphysical theology. This intention of faith is the unifying theme of Christian theology, one that undergoes as many variations and epochal shifts as the being-question does. One might of course undertake a purely philosophical critique of the Christian theological tradition as part of the critique of metaphysics as such, but such an assessment of the purely philosophical factors in Augustine or Aquinas might have little direct bearing on the theological critique of their language of faith, a critique which studies the philosophical factors from a quite different angle. Thus, it is possible that certain metaphysical expressions of Augustine might be judged from a Heideggerian perspective to reveal a forgetfulness of the question of being, while from the perspective of the theological critique they might be very positively assessed if they had been effectively used to reflect the truth of revelation. Thus, the history of faith and the history of being cannot be systematically correlated, nor do they fall under the jurisdiction of a single discipline. Their historical interplay has often given rise to syntheses of faith and philosophy, but retrospectively these appear as inherently instable amalgams. Today faith and philosophical questioning go their separate ways, each bringing a different set of hermeneutical concerns to the past they share.

It might be objected here that it is impossible to separate the "truth of being" from the "truth of revelation" in this way. Some would claim that all revelation takes place against the background of the openness of being, and that faith can be correctly apprehended only as a modification of human understanding of being *(Seinsverständnis),* and that, therefore, the critique of Augustinian or Thomist metaphysics in light of revelation cannot bypass, but must presuppose, a reopening of the question of being as these thinkers (mis)apprehended it. Others would take a converse position. They would claim that any "truth of being" conceived as independent of, or antecedent to, the truth of revelation must bring the absolute character of the biblical message into doubt. Therefore, the "truth of being" must be redefined from the vantage point of biblical revelation. The ethical responsibility of human beings before their creator is a phenomenon more fundamental than the openness of being. We truly appraise the openness of being only when we recognize it as a gift of that creator, something Heidegger himself obscurely indicates when he speaks of being as what is *given.* Any abstraction of the thought of being from this ethical-religious context is idolatrous.[3] Hence, one cannot separate the two questions of the truth of being and the truth of revelation, treating Augustine, for example, as one who had little inkling of the former while being a privileged witness to the latter. Both groups of objectors would claim that the effort to differentiate the theological critique of metaphysics in view of the truth of faith from the broader philosophical critique of metaphysics amounts to a treacherous "double truth" theory which must involve a fundamental incoherence.

As a provisional reply to these objections I observe that, given the historical shape of the metaphysical and the theological traditions as we have them, a conflation of the philosophical and theological quests is not only impracticable, but would be bound to blur the contours of both, as the alliance of faith and metaphysics in the past seems to have done. The philosopher's concern with bedrock phenomena, the most general context of all thinking, belongs to a very different sphere of inquiry from the theologian's concern with the basic "phenomena" of faith, which are only accessible in faith, such realities as creation, providence, salvation, grace, the Kingdom of God, the Holy Spirit, the communion of saints. The vision of faith can be thought through on its own terms without the assistance of a prior meditation on being. The effort to translate it into ontological terms or to use it to solve ontological riddles would distort its own authentic "phenomenality." There may indeed be remoter attunements and alignments between the vision of faith and that general context with which the thinker of being is preoccupied, but our grasp of these is too tenuous to provide an orientation for the historical critique of metaphysical theology. Only by carefully differentiating the concerns of the theological and philosophical quests, despite their historical intermingling, can we hope to attain their respective goals. Each goal is an end in itself, and can never be reached if it is thought of as a stepping stone to something else. Fidelity to these distinct historical paths is the only way to release the dialogue between philosophy and faith from the premature amalgamations and subordinations of the past and obtain some minimal, perhaps ineffable, clarity about the elusive issue of their mutual relations.

The test case for this differentiation of the concerns of philosophy and theology is Aquinas, who constructs his entire theology in function of the nature of God as "being itself" ("ipsum esse abstractum, ipsum esse subsistens")[4] and as such the first cause and final goal of all beings. There are frequent critical references to "Christian philosophy" in Heidegger; he sees it as a square circle, falsifying both the questioning of Aristotle and the faith of St. Paul.[5] Yet the consistency of Aquinas's ontological-theological vision is not so easily dismissed. It is at least clear that Aquinas's theology of creation radicalized and deepened his properly ontological insight, allowing him to give an unprecedented metaphysical depth to the notion of "being," and that his metaphysics, on the other hand, has an effect on his theological grasp of the biblical revelation which is not always an inhibitive one. However, in the twofold deconstruction, philosophical and theological, which his work invites, one may expect a decentering of both his ontological hermeneutic of revelation and his theological vision of being to take place, both being seen as impositions of an extrinsic paradigm on the phenomena themselves. Revelation translated into the language game of being, or ontology grasped in terms of the language game of revelation, constitute what appear more and more to be highly problematic discourses, syntheses which must be replaced by a dialogue respecting the pluralism of the differing concerns of faith and philosophy. Faith and philosophy converged luminously in the thirteenth century, and seem to have been moving apart again ever since. We can neither recapture that convergence nor treat it as a simple illusion; perhaps we should look back to it as a kind of first love which can survive only as the spirit of dialogue, an identification which develops into a differentiation. Neo-Thomists are perhaps untrue to the spirit of Thomas himself when they bewail the breakdown of the synthesis of faith and philosophy, for within his synthesis Thomas is always trying to allow the largest space for the autonomous deployment of the proper concerns of faith and philosophy respectively, and this space can today be preserved only in pluralistic dialogue.

The theological overcoming of metaphysics is in simple dependence on the philosophical one insofar as the definition and delimitation of metaphysics is concerned, and remains close to the philosophical critique, too, in its identification of the limits of metaphysics, though concerned with transcending those limits towards a different goal. Heidegger defines metaphysics historically and systematically. *Historically,* metaphysics originates in ancient Greece and plays a determining role in Western culture through a series of historical epochs culminating in contemporary technology. The Semitic world had no notion of metaphysics, before the advent of hellenization in the later books of the Bible. Chinese and Indian thought is not properly to be described as metaphysical either; its concerns and procedures differ vastly from those of the West. All the intellectual activity of the West—the arts and sciences, ideologies and institutions, principles and customs of our culture—"claims to gather itself together at its own proper summit precisely as philosophy" (Jean Beaufret),[6] philosophy here being rigorously synonymous with metaphysics. Thus, the history of metaphysics is the central core of Western history in general. There may be attunements and alignments between metaphysics and other traditions of reflection based on different principles, those of Israel, India, China, or Japan, and as the West reappropriates critically its own identity it should be able to enter into a more serious dialogue with these traditions, no longer locating them imperialistically on its metaphysical map. Christian theology has effected a metaphysical amalgamation of Semitic and Hellenic in the past. With the overcoming of metaphysics this amalgamation is undone and a space of dialogue opens up instead. Many questions could, of course, be asked about this Heideggerian view of the historical identity of metaphysics. Of particular interest to us is the question whether the history of Christian theology has been simply determined by the epochs of metaphysics or whether Christianity has also been carried by another history, the history of the biblical revelation reappropriated again and again in faith, a fundamentally Jewish history which has inspired a tradition of resistance to the general metaphysical dispensation.

Heidegger's *systematic* definition of metaphysics presents it as the deployment of the Greek problematic of the being of what-is, a question which has never ceased to haunt Western philosophers even when, like Nietzsche, they have seemed to shake it off impatiently. The West has remained faithful to its intellectual vocation of thinking the being of beings, but its thinking has from the start taken a form which falls short of the "truth of being." This is because of the "onto-theo-logical" pattern of metaphysical thinking, which seeks to locate being in a "logical" way, as the ground or cause of beings, either in the sense of that which beings as such have in common (ontology) or that source of being which grounds the unity of beings as a whole (theology).[7] The very words "being" and "beings" have become the hallmarks of the metaphysical forgetfulness of that originary openness in which things come to presence, the world as phenomenologically given, so that in his later writings Heidegger replaces "being" with "world" and "beings" with "things" in an effort to underscore the phenomenological bearing of his thought. The various names for being throughout the history of metaphysics are interpreted by Heidegger as indices of successive onto-theological dispensations—Platonic Form, Aristotelean *energeia,* scholastic *ens creatum,* Cartesian subjectivity, Kantian objectivity, Hegelian Spirit, Schelling's Will, Nietzsche's Will to Power, and the technological grasp of being in terms of its exploitability (which Heidegger calls the *Ge-stell*). Each of these expressions names the essence of being as accessible to a given epoch.

Metaphysics is also characterized for Heidegger by a series of hierarchical oppositions, deriving from its onto-theo-logical structure, such as the Platonic opposition of the intelligible and the sensible or the oppositions of thought and its expression, literal and metaphorical, reality and appearance, rational and irrational, being and becoming, ought and is. For Heidegger these oppositions are no longer normative and he attempts to forge a speech which lies beyond them. Merely to invert the hierarchy, as Nietzsche did, is not to overcome it. Rather, these oppositions must be recalled to a prior context which reveals their inadequacy. Is the beauty of a rose as phenomenologically apprehended appearance or reality, substance or accident, intelligible or sensible? These metaphysical alternatives are inapplicable. Is the statement "Language is the house of being" metaphorical or literal? This distinction is overcome in a language attuned to the authentic phenomenality of things.

If one uses the traditional categories and oppositions one can think fruitfully, logically, and correctly in terms of them, and one's thought can be concerned in a certain way with the question of being, can even be part of a certain "mittence" of being *(Seinsgeschick)* and have a worthy place in the history of being *(Seinsgeschichte)*. Metaphysics is thus "true" as far as it goes. But in the light of a more radical apprehension of the phenomenality of being these traditional categories are seen to lack final adequacy. Each of them must be recalled to its phenomenological equivalent. For instance, "reason" must be traced back to its roots in the disclosive character of being-in-the-world (*Erschlossenheit, Being and Time,* Section 44); "absolute reason" and "pure reason" are in reality the product of a certain historical development; the step back to the prior phenomenological context demystifies them and makes us less dogmatic in our use of such epithets as "rational" and "irrational."

The "step back" is a phenomenological return to the things themselves, but one mediated by history. We have no experience of the things themselves that is not already an interpretation of them; *Dasein* is hermeneutical from the start. The contemporary technological mode of being-in-the-world is informed by the whole tradition of metaphysics. A rigorous historical differentiation and desedimentation of the sources of our interpretation of the world is needed in order to clear the ground for a more originary apprehension of being. Heidegger does not exclude, however, the possibility of leaving behind the historical side of the "step back" at a certain point in order to think the things themselves in the simplest way: "To think being without beings means: to think being without regard for metaphysics. Now such a regard also still prevails, however, in the intention of overcoming metaphysics. Therefore, it is a question of leaving off from overcoming and leaving metaphysics to itself."[8] "Thinking then stands in and before that which has sent *(zugeschickt)* the various forms of epochal being. This however, the sender *(Schickende)* as the *Ereignis,* is itself unhistorical, or better, undestinal *(geschicklos)*."[9] But if it is true that the essential truths of Christianity "ride time like riding a river" (G. M. Hopkins), then it seems that the theological equivalent of Heidegger's step back should rather be presented as the step out of a false history into a true one, the replacement of an abstract conception of divine providence by gospel-inspired historical engagement.

God and Being

All the effects produced by metaphysical language within Christian theology can be interpreted in terms of Heidegger's account of metaphysics as onto-theo-logy. But, again, it is not necessary for the theologian to worry about the adequacy of Heidegger's account, since theology is not concerned with understanding the systematic and historical dynamics of metaphysics as such, but merely with the way in which metaphysics has solicited the discourse of faith. Generally speaking the operations of metaphysical reason within the discourse of theology have been simpler than in purely philosophical

writing, because the problematic aspects of every philosophical concept are carefully developed by the philosophers, whereas theologians are too intent on using philosophy for their own specific
questions to allow their progress to be impeded by the purely philosophical problematic. The Fathers occasionally look down with pity
on the confusions and divisions of philosophy, but their own resolution of philosophical questions concerning God, world, soul, or freedom is rarely achieved through a thorough consideration of the
philosophical issues; even when such a consideration is undertaken it
is guided by the revealed answer from the start; the reasoning is
apologetic (which is not to say inferior or dishonest) and does not
require a total exposure to questioning as philosophy does. Theology
always begins from faith, and this sets limits to the degree of its
participation in the specifically philosophical problematic. For a
theologian to be also an accomplished philosopher is a very rare
achievement, because of the very different concerns involved. Since
theology, in using metaphysics, generally retains only the bare bones
thereof, because it has taken it out of its element of questioning and
inserted it into the foreign horizon of faith, the study of metaphysics
within theology usually has to do with simplified, dehydrated speci-
mens of metaphysical thinking, which nonetheless succeed in communicating a metaphysical shape to the whole discourse of theology.
A theologian need not study Plato or Aristotle to be influenced by
the shaping and ordering power of metaphysical reason. Any Western thinker is predisposed to this ordering, even if its vehicle is the
philosophy of the marketplace rather than the academy. A critic of
metaphysical theology can thus easily detect the presence of metaphysical structuring in all Western theologians, generally in a more
massive and less self-critical form than in professional philosophers
(though faith provides a different source of critical sensitivity). To
observe the effects of this structuring on theological discourse it is
not necessary to spend much time on the inner dynamics of metaphysics itself (which few theological discourses interestingly illustrate). They are better analyzed in function of the concern of faith at
whose service they have been placed. Their relation to the question
of being is of little theological interest.

Heidegger's interpretation of the ontotheological constitution of metaphysics is of direct interest to the theologian only insofar as the god who necessarily figures in philosophy (because philosophy "according to its nature, of its own accord, desires and determines that and how the god comes into it")[10] has been identified with the God of biblical faith, both through natural theology (whose findings are referred directly to the God of whom the Bible speaks) and through the use of a metaphysical hermeneutic in revealed theology (above all through the theologoumenon derived from the Septuagint translation of Exodus 3:14, whereby God is being itself, the one who most truly *is*). Theology will use Heidegger's analysis, without "verifying" it, to understand one moment in the dynamics of Christian theologies, but while the whole history of Christian theology reflects the ontotheological structure of metaphysics this structure has largely been robbed of its intrinsic meaning by the dominant concern of theology with the truth of revelation. When it figures in the discourse of faith metaphysics undergoes a suspension or deflection of its own intrinsic concern with the questioning of being. Not only is the originary form of that questioning repressed, as has already happened within metaphysics itself, but even the ontotheological style of questioning, with its concern with the causes, principles and ends of things, is curbed and inhibited by the fact that faith already knows the answer to these questions, so that the process of questioning is short-circuited. Even when Christian theologians allow wide scope to the autonomous play of philosophy within their systems, that philosophy is always being surveyed from the vantage point of faith and "being as such" and "beings as a whole" are always apprehended as "created being" and "the totality of creatures." This dominance of a concept of being as *ens creatum* has limited the contribution of the Christian philosophers to the deployment of the ontological problematic.

By handing over Christian theology, insofar as it is metaphysical, to the Heideggerian critique of ontotheology, the theologian cannot hope to throw new light on the question "Whence does the ontotheological essential constitution of metaphysics have its origin?"[11] For that constitution was already well developed before the advent of Christianity. What the theologian can hope to gain is a release of

theology from the unquestioned sway of ontotheology. Theology in
the past has used ontotheology as a reliable frame of reference, and
has, in turn, been shaped and bound by it. Efforts have been made,
e.g. by A. Ritschl,[12] to maintain the biblical names of God at a
higher level than the ontological ones, so that while it is correct to
say that the first cause, last end, infinite being of ontotheology are
God, it would not be correct to define God exclusively in these terms.
But give metaphysics an inch and it takes a mile. The biblical
conception of God has always been tightly restrained by the metaphysical one and has been allowed to function only within the
rational limits metaphysics has prescribed for it. A piety oriented to
God as first cause and final beatifying goal and to the infinite
perfection of his attributes may be seen as demythologizing the
biblical Yahweh, but at the cost of an increasing repression of the
existentiality of faith. The Trinity itself was subsumed under this
metaphysical account of God as its internal, strictly mysterious side,
inaccessible to pure reason. Where reason located the divine substance or *esse,* faith discerned within this substance a revealed tri-
adic structure. The effort to relate the Trinity thus situated to the
biblical manifestation of Father, Son, and Spirit was never entirely
successful, whether it took the form of the very guarded theology of
the missions of Son and Spirit worked out by Augustine and Aquinas, or whether an effort was made to import into the Trinity a
richly imaginative and partly biblical, partly Neo-Platonic imagery
of fecundity, self-diffusive goodness, communication, communion in
love, and organic wholeness as in Bonaventure. The inhibiting structural effect of ontotheology barred access to the biblical phenomenality of God.

Theology, then, accepts the critique of ontotheology as an element in the quest for an authentic language of faith, but it leaves to
philosophy the task of following through the fundamental implications of that critique in view of the question of being. Just as the
participation of theologians in the project of ontotheology, even in
the Medieval period, was always short-circuited to some extent by
the doctrine of creation, so their participation in the philosophical
analysis and critique of ontotheology is limited by their specific
interest. Perhaps there is an analogy with the differing approaches a

student of myth and a demythologizing biblical exegete would take to mythological elements in scripture. It is not within the exegete's competence to verify the findings of the student of myth or to propose a redefinition of the essence of myth, though there is a specifically theological critique of myth insofar as it has entered the discourse of faith. Similarly, the specifically theological critique of metaphysics in view of the "matter itself" of Christian faith is facilitated if one first renders to philosophy what belongs to philosophy. But this division of labor can be very problematic in practice.

What makes a clean differentiation of the questions of philosophy from those of faith most difficult is probably the biblical doctrine of creation. Obviously within a metaphysical horizon this doctrine, itself metaphysically apprehended, has clear ontological import. It fixes the status of all beings as "created being" dependent on God for their being. At this level one cannot surpass Aquinas's luminous formulation of these consequences. But even if we follow Heidegger towards a more radical phenomenological apprehension of the presence of things, philosophical thinking still seems subject to direct control by the biblical claim, for to "let beings be" in the biblical perspective can mean nothing less than to let creation praise its Lord. Thus, as the only true metaphysics for the scholastics was one founded on the doctrine of creation, so the only authentic thinking of being is one which attends to the goodness of God's handiwork in a spirit of gratitude and praise, and Heidegger's ruminations must be seen as a relapse into paganism. But it may be that the imposition of this creational perspective on other possible phenomenologies of being has an impoverishing and stylizing effect, and that it, in fact, remains an intrinsically metaphysical gesture. By locating the world in relation to its creative origin we override the plurality and opacity of the world as phenomenologically accessible, the world as manifest in the works of such artists as Cezanne, Rodin, or Proust—a region for endless questioning and exploration which cannot be transparently identified as God's creation. The notion of creation thus loses its clear metaphysical contours and becomes one moment within our general experience of world. In faith we lift our minds to the thought of God as creator of all, but this quasi-mythical representation must be measured critically against our experience of the phenomenon of world. This brings us back once again to a dialogue rather than a synthesis between faith and philosophical questioning. Faith is not the answer to our (Greek) questioning of being, but co-exists with it in dialogal tension.

The identification of God and being in Christian theology also makes the effort to delimit metaphysics and its overcoming from specifically theological concerns problematic. But what is the status of that identification? In a dialogue with some Zurich students in 1951, Heidegger was asked: "Can God and being be identified?" His reply is worth quoting in its entirety:

> This question is put to me almost every two weeks, since it understandably troubles theologians, and because it is linked with the Europeanization of history which already begins in the Middle Ages, namely through the fact that Aristotle and Plato have infiltrated theology and even the New Testament. This is a process whose immense scope cannot be overestimated. I have asked a Jesuit who is kindly disposed to me to show me the places in Thomas Aquinas where we are told what *"esse"* really signifies and what is to be understood by the proposition: *"Deus est suum esse."* Up to the present, I still have not received a reply. —God and being are not identical. (When Rickert opines that the concept "being" is too loaded, he is taking "being" in a quite narrow sense to mean actuality as distinguished from values.) Being and God are not identical, and I would never attempt to think the essence of God by means of being. Some of you perhaps know that my background is theological and that I have still kept an old affection for theology and understand something of it. If I still sought to write a theology, an idea to which I am sometimes inclined, then the word "being" ought not to figure in it. Faith does not need the thinking of being. If it needs it, it is already no longer faith. Luther understood this. Even in his own church people seem to have forgotten it. I think very modestly of being in regard to its suitability for thinking the essence of God theologically. With being one can do nothing in this area. I believe that being can never be thought as the ground and essence of God,

but that, however, the experience of God and his revealedness (insofar as it encounters man) takes place in the dimension of being, which never means that being can be accepted as a possible predicate for God. Here we have need of quite new distinctions and delimitations.[13]

St. Thomas locates the meaning of *esse,* the act of being whereby all beings exist, in the context of an Aristotelean system of concepts, which has been modified under the influence of Neo-Platonism and the biblical doctrine of creation. Heidegger would say that all these concepts have lost the phenomenological import they still carried in Aristotle (though even there it is fading), and that this is true in particular of the radicalized notion of being. Thus when he asks his Jesuit friend to find the passages where Thomas tells us what *esse* really signifies, he is asking for the phenomenological import of the notion in Aquinas. It is now widely agreed that Thomas's distinction between being and beings is a metaphysical construction, which has little in common with Heidegger's phenomenological differentiation of being and beings ("world" and "things"),[14] whatever the possibilities of retrieving a phenomenological sense of being in Aquinas by reading between the lines of his texts.[15] Was Heidegger's Jesuit interlocutor Johannes Baptist Lotz, who in a 1959 *Festschrift* essay "seeks to answer some questions which Heidegger himself put to the author long since?"[16] Lotz ventures this account of the Thomist notion of being:

> For Aristotle being is still veiled in beings, so that even the divine appears only as the most excellent kind of entity; Thomas Aquinas accomplished within Western philosophizing the hitherto greatest and as yet unparalleled unveiling of being (*Enthüllung*), whereby he also breaks through to the idea of God as subsistent being. . . . In Aristotle (the ontological difference) is still quite hidden, does not yet really open up; Thomas Aquinas lives in its unfolding (*Aufbrechen*), thinks fully from the difference and in it. . . (Nor does) the difference as such remain unthought. . . . In his own way Aquinas *really thought* the ontological difference itself and so wrested

it from forgottenness. Yes, we dare to say that in the thinking of this difference he advanced farther than anyone else.[17]

I would say rather that, insofar as the truth of being is accessible within metaphysics, Aquinas may have given the most perfect artic- ulation of it possible, but that because he remained within meta- physics he had no access to the *phenomenological* apprehension of being and beings in their difference. In his system everything centers on the act of being, and this gives it a transparency and a dynamic cast not to be found in the other scholastics, who are generally more oriented to form and essence than to act and being. But does Thomas's metaphysical lucidity about the nature of being amount to a phenomenological apprehension of the presence of being? In my opinion it does not, though like all great metaphysicians he offers material for such a phenomenology.

Thomas's focusing of God as the one whose essence is his being and as *ipsum esse subsistens* is also a perfect realization of the aspirations of metaphysical theology. It is a consequent articulation of the biblical notion of God as it can take shape within a horizon defined by metaphysics, preserving both the reality of the divine attributes and the ineffability and incomprehensibility of the divine essence. It is hard to detect the point in Aquinas where the intrinsic dynamic of ontotheology stops and its assumption into a biblically influenced theological ontology begins. Such a point can perhaps never be clearly identified, since the God of metaphysics has never in practice been a purely rational construction. Even in Aristotle and Hegel the God is as much a product of the cultural beliefs of the time as of the process of pure thinking. If metaphysics is always to some extent "its time grasped in concepts" (Hegel) then Heideg- ger's strictures against Christian philosophy as a "square circle" may be open to revision insofar as they stem from a purism which history everywhere belies. Nonetheless he may be right in claiming that intrinsically and "constitutionally" the God of metaphysics is a product of the grounding, totalizing ambition of metaphysical rea- son and is thus just as problematic as that ambition is, and that, in contrast, the God of the Bible is intrinsically independent of all such grounding reason and need not be identified with its products. From within the horizon of metaphysics it is necessary to identify one's God with the God of metaphysics; not to do so would be to subvert metaphysics and to sink into irrationality. Thomas accepts this intellectual necessity and turns it marvelously to the service of the biblical God. But for us it is no longer a necessity; for us to continue to treat it as a necessity would, in fact, be idolatry. In locating God in the incircumscribable dimension of being as pure act, Thomas guarded faith from idolatry, from any premature comprehension or hypostazisation of God.[18] But for us that very language of being appears as a construct of metaphysics, and therefore as suffering the same limits as metaphysics as a whole, so that it can no longer serve as the vehicle of a topology of the biblical God. The metaphysical treatment of the biblical images of God is seen as sheltering the Western Logos against their unrecognized subversive force. That force is retrieved not by a relapse into biblicism, but by reopening the conflict between biblical and metaphysical representations in such a way that we are impelled beyond both. The true face of God emerges from the mutual deconstruction of the God of Abraham and the God of the philosophers. The metaphysical regime in Christianity might be compared with the laws and rites of Judaism which Paul and John saw as surpassed and fulfilled in a new covenant of grace, although these have been a necessary way of worshiping God in their day. Their obsolescence meant that a return to them would be idolatrous, though their original purpose was to overthrow idolatry. Such revolutions are not uncommon within the history of religions; for instance, in the progress in Hinduism from polytheism to the *advaita* ideal of unity with an impersonal Brahman, or in the progress through the various refinements of Buddhism to the most purified forms of Zen. The highest intellectual religiousness in Christianity to date has been shown in metaphysical theologizing, but the projects of metaphysical theology are no longer a convincing expression of a serious religious mind; they no longer bear the mark of faith and its struggle. Now "faith seeking understanding" must look in another direction, for ever since Hegel the religious status of speculation has been increasingly discredited. Kierkegaard divined this well, and most of his strictures apply perfectly to the speculative

theologies, whether Neo-Thomist, Neo-Hegelian, or Process, which
have been produced since his time.

The thinking of faith and the effort to explicate God ontologically
have moved apart. But why should they not come together again on
new premises, through a synthesis between faith and Heidegger's
thinking of being? Heidegger's rejection of this possibility is strong:
faith does not need the thinking of being, and if it did it would no
longer be faith. The precise import of this, at first sight, abrupt
declaration can be appreciated only when we grasp the historical
sweep of Heidegger's remarks. The "Europeanization" of history of
which Heidegger speaks is the universal triumph of Greek metaphysics, which we experience today as global technology. This
begins in Medieval scholasticism with the subjection of scriptural
language to the categories of Aristotle and Plato, a process Heidegger once described as "a depravation of the genuinely theological
content of theology."[19] Heidegger sees Luther as a prophetic liberator of the biblical revelation from the yoke of Europeanization, as
the instigator, or rather retriever, of a counter-history which makes
the Gospel again independent of the destiny of Western metaphysics. Metaphysics has been the medium of a strong, critical interpretation of scripture throughout Christian history. Yet at the deepest
level the modalities of the divine presence to which scripture attests
seem to elude and subvert metaphysical mapping. Despite their
historical critical function, ontological categories of understanding
seem intrinsically foreign to the specific concerns of faith. Yet without faith's long symbiosis with metaphysics their radical alterity
could not have become so evident. Heidegger points us in a Semitic,
prophetic direction, which would demand a renunciation of these
categories. Not only are they unnecessary to the self-understanding
of faith, but in using them as props, faith loses its own intrinsic
coherence. Were faith now to use instead Heidegger's more originary understanding of being the result would be the same as in
scholasticism, namely, an accommodation of faith to questions and
ways of thinking foreign to its own historical mission.

This is still somewhat unsatisfactory, and is made more so by the
reminder that God can be manifest only "in the dimension of being."
A liberation theologian would say that the manifestation of God

must take place in the dimension of socio-political struggle, and would appropriate the language of such struggle for the biblical revelation. Why, then, may the language of "originary unconcealment" not be appropriated in a similar way? One might argue that in both cases such appropriation is doctrinaire and distorting, and that a dialogue in pluralism is the more fruitful relationship. The premature imposition of system has crippled Christianity in the past. Heidegger's dread of it reflects his respect for the phenomena accessible to thinking and those revealed to faith, in their ever-threatened integrity and difference.[20] It seems that "progress" in religious insight largely consists in such slow differentiation of faith from its sacralized historical embodiments and accompaniments. "Neither on this mountain, nor in Jerusalem. . . ."

Uncertain Margins

It would be naive to imagine that we could solve all the problems of our project simply by taking over the Heideggerian definition of metaphysics here sketched. It seems to me that the question "What is metaphysics?" continues to sound as a real question through all Heidegger's writings; he never attains a fixed, doctrinaire answer. Jacques Derrida is particularly sensitive to the mobility of this problematic, confessing (in an interview with Richard Kearney) that he knows less than ever what metaphysics is after years of studying its classical texts.[21] "The very unity, in any case the assembled homogeneity, of an onto-theology always seems to me problematic and today more than ever. The concept of onto-theology, if it be admissible, still depends on a unity or an assemblage of the destination . . . of Being (*Geschick des Seins*) that seems to me to situate the urgency of a question (in Heidegger, with or without Heidegger, I don't know)."[22] If I understand him correctly, Derrida seems to be saying that the apparent unity of the ontotheological tradition may itself be an ontotheological effect, that this unity itself must be questioned, deconstructed, so that the full complexity of the underlying processes may come to light. Now, the theologian, once again, need not worry about this task of deconstructing metaphysics radically. But the unity of Christian metaphysical theology and of its history may be fruitfully questioned along these lines. This unity is undermined even more radically than that of metaphysics by the co-existence of the biblical and philosophical elements. The history of theology cannot be presented as the unfolding of a single question (in the way that Heidegger presents the history of metaphysics) because it is from the start a series of clashes between rival principles, principles which reappear in very different forms throughout this history and which we may very vaguely denote as "faith" and "reason." If the deconstruction of metaphysics means showing that metaphysics has its "other" inscribed within its treacherous margins and borders, which it can never satisfactorily integrate into the medium of the pure concept, then the deconstruction of metaphysical theology has a particularly salient clue to work on, for the "other" in this case, the specificity of faith, of the God of Abraham, is always struggling to escape from the rational structures imposed on it, from the God of the philosophers. The stability of metaphysical theology is maintained only by the construction of powerful amalgams of faith and philosophy, such as the classical doctrine of the Trinity, an unquestioned cornerstone of all theology from C.E. 400 down to recent times. It is these amalgams which unify the history of this theology, and they are particularly vulnerable to deconstruction, though even more heavily protected against it than the dominant structures of metaphysics have been. The buried truth of these doctrines is emerging in our time through a new activation of the tension between faith and metaphysics, which they have so successfully stilled for so long.

Another reason why Heidegger's definition of metaphysics is one we cannot comfortably take over is that his definition remains a very open-ended one, since metaphysical reason is co-extensive with our language itself. If, as Heidegger finds, "metaphysics still hangs on to us, and we cannot shake it off,"[23] this is largely because of the way it shapes our speech. For instance, when one refers to the beauty of a rose, one instinctively thinks of that beauty as a quality attached to the substance of the rose, or perhaps, in more Platonic moments, as the universal form of beauty in which this rose participates. Even if we do not use the words, the notions of substance, quality, form, participation, foundation, cause, purpose, source, origin, final goal, subject, and object, as they have been defined in the metaphysical tradition, underlie most of our thought and speech, while even such homely words as "soul," "body," "inner," "outer," "values," "freedom," "world," "nature," "life," and many others are charged with metaphysical associations. Indeed, in naming anything at all we do so in terms of a presupposed metaphysical understanding of what makes it to be. This is especially true of the language of our technological world. Our language binds us within the limits of metaphysics. Poetic speech, naming things and the world in a more originary way, can provide glimpses of what this metaphysical framework conceals, but in everyday discourse metaphysics remains firmly in possession. (Even Hölderlin, in his prose writing, thinks metaphysically, though as a poet he has left the sphere of metaphysics; Rilke, on the other hand, remains bound to the metaphysics of subjectivity.)[24] This situation directly affects our language about God, and largely explains why it is so empty and conventional. Indeed, the situation may make language about God quite impossible, since the only God it permits us to name is the God of metaphysics: "To this God man can neither pray, nor can he offer him sacrifice. Before the *Causa sui* man can neither fall on his knees in reverence, nor can he make music and dance before this God."[25]

In everyday speech we make distinctions between *appearance* and *reality* which reinforce the Platonic paradigm, undermining the authentic phenomenality of what *appears*. A speech which would bring phenomena to presence authentically, a speech attuned to the clearing, would abolish the appearance/reality dualism and replace it with the phenomenological duality of unconcealedness/concealment. The distinction between "world-as-it-appears-to-be" and "world-as-it-is-in-itself" would be overcome in a poetic naming of world as a wresting from concealment, which cannot be conceived as a play of appearances with a "reality" hidden behind it. Analogously, an authentic language of faith might overcome the dualism between God or the Trinity as revealed and God as he is in himself and replace it with the duality of God as given in the experience of faith and love and the self-concealment intrinsic to that givenness, which is also part of His revelation. The phenomenality of God, like the phenomenality of being, forbids us to reduce what appears to the status of "mere appearance." Whatever the philosophical difficulties of Heidegger's appropriation of Goethe's maxim, "Look for nothing behind phenomena: they themselves are what is to be learned,"[26] it clearly resonates with the theological ambition to close the gap between God-in-himself and God-as-revealed which has been so much part of Western religious thought. Barth's identification of the Trinity with revelation (phenomenologically differentiated as revealer/revelation/revealedness) is a master stroke of such a reduction to phenomenality within theology, though unfortunately hampered by Barth's simultaneous retention of the classical metaphysical perspective. (Even the triad of revealer/revelation/revealedness is itself still metaphysically shaped, a synthetic construction of the phenomena from a point behind the scenes, which cannot do justice to the plurality of New Testament models of revelation.) The trouble with the appearance/reality disjunction is that it is not a philosophical theorem, but our natural, habitual way of thinking and speaking. To overcome it would demand a transformation of language which, at present, only a handful of poets can hope to achieve. Analogously, the attunement of speech to the phenomenality of revelation is a task which goes against the grain of all conventional religious language.

The habitual structures of Western speech are metaphysical, so that only a supreme critical vigilance over against our entire inherited discourse, and a creative freedom of speech reached by a venturesome "leap" to a new way of thinking can free language, including religious language, from the spell of metaphysics. For the theologian this leap can be facilitated by the espousal of the language of scripture (not of course in a simple biblicism) as the language of Heraclitus and Hölderlin enables it in Heidegger's case. Release from one language to another can never be a matter of starting from scratch, but rather of reactivating buried possibilities of the tradition. Although there is a fairly substantial analogy in this regard between Heidegger's search for a language of being and the theologian's search for a language of faith, the difference between the two quests is shown by the impossibility of using any of the terms of one language for the other. When theologians use Heideggerian terms they invariably either rob them of their phenomenological bearing or end up paraphrasing Heidegger in oblivion of the specificity of faith.

The renewal of the language of faith, like the renewal of the language of thinking in Heidegger, is not merely a recovery of the past. It is also a genuinely new beginning, necessitated by an exhaustion of traditional language and by the impossibility of relying on the metaphysical coordinates of that language. But the new beginning reactivates the past, rearranges it in a new constellation, in much the same way as a creative breakthrough in the arts changes our relationship to the tradition, declaring certain aspects of it to be dead (e.g., *Ulysses* implies the death of the conventional novel) and bringing others to life (e.g., *Ulysses* provides a new hermeneutic framework for rereading Homer). The new beginning which thus reactivates tradition is not something that can be calculated; it comes as a gift. Negative vigilance against conventional religious language and its metaphysical framework, and even a positive appreciation of the elements of tradition which escape this framework, cannot of themselves suffice to bring about a renewal of the language of faith, but they may create the conditions in which such a renewal is possible. In awaiting the renewal, faith may be condemned to long, bleak periods of inarticulateness in which all glibness is silenced. It may be the theologian's task to reduce the traditional eloquence of Christianity to this provisional state of nakedness as a stage in the discovery of a new language of faith.

So far we have defined metaphysics in theoretical and linguistic terms, giving perhaps the impression that the "overcoming of metaphysics" is merely a matter of refining our thought and speech. But there is one further aspect of the issue to be discussed: the relationship between metaphysics and those more obviously oppressive structures whose overcoming is a more immediately urgent task— structures of social and economic oppression which our refinements of philosophical and theological diction may reinforce by ignoring them. Has metaphysics anything to do with these structures? Is the theological overcoming of metaphysics a liberation theology? In answer I should say that there are complex alignments between the

overcoming of metaphysics in theology and the concerns of liberation theology, but no simple, systematic correspondence. The different concerns can have a mutually fertilizing dialogal relationship.
Liberation theology has contributed greatly to the retrieval of the
phenomenality of the biblical God as liberator of the oppressed. The
theological overcoming of metaphysics can liberate the discourse of
liberation theology itself from the inhibiting effects of unexamined
metaphysical presuppositions. Each line of thinking can use the
other, but only in function of its own specific methodology, not
entering into the fundamental problematic explored by the other.
Liberation theology cannot directly overcome metaphysics, and the
overcoming of metaphysics has no direct liberative impact. Thus,
feminist themes, questions of justice, peace, human rights, and any
other aspects of the practical interplay between the gospel kerygma
and the signs of the times, can figure in the present essay only
insofar as they illustrate either the nature of the hold of metaphysics
over Christian discourses or the nature of that phenomenality of
revelation towards which the theological overcoming of metaphysics
is underway. No doubt there are many other possible critiques of
Christian theology. But the critique which focuses on the role of
metaphysics, remote as it may be from more practical concerns, and
obliged though it may be to avoid dealing with those concerns in
concrete detail, nonetheless makes an indispensable contribution to
the liberation of theology, by freeing the relationship of faith to its
inherited language and allowing faith to reappropriate that language in a key of critical overcoming. Without this methodical focus
on the specific issue of metaphysics and its overcoming, liberation
theology is in danger of taking hermeneutical shortcuts, sometimes
blindly rejecting, sometimes unconsciously repeating the classic
metaphysical procedures, instead of interrogating them in view of
the intention of faith they both embody and inhibit.

Let these reflections serve as a basic delimitation of our understanding of "metaphysics." Now we must justify our claim that
metaphysics can be overcome and needs to be overcome. It is very
hard to eliminate all ambiguities from a project of this kind, but we
can hope to obtain some basic clarification of what "overcoming"

means by using Heidegger, once again, as our chief point of
reference.

The Path of Overcoming

Heidegger's thought, like Husserl's, is devoted to the "return to the
phenomena" as the most fundamental task of philosophical thinking. Husserl thought he had discovered the absolute foundation of
philosophical knowledge in laying bare the realm of transcendental
subjectivity and what is intuitively given therein. Heidegger thinks
back to a prior context which makes possible even the emergence of
this most basic self-evidence. This prior context is variously named.
It is the clearing, the open, in which beings come to presence or
absent themselves, the un-concealment (*a-letheia*) which has the
character of a wresting from concealment, the originary givenness
which is at the same time a withdrawal and which provides the space
in which thinking is first appropriated to being and being to thinking, the *Ereignis* which is the primal phenomenon manifest in the
interplay of being and time. The central, most characteristic gesture
of Heidegger's thought occurs at the moments when, having analyzed at length some major theme of metaphysics, he brings us to the
point of seeing that there is an aspect of the theme which metaphysics is unable to think and to which we can become attuned only by
the "step back" or "leap" to the dimension of originary un-concealment. In his quest for the "essence" of what metaphysical discourse
names "being," "truth," "actuality and possibility," "identity and
difference," "ground," "nothingness," "space," "time," "thinking,"
and "freedom," Heidegger is again and again led to this point where
the leap to primary thinking takes place. In his earlier writings
Heidegger tends to retain the metaphysical names for the
equivalents of what they denote in the realm of originary unconcealment. Later he shies away from such expressions as "the truth of
being" in speaking of this realm, and seeks a language more intimately attuned to what is to be named, a language perpetually
trembling on the brink of the poetic.

One might raise many questions about Heidegger's project. First,
is this dimension of originary unconcealment capable of being

thought at all? Heidegger himself will cheerfully admit that the
path of thinking he has embarked on may be nothing more than a
Holzweg, a path leading nowhere. Nevertheless, the negative implications of his thinking would still carry great weight, even if his
positive ambition were to prove vain. He has shown that there is a
domain of phenomenality which metaphysics is powerless to apprehend adequately, whether or not his own thinking is a successful
articulation of that domain. One might also ask, second, if the
domain of originary unconcealment has the unity Heidegger supposes it to possess. The domain Heidegger explores with the aid of
the Pre-Socratics, Hölderlin and the landscapes of the Black Forest
may differ *toto coelo* from the originary unconcealment to which a
person of another culture might think back. Heidegger's account of
the unfolding of world in the fourfold of mortals, gods, heaven and
earth sounds too Hellenic to admit of universal application, though
attempts have been made to uncover the same structure in the Old
Testament.[27] Heidegger would claim that his account of "the world-
ing of world" goes to the roots of Western experience and that other
accounts, e.g., Rilke's, fall short of this due to their bondage to the
metaphysics of subjectivity or some other form of forgetfulness of
being. But one wonders if, even within the Western tradition, the
worlds of, say, Plotinus or Mallarme, can be meaningfully situated
in relation to Heidegger's originary unconcealment. Heidegger con-
trols the pluralism of experience by conceiving of the great traditions, whether Greek, Semitic or Japanese, as the rich unfoldings of
single central experiences, the wonder of being, the faith of Abraham, the Buddhist void. But this may be too tidy.

A third possible objection to Heidegger's project is that the
dimension of basic phenomenality which is supposed to be the original element of thinking, from which all philosophy is a secondary
derivation, may really have nothing to do with philosophy at all.
Heidegger's leap may be a leap away from philosophy to poetry.
This suspicion is increased when we find that Heidegger becomes
increasingly more elusive about the links between the dimension of
originary unconcealment and the great philosophical themes,
replacing the distinction between being and beings with that

between world and things and no longer referring to unconcealed-ness as "the truth of being."

The supposed derivation of the great themes of metaphysics from this originary domain of unconcealedness remains highly problem-atic. For instance, one can doubt whether the everyday sense of true and false can be entirely reduced to a model of truth as phenomeno-logical disclosure, or whether there is a real continuity between *aletheia* and what Heidegger presents as chronologically later trans-formations of "the essence of truth"—*homoiōsis, adequatio,* Roman *verum, veritas,* and Cartesian *certitudo.*[28] The same prob-lems surround the attempt to ground the everyday sense of logical negation in the phenomenon of no-thingness lit up in the experience of dread.[29] Again, can the principle of identity be convincingly traced back to the originary togetherness of thought and being?[30] Does the principle of sufficient reason really derive from an origi-nary experience of being as groundless ground?[31] The word "being" itself has a merely referential function in ordinary language, and carries no specific meaning-content of its own, though concrete senses accrue to it parasitically throughout the history of metaphys-ics. Heidegger interrogates these concrete senses of being in view of their actual phenomenological content, what they tell us about the originary coming to presence of things. But is this really the central concern of Western metaphysics? Or is Heidegger appropriating the metaphysical tradition for concerns foreign to it, boldly putting it at the service of his own poetic quest for an encounter with the phe-nomena themselves? Does this not involve him in much inspired eisegesis, as when he hears in Goethe's verse "*Über allen Gipfeln/Ist Ruh*" (Over every peak/Is rest) a successful naming of the phenom-enon of "being?"[32]

The theologian is not required to adjudicate on these and other questions which Heidegger's project raises, but awareness of them can free the theological use of Heidegger from doctrinaire con-straint and can allow the theologian to appropriate what is most serviceable in Heidegger's critique of metaphysics, adapting it to the goal of recovering the phenomenality of revelation, without being troubled by the fundamental problematic of metaphysics which is Heidegger's concern. It is the negative, critical side of Heidegger which is the most direct relevance for theology. His overcoming of metaphysics is neither a simple abolition nor, on the other hand, a speculative restoration. It is meant as a "more originary appropriation" of the metaphysical tradition. The theologian can aspire to reappropriate the tradition of metaphysical theology in a similar way, albeit in function of an "origin" quite different from that which Heidegger claims to be at the source of metaphysics as such. But before examining further this delicate middle way between abolition and restoration, it might be well to reflect on the more indirect relevance to theology of the positive dimension of Heidegger's thought. For the path of overcoming can never be a purely critical exercise. It is sustained by a positive goal, however indeterminate at first, and though the goal is a different one in theology, eliciting different attitudes—attitudes of faith and hope rather than of "thinking" and "releasement"—nevertheless, there are some general features in common between the ethos of overcoming in Heidegger and that which the theologian wrestling with metaphysics must acquire.

In theology, as in radical phenomenology, concern for the matter itself always goes against the grain of easy verbalization and conceptualization. Theologians, too, must learn again to "think into the wind of the matter"[33] which claims their attention. This is a reversal of the direction of thinking which has prevailed in theology since the start of the Christian era, despite so many partial efforts to return to origins and essentials. Heidegger's example would be misleading if followed too slavishly by theologians, and would cause them to miss again the phenomenality of faith and revelation, which as Heidegger himself has frequently pointed out, is utterly different from that of being—so much so that one may entertain suspicions even about the expression "phenomenality" itself. But Heidegger's example can be infectious for the theologian who wishes to develop a strenuous and vigilant method of reflection whereby to discern, amid so many theological shadows, the authentic lineaments of the message of faith. The age pushes us, as it pushed Heidegger, to such strenuous thinking. Necessity is laid upon us. To give weight again to the language of faith and theology each word has to be reforged in the

crucible of such thought. To give back to theology a tone and atmosphere worthy of its subject matter, to restore resonance to its
speech, without empty piety or archaic biblicism, the qualities of
venture, slowness, and strain which mark Heidegger's procedures
are required. It is the opposite qualities of safeness, haste, and ease
which mark most theological discourse today, and that is a measure
of its failure to attain the essential.

Venture marks Heidegger's thought because it involves a step
back from the familiar structures of metaphysics to the uncharted
pre-metaphysical landscape, a leap from beings to being. Slowness
marks it, because of the treacherousness of a language in which
every word can be heard in a merely metaphysical sense. Strain and
even suffering enter into its texture because the move from beings to
being is usually the result of a renunciation or "letting go" which
may not be immediately serene (*gelassen*) or joyful (*heiter*). Thus, it
is anxiety which, losing the security of its foothold in beings, lights
up awareness of being itself, experienced as nothingness (clearly in
something like the Buddhist, rather than the nihilistic, sense), it is
death which "reveals the mountain range of being,"[34] and the
threshold of awareness which lights up the difference of being from
beings is a threshold of pain: "*Schmerz versteinerte die Schwelle.*"[35]
Since for Heidegger the thinker is very much co-implicated in the
matter of his thinking, the authenticity of thought is dependent on
the tone or atmosphere (*Stimmung*) which sustains it. To imitate
Heidegger must theologians then practice a comtemplative nearness
to the wellsprings in all their thinking and teaching? The requirement is inhibitive and would surely lead to much faking. Still theology should bear some relation to the gospel *Stimmung,* to the
dynamic of Christ crucified, or of the Spirit, and should be able to
allow these somehow to provide the orientation of its quests. Such a
theologia crucis or *theologia cordis* will not succumb to a narrow
subjectivism or anthropocentrism (which would be another relapse
into metaphysics) if the theologian works critically through their
inauthentic counterfeits until a style or method is attained which
effectively opens up to view the landscape of revelation. The trouble
with most exercises in the theology of the heart, or spiritual theology, is that they are not adequately self-critical and do not work

hard enough on their language, until it ceases to be a screen. Above all one must be sparing in one's use of the key words of this theology, such as "cross," "spirit," "contemplation," "liberation" or "freedom," for they are so overused and it is so hard to really apprehend what they denote that they easily become an abstract jargon or shorthand. Heidegger's efforts in a quite different area can certainly be of help to the theologian facing the pitfalls and difficulties of the effort to correspond to the truth of revelation. Ninety percent of the theologian's labors consist of the dismantling and renunciation of languages inadequate to the subject matter, so that the specificity of the revealed can emerge in an appropriate contemporary language of faith.

If the theologian weighs and sounds in this spirit the inherited metaphysical language of faith the inadequacy of this language will become apparent. Logical and linguistic analysis might reveal difficulties in that language, which would force us to alter it. But a purely phenomenological approach can suffice to bring out the precise respects in which this language falls short of the "truth of revelation" and can also light up possibilities of overcoming and replacing it. Logical and linguistic critiques can then be used in a more fertile way as instruments of this basic phenomenological awareness. If I see, for instance, that the phrase "two natures in one hypostasis" tends to subordinate the phenomenality of the Incarnation (as apprehended in John 1:14, for example) to the metaphysical horizons in which that phrase was composed and subsequently reinterpreted, if I can clearly measure the gaps separating the biblical horizon from these later ones, appropriating each of them and the history they form from the critical vantage point of contemporary faith, then "metaphysics" has already been overcome in principle and it remains only to implement the critique, using logical and linguistic methods where they can lend it force. These methods do not attack the tradition extrinsically; the tradition bears witness against itself, insofar as faith always implicitly protests against what is inappropriate in the language of metaphysics, and the phenomenological theologian, "listening with the third ear," will orient logical-linguistic and deconstructive criticism in the direction indicated by the latent discontent of faith inscribed in the traditional sources.

The force of logic and reason will always uphold the discourses the theologian seeks to overcome, and one can refute these discourses *on their own terms* only under pain of identification with the heresies they were originally designed to exclude. The overcoming of metaphysics is not a question of proving traditional doctrines untrue, since the direct counterpositions to these doctrines, as old as the doctrines themselves, equally belong to the sphere of metaphysics. It may be, of course, that what was logically overcome as a heresy at a given point in the Church's history could also have been an inarticulate protest against the limits of metaphysics, misleadingly formulated as a denial of doctrine. If so, the overcoming of metaphysics might give new inspiration to the scholarly game of rehabilitating heretics. In any case, the overcoming of metaphysics cannot itself be the inversion of given metaphysical-doctrinal positions. It consists rather in questioning back to the matter itself underlying the doctrines. As this is done, the monolithic logical structure of doctrine is seen to be a secondary defense of something phenomenologically disclosed in the original revelation. The primary speech of faith, represented by such doxological utterances as "My Lord and my God," is then seen to be more attuned to these phenomena than the later doctrinal formulations which defend those phenomena against metaphysically inspired objections. The original phenomena cannot be integrated within the sphere of metaphysics or explained in its terms. To think those original phenomena by abiding in the primary language of faith is to have surpassed the sphere of metaphysics wherein heresies and dogmas are formulated. Dogmas are true within the limits of the metaphysical debate. But there is a prior "truth" which can be reached only by questioning back to the original phenomena revealed in faith. If the world of faith is shaped primarily by the dogmatic structuration of Christian truth, then dogma has become an obstacle to truth, keeping the mind within the metaphysical enclosure and blocking its access to the basic data of revelation which metaphysics cannot grasp. Many theologians do exemplify such a dogmatically structured faith, but a deconstructive reading brings to light the conflict between their latent consciousness of the phenomenality of revelation and the doctrinal structuration to which they were logically bound. As we

reinterpret this conflict we find that these theologians were witnesses to the truth of faith in a way they did not themselves suspect.

This account of the overcoming of metaphysics in theology must
remain for the moment somewhat schematic. The complexities of its
methods and goal will come to light in later chapters. Enough has
been said to show the analogy between the incapacity of metaphysics
to appropriate the original clearing of being and the incapacity of
dogmatic Christianity (whose metaphysical character will become
more apparent as we proceed) to do justice to the original texture of
revelation. The possibility of stepping back from the sphere of metaphysics in both cases has also been indicated. Perhaps these issues
will be further clarified in the following critique of other accounts of
what is meant by the overcoming of metaphysics in theology.

Inauthentic Overcoming

There are many theologians who deal with the crisis of metaphysics
by subscribing to what they would call a "post-critical" restoration
of metaphysics, whether inspired by Hegel, process thinking, transcendental Thomism or a common-sense *entente* allowing us to continue to use metaphysical language without inquiring too precisely
into its justification. There are others who take up the terms of
Heidegger, Wittgenstein and Derrida, but put them at the service,
whether consciously or unconsciously, of classical metaphysical
thought-forms. But avant garde theologians, for whom the overcoming of metaphysics, the end of ontotheology, is nothing less than a
fait accompli, and who consider themselves far removed from the
danger of relapsing into either of the positions just mentioned, can
also find themselves caught unaware in a metaphysics they too
crudely oppose. It seems to me that this has happened to the group of
theologians who present an excessively radical account of Derridean
deconstruction as "the death of God put into writing" and proceed
from there to treat the entire Christian tradition as a series of
mirages or illusions which now blissfully fade into the light of common day.

Jacques Derrida is a difficult thinker, and it is likely that his
work, like that of so many, if not all, major thinkers will give rise to

conflicting interpretations for a long time to come. Again, like so many, if not all, major thinkers, Derrida is caricatured when his views are summarized in a few propositions or slogans. Both of these characteristics are intensified by the fact that all his work takes the form of commentary, dwelling parasitically in the texts of others. In America, literary critics and theologians, currently rushing in where professional philosophers fear to tread, have produced an image of Derrida which is more likely to be an obstacle than a stimulant to the progress of literary and theological hermeneutics. Derrida is acclaimed as a nihilist, abolishing the extra-linguistic referent of language, and an anarchist, replacing meaning with the pure randomness of the freeplay of signifiers without signification, signifiers whose meaning is merely their absolute negative reference to other signifiers. He is thought to be suffering from despair and anxiety, or to be full of Dionysan joy, as he digs the grave of logocentrism and sets loose the utterly arbitrary process of rewriting the texts of the past in light of their now manifest meaninglessness. Such a figure can then, of course, be refuted by those who point out that he uses logic to destroy logic, and that if language were as impotent as he claims there would be no point in his own effort to explain himself.

I can perhaps best convey my own understanding of Derrida, such as it is, by correcting the misleading emphases of one of his most eloquent theological interpreters, Carl A. Raschke, who writes in the following vein:

> Deconstruction shows that the logos of all our latter-day "-ologies," including theology, has become nought but a ritualistic and compulsive defense against *to kenon* ("the void"). What was heretofore a doxology is now a muttering in the dark. . . . Deconstruction . . . is in the final analysis *the death of God put into writing,* the subsumption of the "Word" by the "flesh," the deluge of immanence. . . . The movement of deconstruction has set about to show that the cathedral of modern intellect is but a mirage in cloud-cuckooland. Neither language nor human self-awareness conceals any thread of reference to things as they are. Hence, Derrida tells us, philosophers should not be so pretentious as to maintain they are

writing "about" anything. . . . The referent of a word, i.e., that which is signified by a token of language, consists primarily in an intransitive jump from sign to sign. . . . Meaning in the formal sense is disclosed as *no-thingness*. Meaning is pure movement, the overflowing self-effacement of language. . . . Every quantum of discourse cancels itself in the moment of "expression." It does not express anything except a "space" between itself and what was said before it. . . . "Spacing" is . . . the bountiful and meaning-laden void amid the interstices of grammar . . . the revelation of all substance as emptiness. . . . The divine word . . . is truly made flesh; it reaches its kenotic consummation, its radical otherness, in a theology which is nought but a writing about theology. . . . How can one read theology when its logos has been sublimated into writing? Reading implies that there is something more to be garnered from a text than the affectations of the text alone. . . . Writing . . . is the ongoing enfleshment and displacement . . . of the eternal "Word" by its diffusion within and through time. . . . Theology must write itself into the grave. Deconstruction within theology writes the epitaph for the dead God. . . . Deconstruction is the dance of death upon the tomb of God . . . the flailing of the spades of God's gravediggers. . . . The omega moment of deconstruction is when the *movement* of deconstruction deconstructs itself, when the book that in the modern age became a text . . . is at last transfigured into the uncrystallized expanse of luminosity and intelligence.[36]

(i) What needs first of all to be said, and it has often been said by Derrida himself, is that it is entirely inaccurate to speak of deconstruction as the abolition of the objective referentiality of discourse. Derrida is close to Heidegger in his understanding of the rapport between speech and world, except that his understanding of language is more complex than Heidegger's. For Derrida to deconstruct a discourse is to deconstruct a world: he refers to "the field of oppositions which it (deconstruction) criticizes and which is also *a field of non-discursive forces*"[37] and tells us that deconstruction consists in "overturning and displacing a conceptual order as well as *the non-conceptual with which it is articulated.*"[38] Deconstruction brings about a new opening on world, on "the space of inscription,"[39] "the shining of what is outside the closure."[40] The logocentric structuration of world is not replaced by a total closure of language on itself, but by a subtler and more differentiated referentiality. Hence a deconstruction of theology need not issue in the death of God. It could tend rather in the direction of something like a negative theology, or perhaps simply towards a new flexibility in theological utterance, comparable to that reached in the subtle trinitarian logic of the Scholastics or the dizzying paradoxes of Eckhart or Angelus Silesius.[41]

Does *différance* mean that language is not "about" anything, that "being" and "truth" are no more than an "intrusion within language's closure upon itself?"[42] Derrida, in the passage Raschke quotes, calls the poem of Parmenides "a text which, in positing a certain sameness of 'thinking' and 'being', *remarked* in language the opening, the opening to the presence of being, to truth, to that which has always *represented the breaking open* (*l'effraction,* not merely 'intrusion') in the closure upon itself of language." Derrida does not here deny that the opening of language to world takes place, though he does contest that it is correctly *represented* as "the presence of being." It can be denoted as *différance* however. One may find in this expression the distinct, though indissociable, notions of differentiation and deferral, and one may associate the first with the signified and the second with the referent of a given signifier. The differentiation of the signified will be discussed below. The deferral of the referent is a development of the Heideggerian temporalization of being, the idea, put crudely, that being is not simply present, it is past and future as well, so that its givenness always co-implies a withdrawal or withholding. Derrida is not attempting to prove that speech has no referential power, but that the functioning of reference cannot be supposed to be simpler than speech itself is. Speech does not refer to purely present referents, because the very texture of speech subverts such a notion of pure presence, confirming Heidegger's phenomenological subversion of the present. Derrida shows that language can never simply mirror its referents by looking at the back of the mirror, the materiality of the text, and showing "the impossibility of reducing a text as text to its effects of meaning, content, thesis or theme."[43] The textuality of the text subverts the naivety of its referential pretensions, just as the unconscious sense of language and behavior relativizes conscious intention or the materiality of praxis relativizes the ideological superstructures (not that Derrida is to be "explained" in Freudian or Marxian terms). Where metaphysics provides an invalid shortcut behind language in order to say what language is unable to say, in order to name the "thing in itself," attention to textuality reveals that all naming is already the withdrawal of the thing named, and it is this withdrawal which keeps language going, forcing us to resume the naming process again and again.

A theological application might take the Nicene Creed as an example. The reference of the text to the objects named in it is mediated by the complex historical process of the composition and reinterpretation of the text. If the meaning of the text, as we shall see, can never be pinned down with final definiteness, neither can its reference be brought to a full stop. The referentiality of the text is refracted across the play of reinterpretation which is a necessary feature of the recitation of the text, and it is impossible to isolate an originary meaning of the text which could bring this play to an end. Does this mean that theology, being forced to take the "linguistic turn," is now condemned to be nothing more than mere writing about writing, as Raschke suggests? No. The text continues to refer, but in a complex way, which cannot be surveyed by a vantage point outside the text. A theology which returns to the textuality of the text is thus taking up its abode in the language of faith in just the way that theology should. It renounces the speculative, extra-linguistic vantage point in order to recover the basic reference of the language of faith, to critically articulate the bearing of that language. This is not at all a nihilistic dissolution of the Word of God in pure writing, as Raschke proclaims, but a return to the traditional identity of theology as, in Luther's words, a "grammar working on the words of the Holy Spirit" (*grammatica in Spiritus Sancti verbis occupata*). The theological critique of the language of faith will never come to a full stop with a direct grasp of its referent. But it does espouse reflexively the authentic referentiality of the language of faith as no other theological method can. Such a theology is an art of reading and itself immensely readable (contrary to Raschke's claim that one cannot read a theology whose logos has been sublimated into writing), for it shows very precisely how the Word of God is historically inscribed in language. The Barthian and Bultmannian phenomenologies of the Word of God in contrast give little to read, because they do not take seriously enough the concrete textuality of that Word throughout history.

Derrida has tapped the critical resources of Heidegger's thought in registering a shift in the basic axes of hermeneutics. First, the relation of speech, thought, and reality can no longer be the harmonious likeness (*homoiōsis*) of Aristotle's *De Interpretatione* nor even the graded unlikeness of the fourth century apophatic topos according to which our thought always falls short of the divine reality and our speech cannot match our thought.[44] The language of Scripture and tradition cannot be regarded as a window opening transparently (or even in some controllable "analogical" way) onto the reality with which it is concerned. If we take seriously the materiality of the traditional texts we find that the pure "word" they wish to communicate is constantly reinvolved in the opacity of the play of signifiers and the play between texts ("intertextuality"). Hence, second, the relation between context, text, and commentary is similarly rendered ungovernable. A complete restoration of the context of a text is impossible as is a definitive application of the meaning of the text to the present, a definitive translation. Commentary thus itself becomes part of the play of intertextuality in which no authoritative hierarchy can be established. The text "always reserves a surprise for the anatomy or physiology of a critique which might think it had mastered its game, surveying all its threads at once, thus deceiving itself into wishing to look at the text without touching it, without putting its hand to the 'object,' without venturing to add to it."[45] Reading as mastery must cede to reading as rewriting. It is only so that texts can continue to signify and refer in a real sense.[46]

(ii) The other aspect of *différance,* the differentiation of meaning, no more reduces meaning to randomness than the deferral of the referent constitutes its abolition. For Derrida, according to one critic, words are characterized not by meaning but by "a certain indeterminacy of meaning."[47] This contradictory statement reveals that Derrida is concerned with doing justice to the complexity of meaning, rather than dissolving it in a meaningless play of signifiers (rather, "traces" or "marks," since Derrida questions the signified-signifier distinction and the very notion of sign). Derrida speaks of a "deconstruction, displacement and subordination of the effects of sense and reference" and a "reconstruction of the textual field starting from the operations of intertextuality or the unending referral of the traces to the traces."[48] This is not to reduce the effects of sense and references to mere mirages. A solicitation of the effects of sense and reference in the language of faith, which would undermine their apparent fixity, revealing the process of dissemination to which all linguistic performance is exposed, would not abolish the objectivity of that language, but would relocate that objectivity in an ongoing process of articulation rather than in propositions whose meaning is fully fixed. Since we can never "saturate the context"[49] of a given expression, providing its final and definitive interpretation, and since intelligibility demands repeatability and repeatability implies constant reinterpretation, even so lucid an expression of faith as the Nicene Creed owes its meaningfulness to the unending process of dissemination in which it is irremediably entangled. The "identity" of the Nicene Creed throughout history, its iterability, intrinsically exposes it to an endless play of "difference" which cannot be regulated in advance.

Any suggestion that the play of dissemination is a purely arbitrary process will be discredited if we remember the Hegelian origins of Derrida's thinking. (At the 1982 AAR Convention, Raschke deplored as "blasphemous" any effort to trace a genealogy of Derrida's thinking; yet who more than Derrida, a professor of the history of philosophy at the Ecole Normale Supérieure, has insisted on the necessity of knowing the historical genealogy of any text or question one discusses?) For Derrida, Hegel is the master of the metaphysics of presence, but also "the thinker of irreducible difference."[50] Derrida does not attempt to refute Hegel on his own terms. Since the logos of metaphysics is co-extensive with reason itself—

something much more powerful than what Raschke calls a "ritualis-tic and compulsive defense against the void"—any direct refutation of metaphysics is futile; indeed Derrida loves to deconstruct such would-be deconstructors of metaphysics as Levinas and Benveniste. Any direct refutation of metaphysics is already foreseen and over-taken by metaphysics. "If philosophy has always on its side known how to keep itself in contact with the non-philosophical, and even the anti-philosophical, with the praxis and knowledge, empirical or otherwise, which constitute its other, if philosophy is basically con-stituted according to this reflexive *entente* with its outside, and has always been able to speak in the same language of itself and of something other, can one, rigorously speaking, designate a place which is not philosophical, a place of exteriority or alterity from whence one could still be dealing *with philosophy?* Would that place not always in advance have been occupied by philosophy?"[51] The textual approach solicits metaphysics indirectly, by showing that the author's own understanding of what he is about is only one piece in the machine of writing his text constitutes.[52] Hegel may attempt to reintegrate the irreducible difference his thought discloses into the identity of the absolute idea, but his text betrays the impossibility of doing this. Thus, "despite the relations of very deep affinity which *différance* has with Hegelian discourse, as it should be read, it can at a certain point not so much break with it, for this would have no meaning and no chance of success, as bring about a certain displace-ment of this discourse at once tiny and radical."[53] *Différence* is a more nuanced and open-ended version of Hegelian difference, dif-ference which can't come home again; but it is not pure randomness. In fact, the integrative power of the metaphysical logos remains a strong temptation against which the deconstructionist, attempting to rewrite Hegel in the key of *différance,* has to be perpetually vigilant. If metaphysics could be surmounted once and for all, deconstruction would no longer be a possible art.[54] The Hegelian logos is not overcome by a simple description of its functioning—as metaphysics of presence or compulsive defense against the void—but only by the practice of immanent criticism of the Hegelian text. Hegel is not a master thinker for nothing, and the superior intelli-gences who have surpassed him soon find themselves overtaken unawares by his logic. Declarations of the bankruptcy of the meta-physical logos generally serve as a prelude to the restoration of simple forms of metaphysics—the metaphysics of the void, for example—usually with the aid of a loose "dialectic," such as "the world is the being of God when God is not being deity, or the being of God in the time of not being."[55] But it is a converse error to think one can explain authentic deconstruction in Hegelian terms, as Mark C. Taylor does:

> To dialectical vision, however, this "gay wisdom" appears to be a variation of the unhappy consciousness that seems to be the fate of post-modern man. One can agree with Derrida's criticism of a metaphysics which venerates atemporal being or presence at the expense of temporal becoming without accepting his virtual absolutizing of absence. The metaphysics of presence and the metaphysics of absence *both* end in nihil-ism: the former resolves time in eternity, the latter dissolves eternity in time.[56]

These exercises in abstraction remain quite securely within the met-aphysics of presence, which is neither described nor overcome in oppositions of being and becoming, time and eternity, presence and absence.

Deconstruction is not the reduction of meaning to a mere no-thingness, or to the empty space lit up by the play of signifiers. It is a wrestling with the metaphysical tradition of meaning which, to use Heidegger's terms, it appropriates in a more originary way, by bringing to light the play of dissemination which the stable hierar-chies of metaphysics occlude. To describe this play as "the deluge of immanence" is to categorize it metaphysically. I should think it is indifferent, as Heidegger's thinking of being is, to the religious choices so imprecisely denoted by the words "transcendence" and "immanence," words which are quite unusable in any case outside the sphere of a certain metaphysics. In using Derrida as the spokes-man for a religious ideology one loses his grasp of the complexity of meaning and imposes extrinsically and dogmatically a simplifying category designed to summarize the whole bearing of his thought. This was done with Heidegger in the fifties, when Being and God were combined in various ways, at the expense of the phenomenolog-ical questioning which is the very texture of Heidegger's thought and which refuses propositional summary by its very nature. Decon-struction for similar reasons resists such summary. As a movement within the very specific problematic of Western philosophy and the human sciences at this point in time it cannot be equated with either the Buddhist void (*sunyata*) or the supposed "kenotic consumma-tion" of the eternal Word. These theological interpretations of deconstruction are flights from the complexity of dissemination and restorations of the immediacy of metaphysical meaning in the name of the supposed meaninglessness of metaphysics.

Derrida, like Heidegger, has no ambition to abolish meaning or referentiality. Their common ambition is to appropriate more ade-quately the process which produces the effects of meaning of refer-ence, whether they name this the clearing of world or *différance*. For both this appropriation is a struggle in language against language. Derrida fleshes out Heidegger's struggle in a more radical and sophisticated method of interrogating metaphysical texts (including literary and psychoanalytical ones). It may be that Derrida lacks Heidegger's contemplative sense of the possible goal or goals of a post-metaphysical discourse, and is less able as a result to serenely leave aside the "overcoming of metaphysics" as Heidegger does in his later writings in order "to think being without regard for meta-physics." Derrida is too essentially a commentator, too unconvinc-ing as a direct announcer of philosophical verity—see the false pathos of the final pages of his lecture, "*La différance*"— to be able to "consign metaphysics to itself."[57] That is why his position in history is likely to be that of a footnote to Heidegger. He is a thinker of great critical but little constructive power. Hence, the fragility of the uncritical constructions his theological admirers construct from his dicta. But a theology informed by Derrida's critical alertness and seeking its constructive materials elsewhere, in the scriptures or in the life of the Church, for example, might succeed in recapturing in a more credible form the meaning and reference of Christian dis-course. But this brings me to my third objection to Raschke.

(iii) Raschke uses Derrida and Heidegger as witnesses to a medium of pure illumination, "the uncrystallised expanse of luminosity and intelligence"—a fantasmal phrase amplifying the false pathos I found in certain pages of Derrida, and it is into this medium that he intends to dissolve not only the discourse of metaphysical theology but even the Word of God itself. He writes for instance: " 'Saying' is ontologically prior to the Word of God, which has the status of ontic re-presentation. . . . Any true correspondence to the Saying of the Logos must preclude any attempt to put a 'Christian' stamp on what is revealed. . . . Rather, the 'way' along which Heidegger's suggestion directs us signals a 'venture' back into the pre-Christian world (which is at the same time a post-Christian one). Heidegger insists that we must search out 'the pre-Christian intent of basic theological concepts' (this is an abusive appeal to Heidegger's 1927 piece on "Phenomenology and Theology," whose tenor is the very opposite of what Raschke here defends). . . . Any opening to revelation at a primordial level does not at all signify the earlier Barthian *sacrificium intellectus* for the sake of the Word of God. The Word of God is . . . nothing but a theological construct"[58] It is sad that Raschke here offers a caricature of Barth, the one theological phenomenologist of revelation, who has so much to teach us, and whose message remains undeciphered because his radical return "to the phenomena themselves" became entangled in a restorative counter-movement towards ecclesiastical dogma and biblicism. A sober deconstruction of Barth's thought could lend content to Raschke's critique. As it is he dismisses both Barth and any specificity of the Christian message as metaphysical intrusions on the pure luminosity of the void. The eschatological parousia of Christ is reduced to a Heideggerian advent of being: "The reception of the *parousia* through the event of poetizing does not abrogate the meaning-content of precious theologies so much as it threshes a clearing for the unconcealment of what previously has only been re-presented as the *certum* of faith. . . . The default of God spells the end of theology, but it also demarcates the threshold for the unobtrusive advent of shining divinity."[59] Leitmotifs were never blended so sweetly, but the result is an erasure of Christian theology, dismissed as a "mirage of metaphysical references."[60] The overcoming of metaphysics has lost any inner check and has become a steam-rolling of everything in sight.

There is no basis here for an interesting deconstruction of the Christian tradition. Such a deconstruction would have to work with oppositions within the tradition, the opposition between faith and metaphysics, for example, but the only opposition to which Raschke attends is a massive one between the positivity of revelation (the Word of God) and the general form of manifestations, "Saying," the Void, the advent of shining divinity, luminosity and intelligence, all new names for the Kingdom of God. No doubt the encounter with other religious traditions, especially Buddhism, has led Christians to test the positivity of revelation against the unobjectifiability of spiritual experience, and this may provide a privileged starting point for a differentiated critique of Christian tradition (as does the encounter with questions of social justice and liberation). But it seems that Raschke urges a suppression of the distinct identity of Christianity and of biblical faith and its God, having found the "truth" of Christianity in the discourses invoked for testing it critically—those of Nietzsche, Heidegger, Derrida and Buddhism. Thus, instead of bringing about a fruitful dialogue between the biblical tradition and these discourses, Raschke seems to abolish the former and ends up giving an eclectic exegesis of the latter, whose blending is presented as Christianity deconstructed.

What we learn from Raschke then is that without respect for metaphysics, whose force is that of reason itself, one's attempts to overcome it will relapse into some simple anti-metaphysical ideology long ago integrated by metaphysics, and, second, that without a steady sense of the tradition of faith and a respect for its central claims, one's attempts to overcome metaphysics within theology (or to overcome "the positivity of revelation," a wider topic which will come briefly into view in our final chapter) merely succeed in reducing the language of faith to an eclectic mush. But we have also learned from Raschke a lesson not to be forgotten in what follows: that the overcoming of metaphysics is no simple task, but a delicate problematic full of pitfalls. Nonetheless, as the next chapter will show, it is a necessary task of theology today. Perhaps the chief cause of the debility of theological thinking today, apart from the economical and institutional reasons, is that theologians, even those who have no time for metaphysics, are still under the spell of metaphysical language and have averted their gaze from the problematic here to be explored. At least in this limited sense it is not only possible, but necessary, to overcome metaphysics.

NOTES

1. Thomas Aquinas, *Summa Contra Gentiles* III, Chapter 65, "That God Conserves Things in Being" (Rome: Marietti, 1925), 290. (I have provided my own translations of most texts quoted from languages other than English.) John D. Caputo has undertaken a Heideggerian deconstruction of Aquinas in his *Heidegger and Aquinas* (New York: Fordham University Press, 1983), cf. "Heidegger and Aquinas: The Thought of Being and the Metaphysics of Esse," *Philosophy Today* 26 (1982), 194–203: "St. Thomas' metaphysics is not the opposite of his mystical life, but a concealed, representational—one is tempted to say 'alienated'—way of expressing it" (201). Caputo's gesture here is precisely that which I wish to extend to the entire tradition of metaphysical theology, with a full consciousness of the methodological complexity of the task. My criticisms of Caputo are expressed in a forthcoming review.

2. Cf. "Has the Nicene Creed Become Inaccessible," *Irish Theological Quarterly*, 48, 1981, 240–255; James Mackey, "The Holy Spirit," Ibid., 256–267; Bernhard Welte, *Zwischen Zeit und Ewigkeit* (Freiburg: Herder, 1982) 211–248.

3. These questions are discussed in a suggestive way by the contributors to *Heidegger et la question de Dieu* (Paris: Grasset, 1980) (=HQD); cf. Jean Beaufret, 30–34; Francois Fédier, 43–45; Jean-Luc Marion, 60–71; Maria Villela-Petit, 90–99; Emanuel Levinas, 239–243.

4. "ipsum esse abstractum" = *Contra Gentiles* I, 42; "suum esse subsistens" C.G. II, 52; see *De Ente et Essentia*, ed. M.D. Roland-Gosselin (Paris: Vrin, 1948), 29ff.

5. Cf. "Einführung in die Metaphysik," *Gesamtausgabe* (=G.A.), Vol. 40 (Frankfurt: Klostermann, 1983), 9. "What our question really asks about is for faith a foolishness. Philosophy consists in this foolishness. A 'Christian philosophy' is a square circle and a misunderstanding. There is indeed a thinking interrogative working through of the world experienced by the Christian, the world of faith. But that is theology.

Only periods which no longer believe in the veritable greatness of the task of theology stumble on the disastrous idea that theology has something to gain from supposedly being freshened up with the help of philosophy, if not indeed replaced by it and made more tasty to the need of the day." (ET: *An Introduction to Metaphysics*, trans. Ralph Manheim [Garden City, New York: Doubleday-Anchor Books, 1961], 7). The present essay can escape these strictures only if our use of Heidegger issues in a hermeneutic "from faith to faith."

6. HQD, 23.

7. For Heidegger's analysis of metaphysics as onto-theology see especially "Was ist Metaphysik?" (1929) in *Wegmarken*, G.A., Vol. 9 (1976), 118 (ET: *Basic Writings*, ed. David F. Krell [New York: Harper and Row, 1977], 109): "Metaphysics is inquiry beyond or over beings which aims to recover them as such and as a whole for our grasp"; *Schellings Abhandlung über das Wesen der menschlichen Freiheit (1809)* (lectures of 1936), ed. H. Frick (Tübingen: Niemeyer, 1971): "All philosophy is theology in this original and essential sense that the conceptual grasp (*logos*) of beings as a whole poses the question on the ground of being, a ground which is called *theos*—God" (61); *Identität und Differenz* (Pfullingen: Neske, 1957) (With an English translation by Joan Stambaugh, *Identity and Difference* (New York: Harper and Row, 1969).

8. *Zur Sache des Denkens* (Tübingen: Niemeyer, 1969), 25. (ET: *On Time and Being*, trans. J. Stambaugh [New York: Harper and Row, 1972], 24).

9. Ibid., 44 (ET, 41).

10. *Identity and Difference*, 123, 56.

11. Ibid.

12. Cf. Albrecht Ritschl, "Theology and Metaphysics" (1887) in *Three Essays*, trans. P. Hefner (Philadelphia: Fortress, 1972).

13. *Vortragsausschuss der Studentenschaft der Universität Zürich: Aussprache mit Martin Heidegger am 6 November 1951* (Zurich, 1952), 11, and HQD 333–334.

14. Cf. for example Josef Van de Wiele, *Zijnswaarheid en Onverborgenheid* (Louvain: Leuvense Universitaire Uitgaven, 1964), 367–422.

15. Caputo, art. cit., note 1, detects a movement in Thomas's thought towards a point at which "all objectivism and representationalism have melted away. . . . At this point for St. Thomas, metaphysics is something to be overcome" (201).

16. Johannes Baptist Lotz, "Das Sein selbst und das subsistierende Sein nach Thomas von Aquin," *Martin Heidegger zum siebzigsten Geburtstag* (Pfullingen: Neske, 1959), 180–203 (180).

17. Art. cit., p. 182.

18. "In the course of that long history in which 'ontology' and 'theology' have exchanged their 'idioms,' two movements intertwine, which it would be useful to disentangle. The attraction of being towards the divine or the god has most often attracted attention. But one should do justice to the inverse attraction. In the work of St. Thomas, this second movement, complementary to the first, is all the more remarkable in that our theologian, when he commentates the Philosopher, has rather a tendency to defend being against its absorption in God. This polarization of the Christian God by being, by pure *Esse* or the 'virtus essendi,' has seemed to some a betrayal of the faith. Instead of being angry they would have done better to try to understand. Aquinas was careful to explain himself on this topic. If he retains being as a privileged denominator, itself subjected, indeed, to the enigmatic Tetragram, it is because being appears to him as 'uncircumscribed' and 'incircumscriptive,' and as such 'liberative' in regard to that which might reduce religious and theological discourse to apparently 'regional' or localized terms. Thus being presents itself as a 'reductor' of the theological" (Stanislas Breton, HQD, 256–257). I should say that Thomas represents an intra-metaphysical victory for the freedom of Christian faith, but that this freedom can today be maintained only in the overcoming of Thomism.

19. Winter seminar of 1950–1951 (HQD, 333).

20. N. Petruzzellis, "Heidegger tra Ateismo e Panteismo," *Doctor Communis* 25 (1982), 265–281, answers Heidegger's question to his Jesuit sympathizer by referring to *Summa Theol.* I, q. 13, a. 2 where John Damascene is quoted: God "has being itself as a certain sea of substance, infinite and indeterminate," and by reminding us that infinity for Thomas is negative not privative, that God is indeterminate for the human mind, not in himself, that God is the absolute and all-sufficient being, the Necessary who rules our contingency and the Principle which explains it. It is Heidegger, says Petruzzellis, who cannot define being, and can only say: "Es ist Es Selbst" (*Letter on Humanism*), 272. Obviously Petruzzellis has misunderstood the phenomenological point of Heidegger's question. None of the ideas he adduces serve to define

the originality of the Thomist conception of being (they are common-
places of metaphysical theology), far less to uncover its phenomenological correlates. "The Supreme being, the Principle and the cause of all
beings is properly that which religious consciousness understands by
God" (266)—here the language of ontotheology is equiparated with
that of faith. God is brought within the sphere of a totalizing rational
system structured in terms of cause, explanation and being. It is just
this which both the phenomenological and the theological recovery of
origins call into question. Perhaps many of the inconsistencies Petruzzellis finds in Heidegger and his interpreters might be resolved by a
differentiation of the metaphysical and the phenomenological kinds of
discourse. For instance: "If there is a God (=metaphysical), he cannot
be absent (=phenomenological): an absent God is a finite God who
lacks something, a non-God, whereas infinity and omnipresence are,
according to Christianity, characteristics of divinity which cannot be
suppressed (=metaphysical)" (271).

A more sympathetic critic of HQD (Thomas J. Wilson, *Milltown
Studies* (Dublin, 1983), 102–106) suggests that "ontology determines
theodicy. This must also hold for Heidegger and the conclusions it
warrants should outweigh even self-interpretations or personal statements of the author" (106). He claims that the analogies between the
procedures of philosophy and theology in the overcoming of metaphysics must "somehow be ontologically grounded" and that Heideggerian
phenomenology grasps the divine as "part of the Being-process," thus
founding a "natural theology" (105). Certainly Heidegger explicates a
certain experience of the divine and its absence, especially in his
Hölderlin studies. This is less a natural theology than the religious
aspect of the modern struggle with nihilism. The recovery of God is
correlated in this historical experience with the remembrance of being.
Conversely when Heidegger says (in his *Spiegel* interview) that "Only
a God can save us" he has in mind the preservation of being from the
threat of being eclipsed and dominated by beings, the preservation of
human being as such, human being as mortal: "We understand *save* in
this elevated and absolutely ontological sense" (F. Fédier, HQD, 41).
These thoughts do not seem to me to provide a framework into which
the content of the Christian revelation could be poured, but rather they
designate the contemporary dialogue partner of that revelation in the
West. Much more is demanded in this dialogue than the raising of "the
same material reality to the level of the supernatural" (Wilson, 105).
The contrast of natural and supernatural, eminently metaphysical, is

perhaps not helpful in a phenomenological context, though Heidegger seems to use it on one occasion (HQD, 335); on that occasion Heidegger also remarked: "The provocation which comes from philosophy can always be only an indirect one" (Ibid.=*Anstösse: Berichte aus der Arbeit der Evangelischen Akademie Hofgeismar*, Vol. I (1954), 33). I have similar misgivings about Maria Villela-Petit's view that Heidegger's threshold thinking of divinity is to be completed by faith's encounter with a God experienced as personal (HQD, 95–97). The "personality" of God is a theme exposed to critical interrogation in the dialogue between faiths, or between faith and contemporary agnosticism.

21. Richard Kearney, *Dialogues with Contemporary Continental Thinkers* (Manchester University Press, 1984), 114. In the same interview, Derrida claims that the "original heterogeneous, elements of Judaism and Christianity were never completely eradicated by Western metaphysics. They perdure throughout the centuries, threatening and unsettling the assured 'identities' of Western philosophy. So that the surreptitious deconstruction of the Greek *Logos* is at work from the very origin of our Western culture" (117).

22. Letter to John Leavey, *Semeia* 23 (1982) ("Derrida and Biblical Studies"), 61.

23. M. Heidegger and E. Fink, *Heraklit* (Frankfurt: Klostermann, 1970), 124.

24. cf. Hölderlin's "Andenken," G.A., Vol. 52 (1982), 119–120; "Wozu Dichter?" in *Holzwege*, G.A., Vol. 5 (1977), 269–320 = *Poetry, Language, Thought*, trans. A. Hofstadter (New York: Harper and Row, 1971), 89–142.

25. *Identity and Difference*, 140, 72.

26. Heidegger, *Basic Writings*, 385; cf. Dilthey to Husserl (1911): "we agree in regard to the effort needed to reach a universally valid foundation for the sciences of the real, in opposition to constructive metaphysics, and against every assumption that an in-itself lies behind the reality that is given to us" (P. McCormick and F.A. Elliston, *Husserl: Shorter Works* [University of Notre Dame Press, 1981], 207). There is a Kantian pathos here, though it is directed against Kant himself. On the problem of phenomenality in Kant, see G. Granel, *L'équivoque ontologique de Kant* (Paris: Gallimard, 1970). For Heidegger the hiddenness, the withdrawal of Being is essential to its phenomenality: see *Sein und Zeit*, G.A., Vol. 2 (1977) (ET: *Being and Time*, trans. J. Macquarrie and E. Robinson [New York: Harper and Row, 1962]),

paragraph 7, and the further developments in the discussion of Being and Seeming (*Sein und Schein*) in *Einführung in die Metaphysik*, 75ff (ET, 98ff). (Cf. Jean-Francois Courtine, "La cause de la phénoméno-logie," in *Exercices de la Pensée* 3/4 [1982], 65–83). Derrida's crusade against the "transcendental signified" belongs to the same tradition, whose device might be: "The real is the phenomenal and the phenomenal is the real." In both Heidegger and Derrida "phenomenal-ity" no longer refers to something "given," which only demands to be brought into view in a purified apprehension. Instead phenomenality has become the locus of a hermeneutical struggle. In Derrida phenomenality has been more radically apprehended as textuality (following on Heidegger's insight that language is what brings all phenomena into presence), so that the principle of phenomenality now means that "there is no outside of the text." For both thinkers the only way to reality is through abiding in phenomenality (language, textuality) and any effort to think of a noumenon lying "beyond" this realm shows itself to be impossible. The noumenal has held sway in theology more than anywhere else. It needs to be replaced by the hermeneutical struggle for the phenomenality of God.

27. See Maria Villela-Petit, HQD, 87–88.
28. For a recently published discussion see *Parmenides*, G.A., Vol. 54 (1982).
29. Cf. *Basic Writings*, 99–100: "We assert that the nothing is more original than the 'not' and negation. If this thesis is right, then the possibility of negation as an act of the intellect, and thereby the intellect itself are somehow dependent upon the nothing."
30. Cf. *Identity and Difference*, 85 ff., 23 ff.
31. Cf. *Der Satz vom Grund* (Pfullingen: Neske, 1956).
32. Cf. *Grundbegriffe*, G.A., Vol. 51, 1981, 30–31.
33. *Aus der Erfahrung des Denkens*, G.A., Vol. 13 (1982), 78 ("hart am Wind der Sache") = *Poetry, Language, Thought*, 6.
34. *Vorträge und Aufsätze* (Pfullingen: Neske, 1954), 177 = *Poetry, Language, Thought*, 178–179.
35. *Unterwegs zur Sprache* (Pfullingen: Neske, 1959), 26–27 = *Poetry, Language, Thought*, 203–205.
36. Carl A. Raschke, "The Deconstruction of God" in *Deconstruction and Theology* (New York: Crossroad, 1982), 1–32: 3, 4, 7, 9, 11, 12, 14, 15, 27, 28, 30, 31.

37. *Marges. De la philosophie* (Paris: Editions de Minuit), 392 (ET: *Margins of Philosophy*, trans. Alan Bass [Chicago: University of Chicago Press], 329).

38. Ibid., 393 (ET, 329).

39. "The very idea of institution—hence of the arbitrariness of the sign—is unthinkable before the possibility of writing and outside its horizon. Which is to say quite simply outside the horizon itself, outside the world as space of inscription, opening to the emission and spatial distribution of signs, to the regulated play of their differences, even if these were only "phonic" (*De la grammatologie* (Paris: Editions de Minuit, 1967), 65–66) (ET: *Of Grammatology*, trans. Gayatri C. Spivak [Baltimore: Johns Hopkins University Press, 1976], 44).

40. *De la Grammatologie*, 25 (ET, 14). Cf. *La Dissémination*, 42: "To say that there is no absolute outside-the-text is not to postulate an ideal immanence, the incessant reconstitution of a relation of writing to itself. . . . The text *affirms* the outside, marks the limit of that speculative operation (sc. of Hegel), deconstructs and reduces to 'effects' all the predicates by which speculation appropriates to itself the outside. If there is nothing outside the text, this implies, with the transformation of the concept of text in general, that the text is no longer the air-proof inside of an interiority or a self-identity . . . but another location of the effects of opening and closing."

41. For this suggestion see Robert Magliola, *Derrida on the Mend* (Purdue University Press, 1984), Chapter four; but the trinitarian logic and the mystical paradox invoked by Magliola are themselves in need of historical and phenomenological criticism before their possible contribution to a contemporary language of faith can be completely articulated. Magliola's stinging criticism of Derrida's latent theology might also apply to the latest, and best, exercise in death-of-God deconstructionism, Mark C. Taylor's *Erring: A Postmodern A/theology*, University of Chicago Press, 1984.

42. Raschke, 15, quoting Derrida, *Marges*, 236 (ET, 197).

43. *La dissémination* (Paris: Seuil, 1972), 13.

44. Cf. Aristotle, *De Interpretatione* I, 16ᵃ 3; Athanasius, *Ad Monachos*, 1 (P.G., 25, 692); Basil, *Sermo*, XV (P.G., 31, 464); Augustine, *De Trinitate*, V 1.

45. *La dissémination*, 71.

46. I am indebted to Terry Pulver for several of the thoughts expressed here. My overall interpretation of Derrida owes much to André Schuwer's seminar on "Metaphor" at Duquesne University, Fall 1982.

47. S. Sin, "De-composing in Bad Faith: Its Cause and Cure," *Critical Quarterly* 24/4 (Winter 1982), 25–36.
48. *La dissémination*, 51.
49. Cf. Derrida, *Limited Inc.*, *Supplement to Glyph*, 2 (Baltimore: Johns Hopkins University Press, 1977), passim.
50. *De la grammatologie*, 41 (ET, 26).
51. *Marges*, II-III (ET, xii).
52. Ibid., II (ET, xi).
53. Ibid., 15 (ET, 14).
54. This is why Richard Taft writes: "perhaps it would be better not to refer to such deconstruction as 'post-metaphysical,' a designation which tends to suggest the possibility of escape. . . . Perhaps it would be more to the point to situate Derrida at the 'edge of metaphysics,' a place from which he can disclose the limits and presuppositions of metaphysics, in a way which is itself not *simply* metaphysical, but does so without ever fully escaping from it." "The End of Metaphysics and . . . Language? The Problem of Radical Deconstruction," paper read at Stony Brook Colloquium on "Deconstruction and its Alternatives," May 1983.
55. Robert P. Scharlemann in *Deconstruction and Theology*, 90.
56. Mark P. Taylor, *Deconstructing Theology* (American Academy of Religion, 1982).
57. *Zur Sache des Denkens*, 25 (ET, 24).
58. Carl A. Raschke, *The Alchemy of the Word* (Missoula, Montana: Scholars Press, 1979), 83–84.
59. Ibid., 84.
60. Ibid., 90.

II: FAITH IN CRISIS, THEOLOGY IN BONDS

In the preceding chapter the overcoming of metaphysics was presented as a hermeneutical strategy whereby contemporary theology might establish a more creative relationship to Christian tradition. But this hermeneutic scenario has a *Sitz im Leben* beyond the pleasures of the study, for in speaking of the readability of Christian tradition one is at the same time talking about the transmissibility of Christian faith. Theology exists chiefly to facilitate the communication of faith. Without a sense of this responsibility its hermeneutical exercises are unlikely to be very decisive. The hungry sheep look up: the question is pressed both by those outside the Christian community and, in a muted form, by those within it: Can we believe? What can we believe? When theologians are claimed by that question, cornered by it with no way of escape, they may find that their recourse to the vast linguistic repertoire of Scripture and tradition has become subject to stringent conditions; that even within the community of faith the free circulation of religious jargon is inhibited by a diffuse sense of crisis, a scrupulous skepticism forming the backdrop to all theological labors, so that one is forced to weigh every word to make sure it carries conviction; and that doing theology, whether in the lecture hall or the pulpit or in writing, has become a chastening experience, in which one discovers again and again the impossibility of taking any religious expressions for granted and the difficulty of producing any that do not instantly, by their hollow sound, betray a bondage to convention or spiritual ineptitude. The questions of theology—including Jesus's "Who do you say that I am?"—have become real, unanswered, questions once again and every boldly assertive reply—like Peter's "You are the Messiah"—seems to have become intrinsically problematic. As theology grows into this situation of crisis, it finds itself "on the way to

57

language," earning its words one by one, in the slow formation of a new saying of faith.

But most theologians seem to resist the summons, imposed by this situation, to a Heideggerian descent to the poverty and provisionality of an elemental language of faith. Their eloquence, which is in large part the eloquence of metaphysics, is not easily subdued. Academic theology today is not uncontaminated by the pressures of the marketplace, indeed it is delivered over to those pressures by the institutions which should be defending its integrity—by universities which instill the ethos of "publish or perish," by churches which enter with unabashed vulgarity into the mediocratic fray, by theological associations which become hotbeds of careerism, and by theological journals which prefer established names to questions of faith. It would not be untrue to say that the "unproductive productivity"[1] of theology, marked by an absurd proliferation of exciting projects which dazzle for a few months and then disappear, never to be followed through, is diametrically opposed to the spirit of the *Letter on Humanism.* Nowhere is a question allowed to put down deep roots and given time to ripen and deploy all its implications. At a time when their subject summons theologians to become a community of questioning faith, one finds them instead staging an immense *trahison des clercs,* busily repressing or trivializing the questions which confront them. Indeed, of all the humanities, it seems that theology is the least critical (though it should be the most) of those ecclesiastical, social, and academic conformisms which betray the human spirit and which are in contradiction with faith. In this situation metaphysics functions as an unfailing source of convenient assumptions and procedures whereby one can make a profitable industry out of the deferral of radical questioning. What is the relationship between such a theology and the travail of the contemporary faith? Do theologians "heal the wound of my people lightly" instead of letting that wound be felt in the texture of their discourse as questioning and a struggle with language? Where does theology today exemplify the poverty of faith? Luther's last words—"*Wir sein pettler*" ("We are beggars")—find no echo in most contemporary theological discourse, although they may well serve to express the situation of authentic faith today.

Some of the theologians criticized in this chapter are among those who have done most to make the Word of God audible in a convincing form to the contemporary world and to free the Christian community from conventional or fundamentalist jargon. But even they seem to lack one thing, namely, the ability to free the texture of their thinking from patterns of metaphysical reasoning, which have become unserviceable for the matter of faith. Even when these theologians succeed in acquiring a measure of critical freedom in regard to the residues of patristic or medieval ontology and Hegelian speculation, they are likely to continue to work within the system of a metaphysics of subjectivity, using such categories as "the meaning of life" or "the nature and destiny of man" which fall well within the orbit of the abstract humanism criticized by Heidegger. Even those we think of as defenders of biblical faith against metaphysical absorption—Luther, Pascal, Kierkegaard, perhaps even Bonhoeffer —often reveal a self-understanding which is structured by the metaphysics of subjectivity. These people are a "cloud of witnesses" for those who wish to live by faith today. But we cannot simply assume their existential stance without overcoming the metaphysics by which it was conditioned. This point can be made more perspicuous if we observe the interplay between metaphysics and myth. Metaphysics aims to overcome myth and project a rational understanding of reality in its place. Yet every metaphysics continues to derive its vitality from a latent mythical pattern—a world of forms, a hierarchical order of being, a progress of absolute spirit or of will to power —so many poetic visions whose mythical quality is never finally erased by their rational explicitation. Theology today is still attached to myths of cosmic explanation; those of process theology provide the most elaborate refuge from the questioning of faith. But generally it is the myths attaching to the metaphysics of subjectivity which tempt theology more intimately, for these seem to guarantee the authenticity of faith. Modern Western faith still lives from such founding myths as Pascal's fideistic assurance (an inverted form of the Cartesian myth of certitude), Luther's radical, individualistic freedom of conscience (for we have demythologized his struggle with Satan and Antichrist and his fetishism of biblical authority only to remythologize his "Here I stand" as a sacralization of individual conscience), Kierkegaard's pathos of authenticity, Newman's narcissistically structured projection of an inward God of the heart, and the "I-Thou" myths of personalism and pietism. None of these myths are fully valid for faith today. The metaphysical structures—abstracted individualism, the primacy of interiority, foundational experiences of feeling or conscience, self-sufficient certitude—which they interpose between the believer and the Word of God must be undone. No doubt the overcoming of metaphysics also has its own mythology, but it is one attuned to the signs of the times. If we live old myths, even those of recent centuries, our faith can only appear on the contemporary horizon as a lofty fiction, at home only in the enclaves of an ecclesiastical culture.

The overcoming of metaphysics in theology can find no more logical starting point than that provided by a diagnosis of the unpurged mental and linguistic habits of contemporary theologians, whether these derive from classical or Hegelian metaphysics, from the myths of subjectivity or from an amiable complacency whereby one toys with various metaphysical notions and methods without questioning their credentials. But first, in order to clarify the scope and purpose of the entire enterprise, I should like to dwell a little longer on those urgent questions of faith which raise critical reflection on inherited discourse to a more than academic level, making of it a demanding spiritual exercise, a struggle towards spiritual freedom through a conversion of mind.

The Contemporary Mutation of Faith

Forty years or so ago it might still have been thought that the drama of atheistic humanism took place outside the community of faith. Still more recently the secular, agnostic complexion of contemporary culture could be seen as conferring a diaspora status on the Christian community without essentially altering the nature of their faith. Yet it is becoming increasingly clear that what so many of the thinkers and artists of our time have registered as the default of God (Hölderlin's *Fehl Gottes*) is a situation in which Christians too are obliged to participate. Of course, Christians are still claimed by the tradition of faith and still try to live by it, but the double challenge to faith articulated by Nietzsche—the challenge of radical doubt and the demand that faith be true to life, faithful to the earth—lodges now in Christian consciousness as an inextinguishable wound. It is important that faith should live with this double interrogation, the dark angel with which it must wrestle until dawn, for it is only along the narrow way this interrogation lights up that faith can be transmitted to future generations. That faith should pass the tests imposed by skeptical, questioning post-Enlightenment reason is necessary if it is to testify convincingly to the reality of God. To meet this challenge it must undergo a change in its texture; the primarily affirmative and dogmatic character of all the historical forms of faith must yield to a new dispensation in which faith will have a primarily questioning and dialogal character. Second, faith cannot effectively counter contemporary nihilism (so accurately symbolized in the nuclear threat) unless it renounces its own nihilistic tendencies—the projection of platonic world-negating images of God; the use of gestures and language without an authentic this-worldly empirical correlative; the parasitism of religious interpretations of the experiences of life which overleap their phenomenality; the poisoning of eros; the general inability to earth the life of faith in the Teilhardian mandate: "Put your trust in life and life will carry you forward; but choose always what promotes life."

These interrogations cut faith off from its past—after Voltaire it is impossible to indulge a Pascalian haughtiness towards reason; after Goethe, Blake, and Lawrence it is impossible to sustain the old-style contempt for the flesh and the world. Those traditions have to be more subtly rethought. But the break with the past goes deeper, for the withdrawal of God effects a reevaluation of the entire gallery of historical representations of the divine, and throws us back on an empty space, where once we could rely on secure images of God as Yahweh or Father, first cause or final end. The unconditional assertion of any such image now appears idolatrous, and God comes to be thought of primarily as the goal of a search rather than as the object of an assertion. "I believe in God" then means "I believe in that towards which the traditional images of God point and I am embarked on the search for it in all the experiences of life." Such a faith espouses the iconoclastic movement of biblical language about God (including the Johannine attempt to think God as love and as spirit) and regards no established representation of God as sacred. It is thus free to negotiate the trial of radical doubt and can enjoy a consciousness of being as large as life, true to the world in which it lives, rather than confined within an ecclesiastical hothouse. Conversion to such a faith no longer spells the cessation of questioning, the answer to all the riddles of life, but rather entry onto a larger path of questioning. A community whose faith has this questioning character is thrown into real dialogue with other traditions for the first time, in the realization that the partial and provisional insights mediated by tradition are likely to remain sterile or become distorted unless shared with fellow searchers elsewhere.

The radical awareness of the historicity of its representations which such a questioning faith enjoys is what makes the simple maintenance of any of these representations appear idolatrous. Jean-Luc Marion claims that "To every epoch there corresponds a figure of the divine which is fixed, each time, in an idol."[2] For Marion to think God as love is to escape this condition of idolatry, but surely even the phrase "God is love" is always shorthand for a set of historical representations, and so also exposed to idolatrous interpretation. Marion's own account of God as self-giving love lacks historical texture, savors of the false infinite and can easily be classified as a speculative idol. If every representation of God captures only a human historical experience of the divine, then to let one's faith be limited by any such representation beyond the period of its historical effectivity can be called idolatrous. Faith can attack the Molochs and Belials of the world only if it is constantly shattering its own language against a more radical apprehension of God as Spirit. Scripture and the Creeds are preserved from idolatry only by constant reinterpretation and recontextualization, and with the awareness of the historicity of all representations this process ceases to be one of merely local amendment and develops into a conscious ongoing struggle with tradition. In regard to the very elements of its language contemporary faith is obliged to practice a constant discernment and differentiation. Thus the central Christian experience of dying into life seems to be inscribed in the texture of the language

of faith. Sometimes an entire epoch is *retrospectively* declared idolatrous in a prophetic leap forward: Isaiah and Ezekiel, Jesus and
Paul, Luther and Calvin may signal such epochal leaps, and faith
today is undergoing another, in which metaphysical theologies are
revealed as idolatrous for us, however anti-idolatrous in their original context. There is much else of course that faith has to be liberated from, for instance biblical fundamentalism, ideological
unconsciousness, collusion in war and injustice, unreal devotionalism, the limitations of Western culture. Authentic faith is always
being liberated from its own past; it is a constant exodus. But it is
probably the closure of metaphysics which chiefly impels contemporary faith to dismantle the other idolatries, as it was the stability of
metaphysical assumptions which did most to bolster them in the
past.

But can this spirit of questioning be reconciled with the qualities
of affirmation, commitment, and certitude which surely belong to
the existentiality of faith and without which faith would not be
worth transmitting? To be authentic faith must be fully exposed to
questioning, yet to maintain continuity with tradition some core of
certitude must survive this process; if the tradition dissolves into
mere questions it has ceased to be a tradition of faith. The paradox
or miracle of the contemporary narrow way of faith is to be sought
precisely in the fact that its certitude does survive, in a greatly
chastened form. This chastened faith is the medium in which the
specifically biblical experience of God is available today. Agnostic
questioning may have its own intimations of the divine, for instance
of that quasi-Eckhartian divinity of which Heidegger claims that it
is "nearer to thinking than to faith."[3] The legitimacy of such
inklings need not be denied, but they cannot replace the decisive
autonomy of biblical faith any more than that faith can exclude
them. More than ever before biblical faith today grasps itself historically as one strand in the wider religious quest of humanity, a strand
for which a unique importance may certainly be claimed, even
though the terms in which it is claimed must inevitably undergo a
sea-change in the experience of dialogue.

The certitude of faith today is such that it consigns one to questioning and dialogue; every credal assertion is set in the context of an

ongoing search and subordinated to the dynamics of this search. As inherited dogmatic reflexes melt more and more into this questioning texture, authority's function of commanding belief (which has proved impracticable in its traditional forms) is also subordinated to the larger task of keeping open the process of questioning and dialogue and exemplifying it at the highest level. Thus the dogmatic and denominational heritages of faith fall into a new perspective in which they cease to be obstacles to valid religious insight. As dialogal concern with the "matter itself" of faith reduces all assertive discourses to their humble place within this dialogue, the certitude of faith is weaned away from secondary objects and focused more singly on the essentials of the biblical kerygma as currently accessible. How one might determine what these essentials are is a question I shall return to in Chapter Five. In the new hermeneutics this questioning faith makes possible, the primarily affirmative language of Scripture and tradition is retrieved as a fund of latent questions, as the painful historical tracing of the outlines of humanity's question about God, in and across which faith can also hear God's question to humanity. Certainly God asserts, being, as Barth says, the Yes to humanity's No and the No to humanity's Yes; but such assertion too melts into a deeper texture of questioning, which in the case of God we call mystery.

The struggle of such questioning faith with its past is largely a struggle with language, and the services expected from theology always entail a linguistic responsibility, which the linguistic philistinism of much academic theology poorly prepares it to meet. It might seem that the unguarded use of such terms as "immanent," "transcendent," "substance," "person," "supreme being" in speaking of God, or, to take another example, such terms as "value," "principle," "meaning," "cause," or "purpose" in connection with the efficacity of faith or of grace, is an innocuous convenience not meriting a determined critique. But it may be that such words imply horizons of understanding, a depth grammar, fundamentally though unconsciously opposed to those of authentic faith, and that their seeming naturalness indicates a deep-seated "forgetfulness of revelation." How sinister should it be deemed that when I say "God is utterly transcendent" I am almost certain to be found parsing the mystery of God with a Platonic grammar (the transcendence of the intelligible world over the sensible) because two thousand years of Christian Platonizing prevent my words from being understood in any other way? Am I reducing God to proportions which either make God less than life-size, so that speech about God lacks resonance with experience, or else forcibly imposing this abstract absolute on the texture of life and/or history? I might wish to open up a counter-metaphysical meaning for the word "transcendence" and to declare, for example: "let 'transcendence' stand for the unmasterable, eschatological future of God." Such academic rechristenings may produce a new space of discourse for a while, but when the effect wears off they are likely to be seen as factitious efforts to revive last year's language. Heidegger's success in opening certain words to a trans-metaphysical meaning—words like "house," "mountain range," "thing," "saying," each of which thought appropriates in a non-metaphorical meaning of being, and also technical words like "*Wesen,*", "*Sein,*" "*Dasein*" which are made to stand for the underlying concrete phenomenality their technical use occludes —was not the result of academic tinkering; a durable transformation of language has deeper roots: "What *remains* however, the poets establish" (Hölderlin).[4] Theology has been too fertile in models and metaphors for God. Part of the reason for their unconvincingness is that they lack the tension of overcoming; their counter-metaphysical thrust is not lucidly established; indeed they are often embedded in a discourse which continues to be shaped by conventional metaphysics and this belies their claim to more than a secondary, illustrative status. Even those who have tried to retrieve divine transcendence in a consciously counter-metaphysical language, such as Emmanuel Levinas (God as "infinity" or "alterity" which cracks open the "totality" or "identity" of the unconverted consciousness for which Western metaphysics provides the most imposing rationale) or Jean-Luc Marion (the paternal "distance" measured by the cross of Jesus), do not perhaps quite succeed in setting language on its way to a more responsive openness to the phenomenality of the biblical God; a certain abstract rigidity still marks their constructions, perhaps a necessity of their strategies of opposition or perhaps because, writing as philosophers rather than theologians, they have

still not attained a sufficiently thorough immersion in and critical
engagement with the riches of historical Jewish and Christian diction. Only through tradition, tradition is conquered; only from
familiarity with the resources of the language of faith to the point of
saturation can one undertake its transformation.

Faith's struggle with language takes diverse forms according to
the particular language the believer speaks and in this realm Stanislas Breton's saying that "a language is a destiny" has a particularly
pungent application. The languages of Western theology all seem to
be past their prime as mediums for the articulation of faith. The
rather bloodless Latinized Christian diction of English seems
exhausted, but the preservation of a native Germanic vocabulary for
religious things in modern German somehow does not seem to help
matters very much, while the Latin languages (French, Spanish,
Italian) seem positively to enfeeble every biblical reality they
attempt to express. As for the mission languages, perhaps the major
challenge of inculturation is to activate their native resources under
the impact of the biblical kerygma, as Paul activated those of Greek,
Augustine those of Latin, or Luther those of German. Any such
activation brings with it a reshaping of the kerygma through the
genius of the language; it is perhaps largely through fear of such
unpredictable transformations that the Gospel is still being
preached in translatese. But even in Western languages the metaphysical shaping of the Christian message has impeded the testing
and transforming of its diction. The opening of words has been
short-circuited by theological circumscriptions of their reference.
"Grace," for instance, as biblical event calls on language to produce
poetic ways of saying it; but when it is defined by theology any such
linguistic performance is discouraged as unnecessary. Experiences
of grace become exemplifications of the predefined metaphysical
principle and the effort to find words for the specific phenomenality
and irreducible variety of such experience is abandoned. The result
is that the language of faith today is an inflated currency, depending
too heavily on token words whose experiential cash value has
become extremely elusive—indeed when theologians begin to
explain the meaning in experiential terms of such words as "faith,"
"hope," or "love" the inflationary situation becomes even more

apparent. The language of the liturgy unconscionably wallows in this inflation. Against it must be pitted the effort at a more pristine or originary saying of faith.

To neglect this linguistic task in favor of "substantive issues" would be to underestimate the degree to which the vitality of faith depends on the soundness of its language. Furthermore, faith's discontent with its language unleashes an energy of questioning and reformation which goes far beyond the merely linguistic. In contesting a word one may find oneself subverting an institution or changing a way of life. In pulling the smallest thread in the tapestry of logocentric theology one may unstitch the whole. As the prophetic believer or community of believers strives for a language of Spirit which is larger, but not looser, than that prescribed by the Western Logos, opening the jargon of the dogmatic tradition (in a way that best preserves the truth of this tradition) into a language more fit for a pneumatic questioning style of faith, the theologian is challenged to follow suit at the systematic, reflexive level, coordinating the emergent languages of faith and critically defending them against metaphysical reabsorption or marginalization. If prophetic speech were thus established, both through its practice and its theoretical explicitation and defense, as the primary language of Christianity, the authority of the Church would become again that of a word eliciting dialogal response rather than imposing theoretical claims. The primacy of the prophetic demands that the norms of metaphysical reason fall away, as tonality disappears from music or representation from painting, causing in each case a disorientation which spells the emergence of a more intrinsic orientation, so that music becomes more purely music, painting more purely painting, theology more purely a discipline of faith.

God as Concept

Many contemporary theologians will admit that the traditional discourses have lost their force and need to be rerooted in something more primordial, whether that be religious experience or the biblical kerygma or the historical struggle of humanity. But generally each such effort to return to the primordial is still so structured by the

characteristic procedures of metaphysical reasoning that it remains
subject to the same misgivings as the system it is designed to replace.
The return to "religious experience" is usually no more than the
replacement of one metaphysical *arché* by another, and fails to
articulate that aspect of the experience of faith which eludes all
integration into a metaphysical system. Such phrases as "ultimate
concern," "the beyond in our midst," the "feeling of utter dependence" continue to stylize the experience of faith in such a way as to
make it the foundational principle of a totalizing worldview rather
than concrete engagement with history led by the ever-new address
of the Gospel kerygma. Yet theologies which appeal to the kerygma
or to history also tend to remain entrapped in metaphysics in their
aspirations, procedures and results. Jürgen Moltmann and Wolfhart
Pannenberg provide the most instructive examples of this in recent
years. Both proclaim an encounter between the Gospel and history
but both end up wandering within the recesses of the Hegelian
system. Why? Is it because of a failure to abide with and in the
biblical word and to abide with and in the historical situation which
interprets that word and is interpreted by it? One cannot abide in
the biblical word without abiding in the situation it addresses, and
one cannot do either without overcoming the metaphysical habits of
mind which bring both word and situation within the ontotheological grasp. One cannot abide in the wisdom of the cross without
finding the cross in the unresolved agony of contemporary history
and without splitting open those theological systems which make the
cross into a structural principle of speculative progress. One cannot
enter into a biblical confession of faith, e.g., "My Lord and my God"
(John 20:28), by using it as the foundation for ulterior speculative
refinements, but only by going back to its roots (by espousing, to
begin with, the entire contemplative context of the Fourth Gospel
whence John 20:28 derives its sense) and by attempting to find
equivalents of these roots in the reality of experience. We must read
our tradition backwards, in the direction of its underlying convictions, overcoming the layers of metaphysical rationalization and
institutionalization under which these convictions lie buried, letting
ourselves be stripped of all the conveniences of our present doctrinal
vocabulary in order to retrieve some authentic elements of belief. To

accomplish this work theologians need a keener awareness of the metaphysical texture of their language and a willingness to play with that texture ironically and subversively, to solicit it in the name of what always eludes it, the spiritual resonance of the scriptural words.

Theologians sometimes have an inadequately trained ear for the inauthenticity of metaphysical religious language. A study of this all-important question of tone would, however, take us too far afield, through the dreary career publications of professional journals for the study of religion, all striking the vacuous "scholarly" note, poor substitute for a thinking rooted in faith. Instead, I focus on the conceptual aspect of what modern theology is making of two basic Christian topics, "God" and "Christ." "God" is still being treated as a metaphysical concept as can be seen from such writing as this:

> The concept God is the central and clearest expression of the general metaphysical character of religious language itself. Where God is conceived radically (as in such monotheistic religions as Judaism, Christianity and Islam), God is conceived metaphysically. In Ogden's . . . language, which I see every reason to endorse, God is conceived as "the ultimate creative ground of anything that is so much as even possible, and hence to be in the strictest sense necessary, not merely a being among others, but in some way 'being-itself.' In fact, the God of theism in its most fully developed forms is the one metaphysical individual, the sole reality whose individuality is constitutive of reality as such; the sole being who is, therefore, the inclusive object of our faith and understanding."[5]

Apart from the question of tone, what is wrong with this? One might ask, first of all, if it really has any reference to the God of the Bible. Is God metaphysically conceived in Scripture? Is God conceived at all in Scripture? Do we find concepts and metaphysics in Jewish and Christian "theism" before Philo and Justin? And is their entry at that point not synonymous with the synthesis between the biblical God and the God of metaphysics, a synthesis whose questionability Tracy and Ogden have no means of addressing? The very fact that Tracy and Ogden, in continuing to use metaphysical language about

God, feel obliged to subject it to rather bizarre modifications is a sign that such language is no longer self-evidently suited to the God of faith. It has lost its grip on the believer, and theologians have apparently lost their grip on it. To speak of God's "individuality" as "constitutive of reality as such" and of "the ever-new event of God's own self-creation in response to the free self-creations of his creatures . . . the unique process of God's self-actualization, whereby he creatively synthesizes all other things into his own actual being as God"[6] is to compose a metaphysics whose conceptual rigor and biblical warrant are simulated, and which cannot serve to root the believing mind in the thought of God. Tracy summarizes this factitious reconstruction of the God of Abraham thus:

> We affirm that God has both a concrete pole which is eminently social and temporal, an ever-changing, ever-affecting, ever-being-affected actuality, and an abstract pole which is well-defined—if "concretely misplaced"—by traditional Western reflection upon the metaphysical attributes of the wholly Absolute One.[7]

The bird's eye view on God which allows this extrinsic synthesis of classical metaphysics with the metaphysically interpreted biblical narratives of passion and change in God does not seem to be subjected to a really searching epistemological or linguistic critique by the writers who espouse it. The ascesis of religious language in our time, whereby talk of God is reduced to its purified essentials, namely to what can be said in the call of prayer or in loving blessing of another or in prophetic engagement for peace or justice, is ignored in the constructions of process theologians. They are insensitive to the embarrassment attendant on all direct dogmatic and speculative speech about God. If they "turn to the subject" it is in order to find a new set of abstractions, "process," "sociality," and "time" from which to construct a speculative model of God, which to my mind bears less convincing witness to God as Unchanging Love than the old language of "being," "aseity," and "eternity." The phenomenological situation seems to be this: when God becomes an object of discussion or of speculation God has ceased to be God. The only valid speech of God is that which names or invokes God in a situation of faith. The simplicity of this naming delivers us from the fantasms of speculative talk of God, and thus, in the phrase of Eckhart, God delivers us from God. Theology should abide in the poverty of faith's context-bound naming of God, in increasing awareness of the human-all-too-human status of even this elemental language, and should thence defuse those explanatory projects which leave this element behind. As the philosophical and religious impossibility of every other path becomes apparent, and as every effort to revitalize metaphysical treatments of God with the aid of dialectical, or personalist, or existential, or process terminologies is worked through and revealed to be bankrupt, theology is forced to descend to the true limits of its language, wherein is its true wealth. "Thou art my God, to Thee do I call all the day"—we must think our way into the poverty of such utterances, not supplementing it from adventitious resources. Escape from this poverty is easy; but only when claimed by it does theology become the science of faith.

To retrieve and understand the simple is the highest task of theology, one which can imply the upheaval and reconstruction of all its inherited categories, and of the world around it. This is the very opposite of the metaphysical effort to integrate the data of biblical faith into an over-arching speculative vision. "This major modern discovery"[8] (namely, that God has both a changing and an unchanging, a concrete and an abstract pole) "can aid us to understand in strictly conceptual terms . . . the God of Abraham, Isaac, Jacob and Jesus Christ"[9] and make the New Testament's summary limit-metaphor *God is love* "both conceptually coherent and existentially meaningful."[10] Pascal vigilantly opposed "the God of Abraham, Isaac, Jacob and Jesus Christ" to the "God of the philosophers." Here Tracy uses Pascal's version of the divine name to bring about the opposite of what Pascal sought, quite erasing the contrast between the naming of God in the situation of faith and the philosopher's quest for a conceptual grasp of God. Has Tracy really transcended this opposition?[11] An even more startling piece of literary insensitivity may be suspected in the offer to make St. John's words

"God is love" (I John 4:8, 16) conceptually coherent and existentially meaningful. Has the interpreter, aided by the tawdry conceptuality of processism, so penetrated the world of Johannine contemplation as to be able to confer on the words "God is love" the coherence they lack? What if Johannine contemplation is intrinsically irreducible to Western criteria of conceptual coherence and existential meaningfulness, and calls these criteria themselves into question?

Having metaphysically explicated the sense of the Johannine words, Tracy proposes to go on to supplement this conceptual explication with "symbolic forms of expression that might allow that insight to resonate more fully to the deepest sensitivities of our present multi-dimensional cultural situation."[12] Such supplements might be less necessary if he had begun by allowing the biblical "metaphor" itself to unfold its contemplative import. Of course in labelling the expression "metaphorical" he has imprisoned it within metaphysics from the start. "God is love" can only be either a "literal definition" or a "poetic metaphor" as long as one interprets it metaphysically; the possibility that it speaks of a dimension irreducible to metaphysical explication is one to which Tracy does not advert. That is why his distillation of the metaphysical essence of the scriptural expressions leaves him with a sense of something missing, which obliges him to revivify the non-conceptual elements his conceptualizing hermeneutic leaves over, now circumscribed and domesticated as "metaphorical" pedagogic devices. (No doubt he would say that this happens at the level of "communications" the last of the eight "functional specialties" into which Bernard Lonergan divides the work of the theologian.) The unquestioned primacy of the conceptual thus reduces the language of Scripture to a pasteboard imitation of itself. The pastoral and catechetical consequences of this disembowelling of Scripture can be imagined. Indeed, the relation between pastoral conventionalism and theological metaphysicizing is a harmonious symbiosis, each reinforcing the other. In the academy we subject the word of God to the "what" and "why" questions of Western metaphysics, and easily find the answers, which are largely predetermined by the terms of the questions, by the intrinsic structure of metaphysical reason. In the parish church the questions may be more homely, the answers more pat, but often the same metaphysical impediments to letting God be God are at play. As long as a preacher thinks that the essential Gospel is a set of principles, and the rest its metaphorical clothing, then God remains a concept to be applied rather than one whose cause, will, Kingdom, or presence is to be found concretely inscribed in the texture of our lives and struggles. Christ is another name for that concrete inscription, and he too has been reduced to a concept.

The Christ of Metaphysics

Faith names Christ variously, and each confession is born from the praxis and struggle elicited by a particular historical context. Metaphysical theology, however, wants to construct an account of Christ independent of faith and of historical context, an account which can be indifferently repeated in any historical context. But it may be that the limits of our language are such that this can never be done. This would mean that we must reread the great confessions of Nicea and Chalcedon as witnesses of faith in a moment of historical crisis, rather than as metaphysical definitions of the being of Christ which could be meaningfully repeated independently of the concrete historical tradition of faith which carries them and reinterprets them. If we attempt a metaphysical definition of Christ, e.g., "the second person of the Trinity, co-eternal with the Father, incarnate in time," our language crumbles due to the impossibility of defining any of the terms we are using. What can "second" or "person" mean in God? Since we know nothing outside of time, and have nothing to oppose it to, the word "time" is as obscure as the word "reality." The word "eternity" has no assignable sense at all when we cease to imagine we can grasp the essence of time by rational analysis (so as to define eternity by contrast). The language of Nicea and Chalcedon is metaphysical in that it supposes a total explicative scheme in which God and creation, time and eternity, the human body and soul, and their various relations can be systematically surveyed. Reading our tradition backward we would reduce these conciliar doctrines to their phenomenological foundation in the biblical narratives and interpret them as preservations of the integrity of those narratives within the constraints of metaphysical discourse. Narrative is of course a medium of communication much less adapted to Western reason than the metaphysical system which Christian theology for so long aspired to become. But this reference to narrative offers no simple panacea, for neither can the contemporary mind find itself immediately at home in the world of any of the biblical narratives. Nonetheless it has become more and more clear that our faith is no longer capable of naming Christ metaphysically, not because of a weakening of this faith, but because of an awareness that metaphysical names are no longer its appropriate vehicle. A contemporary Christian who said "I believe with all my heart that Christ is the pre-existent eternal Logos of God" would not, as far as the literal import of the words go, have achieved a particularly satisfactory contemporary confession of Christ, for this vaulting over time and eternity, and the horizon of thought it presupposes, remain unrelated to the many lines of questioning which lead to Christ in contemporary culture. The emergence of a confession of faith in Christ in our times would have to reflect its historical matrix more intrinsically. Only as Jesus emerges as the word (Logos) of God in and through the travail of our world can it begin to make sense to talk of the divinity of that Logos (cf. John 1:14; 1:1). There is no ecclesiastical shortcut past that contemplative process. In such a situation the divinity of Christ cannot, it seems, be the starting point for faith, but one of its furthest reaches, a dimension almost impossible to thematize. Thus, with the decline of metaphysical christology, we are thrown back into a situation reminiscent of New Testament times (and one in which there is also a certain lightening of the impediments to dialogue with other faiths).

Greek metaphysics had assigned a place to God long before its encounter with the biblical revelation, and the proclamation of the God of Abraham in the West has involved very complex negotiations with this metaphysical God, a tangled history of identifications and differentiations. But Greek metaphysics had also a place for Christ, as a principle of mediation and totality. The Platonic ideas, the Stoic Logos, the Plotinian *Nous* have the function of uniting the many through a single cosmic intellectual principle and of mediating between the many and the one. The two aspects of this function could be correlated with the ontological and the theological dimensions of ontotheology. Ontologically the Logos names the true being and intelligibility of things; theologically he brings them as a totality back to their ultimate ground in the divine. Thus the identification of the biblical God with the God of metaphysics made it inevitable that the figure of Christ would be identified with the mediating principle of metaphysics, and the principles of this double identification (whose roots in the interaction of Jewish and Hellenic in the preceding centuries we need not here examine) are already evident in Philo of Alexandria. From Arianism to Hegelianism, Western metaphysics has made the figure of Jesus Christ its own in various ways. He has functioned as the mediation and reconciliation of the transcendent and the immanent, the absolute and the relative, eternity and time, the universal and the particular. From Athanasius to Kierkegaard faith has resisted this metaphysical absorption of the Messiah, but without ever being able to recover in a lasting way a fully satisfying equivalent of the New Testament perspectives. Metaphysics was kept at bay, but not overcome. The place of Christ in the theologies of Augustine or Aquinas is still largely dictated by a desire for ontological coherence. Though they observe the rules of orthodox faith one has the impression at times that they continue to play the metaphysical game of finding connections and providing mediations between different spheres of being, but now in a higher key, as part of a spiritual exercise and with a constant supplementation of biblical "metaphor" and piety. This tradition is so strong that contemporary theologians inevitably gravitate towards its language as soon as they attempt to make any general statements about the meaning of Jesus Christ. By scrupulously confining oneself to a biblical and kerygmatic level of discourse, even at the cost of the intellectual dissatisfaction felt when one avoids metaphysics rather than thinking it through, one can avoid the most ineffective forms of metaphysical christology, and perhaps out of this practical response to the problem a new christological discourse with its own coherence is being formed But this renewal of christological language will not be complete without a conscious overcoming of the metaphysical heritage.

When we become aware of the metapysical shape of all traditional christologies and of the impossibility of dwelling within them
at a time when metaphysics has become questionable, we find our
faith pushed to the edge of dogma. The limits and fragility of
dogmatic utterance become apparent in a new way, so much so that
one can even speak of a "closure" of the dogmatic epoch, correlative
to the "closure" of metaphysics. This does not mean the abandonment of the dogmatic tradition but the emergence of a new deconstructive relationship to it, wherein it is reinterpreted as the history
of the Church's witness to its faith rather than as the building up of a
dogmatic system. The distinction between the activity of bearing
witness in a time of crisis (Nicea and Chalcedon as experienced by
the participants) and the acquisition of an increment of speculative
insight (Nicea and Chalcedon as seen through the lens of scholastic
theology) opens up a path to the figure of Jesus Christ as the one to
whom the Church has always borne witness, rather than as the
object of speculative, dogmatic claims. Unease with the language of
classical dogma thus ceases to be a distraction from faith and
becomes an integral component in its dialogue in its history, for this
unease is no longer tending to a skeptical denial of the dogmas but to
a phenomenological clarification of their significance as acts of
witness at a given historical juncture. Within the horizons of metaphysics Nicea and Chalcedon said all that could be said, and needed
to be said, about Christ. Yet for us the question about Christ and its
answer can no longer be formulated in that particular way. The
question "Who do you say that I am?" (Mark 8:29) continues to
sound, in a pre-metaphysical way, but the metaphysical tradition is
of only indirect assistance to us in our search for the contemporary
answer. It is of most assistance to us insofar as it is a tradition of the
witness of faith; it is an instructive counterexample insofar as it is a
tradition of cumulative speculative insight.

From this perspective we can also see more clearly than before
that there are no *pure* dogmas. Every doctrinal utterance is marked
by the confusions and contingencies of history, and we can never
"saturate the context" of a dogmatic utterance, either by fully
reconstructing its historical context, or by elucidating its terms in
function of the coordinates of a dogmatic system. The residual

opacity of all dogmatic formulations is not troubling to a hermeneutic which reads them as part of a history of witness. The language of the New Testament or the contemporary witness to Christ is no less opaque. In each case one says only what one can say within the language of one's time, nor can one hope to reach a language of ideal clarity with whose aid the entire range of historical languages of witness could be assessed and corrected. There remains only the open play of dialogue between present and past witnessings, and no language of orthodoxy can be constructed which is immune from this historical give and take. Thus the language of dogma is brought back into a living relationship with the other historical forms of Christian discourse, no longer hierarchically dominant over them. It is also reinserted in the contexts of life and praxis from which it originally emerged as a witness of faith but from which it had become divorced, due to the status of dominance conferred on it in the metaphysical structuration of Christianity. Catechetically and pastorally the stories of Nicea and Chalcedon can thus be told as part of the pre-history of the witness to Christ in contemporary faith, even though it is admitted that it is no longer possible to effectively address the mystery of Christ's divinity in this direct metaphysical style. The pastoral difficulties of communicating such an understanding of dogma are probably less than those presented by the classical presentation of dogma at its face value. Nor does the displacement I am here attempting to articulate imply a contradiction of the "binding" and "normative" status of the classical dogmas, though it profoundly changes the modality of our respect for them.

The overcoming of metaphysics in our thinking about Christ has a healing effect insofar as it allows one to articulate one's faith in Christ without being burdened by the wrong kind of relationship to the classical dogmas, either a relationship of forced conviction or skeptical unease. Others have tried to bring a similar integration to the discourse of contemporary faith in Christ by means of a speculative rehandling of the categories of Chalcedon, treating that Council, in Rahner's words, as a "beginning" rather than an "end." This, I feel, is fundamentally misguided. In what other discipline would one use a fifth century document as a "beginning" for speculative work? Is theology the only discipline in which history moves this slowly? The more conscious one becomes of the historical materiality of this or any other dogma, the more one realizes the impossibility of extracting it from its age. The texture of the dogmatic statement points backward to that which it was intended to defend, not forward to higher speculative syntheses. Whenever the dogma is assumed into a speculative system it is rewritten in the terms most meaningful to the maker of that system, and so it is no longer the historical doctrine of the Incarnation that one is dealing with. If one tries to correct this by historical research, the doctrine as historically reconstructed soon comes into tension with its stylized reinterpretation in the later system (just as, *a fortiori*, the original sense of Scripture turns out to be in tension with all later theological uses of it). Once one's hermeneutical inquiry allows itself to be caught in the texture of historicity, there is no way back to the purity of speculation. In this field speculative syntheses are possible only in blindness to history (as in the Scholastics) or through the imposition of speculative patterns of development on history (as in Hegel). The way for contemporary faith to grow in its understanding of Christ is not through systematic constructions which use history only as their point of departure, but through an ever-deepening interrogation of the historical witness, from its biblical origins, so that satisfying perspectives are opened up on its latent drift and its contemporary import. It is only in the context of such a quest for historical self-understanding that the results of past dogmatic conflicts can be theologically instructive today.

A good example of the ineffectuality of speculative revampings of dogma is provided by Edward Schillebeeckx when he attempts to focus the theological upshot of his examination of New Testament accounts of Jesus in the following Neo-Chalcedonian statements:

> Thus, thanks to the hypostatic identification of that in God which *starting from Jesus* is called "Son of God" with Jesus' personal-human mode of being, the *man* Jesus is a constitutive (filial) relation to the Father, a rapport that in the dynamic becoming of Jesus' human life grows into a deepening, mutual *enhypostasis,* with the resurrection as climactic point . . . in

him the one divine consciousness and absolute freedom, as "filially" lived within the Godhead (in perfect unity with the Father), is *in alienation* rendered man, as a humanly conscious centre of action and human (situated) freedom.[13]

Here Schillebeeckx constructs various strange entities on the basis of very fragile deductions from the biblical data, and then puts those entities together in a highly artificial synthesis. Can the biblical notion of the divine Logos be translated as "that in God which starting from Jesus is called 'Son of God'" or as "the one divine consciousness and absolute freedom, as 'filially' lived within the Godhead?" Does the hymnic context of the Johannine naming of Logos admit this literalistic transposition? What warrant is there for this talk of "consciousness," "freedom," and "living" in God? Test these words in the language of prayer and their incongruity becomes manifest: "O God, your consciousness is all-embracing, your freedom is absolute and they are lived filially by your eternal Son" . . . This untranslatability of theological constructions back into the language of prayer reveals their lack of a phenomenological ground. Indeed, one might be tempted to suggest that all theological discourse should be subjected to this test of translatability and that whatever in the language of theology could be shown neither to belong to the primary language of faith, nor to be directly at the service of that language and a necessary defense of its integrity, be discarded. This would imply a great simplification of the theological task and would also bring to light the essential difficulties to which it is exposed. It is not the business of theology to invent and resolve speculative conundrums, but rather to preserve and uphold the force and meaning of the very simple expressions operative in the primary languages of faith. Its task is to hold these languages free from speculative distraction, freeing them from the explicative developments in which they have been for centuries immersed. These historical efforts at speculative explanation cannot be simply forgotten. They serve as a valuable map of the possibilities of that kind of thinking, and a proof of its severe limitations. They also point the way to the more subtle critique and purification of the primary languages of faith which theology today must undertake, a critique led by the questions of faith, not by a desire for metaphysical insight. The data of faith do not demand further explanation, but a constant critical refocusing. The theological critique of the language of faith is at the service of that language, and cannot bring its primacy and adequacy into question. It has no mandate to replace that language or supplement it with a higher explanatory language. Its role is merely therapeutic.

How is this proposed test of translatability to be applied? Take the expression "hypostatic union." Could one say in prayer: "Lord Jesus, whose humanity is hypostatically one with the Word of God?" Could one even introduce this phrase in a credal formula: "I believe in the hypostatic union"? The question bears as much on tone as on content, and the test would demand a fine ear for the appropriate. It seems to me that there is no use for the phrase "hypostatic union" in the primary language of faith. But it can be justified as preserving the integrity of that language, at least at a certain juncture of history, in opposition to the Nestorian and Monophysite interpretations of that language. Perhaps the phrase itself can be retained in theology only as shorthand for the historical defense of the integrity of the primary language of faith at Chalcedon, and has no direct use in contemporary theological discourse, the opposing heresies having died out, along with the very horizon in which both the heresies and their rebuttal were framed. The upshot of applying the text of translatability to the words "hypostatic union" is thus to reveal the secondary, reflexive, and methodological character of the expression as a rule for the use of religious language rather than part of that language itself. Can Schillebeeckx's language be defended on the same grounds? I do not think so. Such a phrase as "the one divine consciousness and absolute freedom" is a speculative doubling of the biblical naming of God which does not serve to retrieve critically the force of that naming, freeing it from misuse, but seems rather to obscure its impact. Most of Schillebeeckx's other coinages also fail the test, being neither part of the primary language of faith (one could not say, "I believe in the resurrection, climax of the mutual *enhypostasis* of Father and Son") nor a necessary defense of it nor a successful critical refocusing. It might be objected that this test of translatability is an unjustified one and that such language as Schillebeeckx uses can be recommended on the grounds of its speculative elegance. But in what terms is this elegance judged? In terms of the speculative drive for a comprehensive explanatory scheme? It does not seem to me that this speculative drive can harmoniously coexist with faith's more basic quest for a convincing language or that the comprehensive explanatory scheme can be superimposed on the event of revelation. Judged from the point of view of faith they are a cumbersome imposition and whatever speculative satisfaction they might generate is as fundamentally inelegant as would be the appearance of rhyming couplets in a treatise on economics. We cannot step outside the horizon of the tradition of faith in the message of the resurrection, so as to consider its metaphysical structure as one of mutual *enhypostasis*. If we really could adopt this metaphysical vantage point it would serve as a controlling framework for our reading of the Gospel narratives, preventing us from entering into the horizons of contemplation opened up by such words as "I and the Father are one" (John 10:30) which we would immediately translate into terms of mutual *enhypostasis*. But why, it may be objected, should contemplation not allow a precipitate of such metaphysical understanding, as a kind of by-product? In fact it is not contemplation but the lack of it which gives rise to such metaphysics. Absorbed in the given, contemplation does not seek to muddy its clarities through the language of secondary rationalization. It is only when the (already secondary and defensive) language of dogma is misinterpreted as a language of speculative insight that one seeks to solve the apparent problems of that language by a further speculative breakthrough. All such breakthroughs in turn generate further problems so that the task of speculation is infinite. Nor can the speculative process be curtailed unless it is stopped at its origins. A contemplative abiding in the message of faith pulls against the speculative urge, revealing even its initial questions to be beside the point. It may be that even the Fathers of Nicea became entrapped in the speculative cast of mind underlying Arianism, arguing with it on its own terms, and that they were not entirely clear in their own minds about the merely defensive status of the *homoousion*. If they had been I do not think they would have made it part of the primary language of faith by inserting it in a Creed (albeit a creed for bishops). If this was a fateful precedent, launching Christianity on its costly though instructive speculative career, or at least officially confirming the speculative direction it had already begun to take, it is a precedent which we today may reverse in light of its consequences, reading Nicea as a defensive footnote to John 20:28 ("My Lord and my God") and reading this in turn from its contemplative context as articulating, in a way that is perhaps no longer unproblematic, the experience of a community of faith.

Perhaps my opposition of faith and speculation is an overly simple presentation of the case. Both faith and speculation can mean different things in different contexts. How faith in practice dethrones speculation is a matter that could be worked out in different ways in many concrete issues. The reduction of speculation to the status of a critical, methodological discourse keeping watch over the words of faith, the thorough subjection of theology to faith, the abolition of the illusion that theology has something positive to *add* to faith, is a therapeutic process as varied in its methods as the diversity of the speculative enterprises with which it has to deal, and as fertile in the invention of new critical strategies and interpretative perspectives as the tenacious vitality of the metaphysical illusion makes necessary. Why is that illusion so vital? In part because it is not all illusion, and is triumphantly sustained by a sense of the logical and rational character of its procedures which have worked so well for two millennia. The illusion resides in the tiny nuance that separates the language of faith from the language of faith as heard by metaphysical ears. The first is the language of the believer for whom faith is an end in itself; the second is a language used by someone whose ulterior intention is to raise that language to the transparency of the concept. The first language commits its speaker in trust to the unexplored paths of grace and providence, to the expectation of the fulfillment of God's gracious promise. The second, though it may be verbally the same, is oriented differently, towards the rational mastery of a doctrinal system in which the Word of God is securely placed, so that it cannot any longer challenge and unsettle the basic horizons of our understanding. For the first language "My Lord and my God" represents an apex of contemplative insight to which one is always underway, though the way may involve a deconstruction of the Johannine categories. For the second the divinity of Christ is an axiom on the basis of which one can build up speculative expositions of the system of Christian truths.

The incompatibility of the two languages, the impossibility of reconciling an ongoing phenomenological apprehension of the faith data with a speculative grasp of their sense by means of a metaphysical scheme, is apparent from the unreality with which Schillebeeckx's Chalcedonian diction infects everything it touches. Even the language in which he refers to the humanity of Jesus is such as to transform that humanity into a remote metaphysical quantity, so that it is no longer the source or vehicle of an address to our faith but rather a screen inhibiting faith, a problematic entity which involves faith in the kind of puzzles which only speculation can untangle— and of course speculation cannot untangle them. When a human being has become problematically human no amount of speculation can make him unproblematically human again. The reality of Christ's humanity is best preserved by cutting off at their source the kinds of questions and the clumsy formulations which tend to undermine it. "Personal-human mode of being," "dynamic becoming of Jesus' human life," "a humanly conscious center of action"—the oddity of these descriptions is that we would never think of using them of another human being. A human so deliberately described is already less than, or only partly, human. The purpose of the descriptions is to "sight" Jesus's humanity in a different way from that in which the humanity of other historical figures is taken for granted. The totalizing grasp of Jesus's humanity takes it out of the open horizon of historical encounter and arranges it in a tidy metaphysical package, which is then easily situated in relationship to the divine mode of being which has been similarly packaged. The terminology of "relation" and "alienation" suffices to tie the two together. Basically what has happened is that the phenomenological reality both of the man Jesus and of God has been lost—along with the phenomenological reality of the brokenness and open-endedness of our access to them in faith—so that what Schillebeeckx links together in his scheme of "relations" and "alienation" are no more than reified abstractions. In cultivating an objective discourse which

can embrace God and humanity, time and eternity, and which can
be spun out independently of the context of the primary utterance of
faith, Schillebeeckx is embarked on the way that leads at best to
some variety of Hegelianism. But the situation or perspective of
faith is irrevocably lost if one allows it to be sublated into the
medium of the Hegelian Concept. Theology, attentive to the danger
Hegel's system lights up, must not allow itself to overleap the situation of faith. There is no higher approach to revealed truth somewhere beyond faith. What may appear to be such invariably turns
out to belong to the all too familiar terrain of Western metaphysics.
Nor can one go half way with Hegel, making the adjustments orthodoxy demands. When one develops accounts of God or Christ which
are no longer intrinsically dependent on the primary language of
faith, but have attained a certain autonomous objectivity, then one
has broken the existential connections of that primary language and
replaced them with the very different stance which speculative
thinking adopts in regard to its themes. One is within the Hegelian
enclosure, and no amount of immanent correction can help one find
the exit. All of speculative christology today moves within Hegel's
orbit, however vigilantly it still clings to its Chalcedonian and Scholastic origins. Rahner, Kasper, Moltmann, Pannenberg and the process christologists seem to have succumbed to this last form of the
enfolding capacity of metaphysics, from which the only escape is
through the step back to the poverty of a faith which is content to be
only faith.

Many other illustrations of this theological malady could be
given. For instance:

> God's knowing and willing in his continuing creative activity
> must be seen as occurring within the divine essence, as imma-
> nent realities whereby that essence is always in "movement."
> In such movement God's essence takes on ever new forms. This
> conception obviously frees the cross of Christ from the static
> juridicism that is operative in satisfaction theories.[14]

In exorcising the dreaded death's head of a "static divine essence"
theologians fail to notice that what is really paralyzing their thought
is the very horizon in which such a conception of God is possible, a

horizon without phenomenological roots in the experience of faith. Unfortunately, in attempting to make God "dynamic" instead they become more than ever entrapped in talk of the divine essence, and find themselves now somehow empowered to tell us all that is going on in that dark place—"knowing," "willing," "continuing creative activity," "movement," "ever new forms." Then the cross of Christ is explained from this height, in exactly the same procedure as in more static versions of metaphysical theology. The Congregation for the Doctrine of the Faith tends to worry about the variations from orthodoxy this revisionist metaphysics produces. Perhaps the real error of such theologizing lies in the incompatibility of its basic horizon with that of faith, an incompatibility no unhistorical return to Chalcedon can possibly correct. It should be noted that it is not Schillebeeckx's faith in the truth and irreversibility of the decision of Chalcedon which misleads him in the passage quoted, but the lack of an adequate method of situating the witness of the Council historically and theologically. Meanwhile, the ultra-conservative claim that the categories of Chalcedon are "notions which have a universal value and can be understood by people of any civilization, of any epoch" and "belong to the intellectual patrimony of humanity, what could be called an essential language permitting all people to understand one another"[15] begs not only the question whether typically Greek notions like *physis* and *hypostasis* can be not merely inserted but integrated into other cultures,[16] but also the more basic one, whether the entire horizon within which the Chalcedonian debate was possible can be convincingly reconstructed in post-Kantian minds.

The following critique of Gutierrez's liberation theology provides another illustration of the malfunctioning of metaphysical perspectives in contemporary theology:

An orthodox understanding of the Incarnation simply cannot be reconciled with a dialectical interpretation of history. No dialectical *tour de force* can integrate the epiphany of the Absolute in time with the vision of history as an ongoing struggle of the oppressed to realize the untested feasibility of liberation. This is so because the Incarnation makes God the primary agent or "Subject" in human history, while the dialectical vision makes "it possible for men to enter the historical process as responsible subjects." If "history is one" in the sense required by the dialectical vision, then the Incarnation must be regarded as myth.[17]

What McCann sees here as "an orthodox understanding of the Incarnation" is in reality a metaphysical one, in which "time" and "history" are sighted from an impossible vantage point beyond them, and in which God then appears as a "Subject" above and beyond history, the timeless "Absolute" for whom history is at most the theater of an "epiphany." The resultant antinomy between human freedom and divine is one of the many false problems to which the confident assumption of a metaphysical vantage point leads. Since we have no fixed, objectified grasp of either human or divine freedom to begin with, but only an ongoing experience of the phenomenological realms of human historical freedom and what the Bible or the Holy Spirit suggests about "divine freedom," it is premature to suppose that there is necessarily a conflict or tension between the two, and in fact the phenomenological data points in the other direction (when God is experienced as freeing and enabling Love). Thus it transpires that it is not the Incarnation which is a myth, but the frozen view of it which holds McCann captive and which Gutierrez effectively begins to overcome, by his reliance on the perspectives opened by Scripture.

The fortunes of the Christ of metaphysics could be followed far and wide throughout contemporary theological literature. Speculative expositions of Gethsemane and Golgotha, or even of Auschwitz, are perhaps the most unseemly consequences of this metaphysical christology, and the clearest mark of its basic fault.[18] One of the ways in which Jesus Christ is revealed to contemporary faith is precisely through his withdrawal from all such systems of comprehension. For a long time the Church has seen Christ as the Logos in which all aspiration after speculative totality and cosmic integration find their point of rest and their rich completion. Yet Christ crucified eludes the role thus assigned to him, and by this withdrawal subverts the culture of ecclesiastical logocentrism. All cosmic and speculative Christs, mediators of the one and the many, concrete universals, omega points, turn out to be hollow idols when confronted with the "wisdom of the cross." The overthrow of Christic triumphalism through the unobtrusive poverty of what can convincingly be said about the Crucified and Risen One today spells a kenosis which has nothing to do with the speculative "alienations" of metaphysical christology. The emptying here is not a Hegelian negation leading to a higher synthesis, but the opening of a way in which faith and the thinking of faith must unconditionally abide. This way of faith feels merely "provisional" and "elementary" to the speculative mind, but the provision of elements, the recovery of basics, is in reality the highest task of theology. Its flight from this task has generated a false wealth of speculation and a correlative impoverishment at the level of the vision and engagement of faith.

Rahner's Foundations

Perhaps the two "systematic theologians" of this century who have most constantly sought to reroot theological discourse in the extentiality of faith are Karl Rahner and Karl Barth. Yet despite the renewal they accomplished, both of them remain inhibited by their inability to focus the influence of metaphysics in their thinking and to overcome that influence effectively. Unless they are subjected to a deconstructive reading their influence on contemporary theology is thus bound to reinforce the same inhibitions and distract another generation of theologians and preachers from the quest for *die Sache selbst*. It is important to try to focus clearly where things went wrong in the projects of these thinkers.

These remarks of Fergus Kerr may serve to launch our critique of Rahner:

> "Le plus profond, c'est la peau," said Paul Valéry: the skin is what is the deepest thing. It would of course be enormously difficult to rethink Christian theology after the spread of such views. Everybody wants Rahner's transcendental anthropology to be true. Certainly very little theological work since Wittgenstein has taken his ideas seriously. For that matter it is not at

all clear that Christianity could now survive without its traditional Platonism. But couldn't it be tried? Doesn't it *have* to be
tried? The work of curing ourselves of the inveterate idea that
we can get outside our world in some more substantial sense
than that we talk about our world would no doubt prove labori-
ous, particularly for religiously minded people.[19]

Kerr claims that a Wittgensteinian reading of Rahner's *Foundations of Christian Faith* would reveal its structure to rest on a
confusion between the trick inscribed in language whereby we can
objectify and surpass any given reality, e.g., "the human condition,"
"the world," "the data of experience," and a real noetic openness to
the infinite. It might be objected that were one to apply a Wittgensteinian suspicion of linguistic traps to the discourse of theology it
might never be able to get off the ground at all. But unless theology
learns at least to live with the constraint of that suspicion, as an
uneasy conscience whose exigencies can perhaps never be perfectly
met, there is little hope that its language will ever credibly match the
skeptical consciousness of its contemporary audience. Faith does not
lessen, but should rather increase, linguistic responsibility. Here I
should like to supplement Kerr's remarks by showing that Rahner
cannot defend his language on the grounds of phenomenological
fidelity to the experience of faith. Its facilities do not reflect a
trusting openness to the mystery of God, but rather a flight from the
poverty of authentic faith.

Rahner's language moves habitually in the dimension of "transcendence," a dimension which provides not only the transcendent
but the transcendental ground of all human activities and which can
also be brought to light in a phenomenological study of human
experience. But the assurance with which Rahner passes from everyday reality to the infinite mystery of God, by means of this remarkable conjunction of the theological, the transcendental, and the
phenomenological, must arouse doubts whether the sturdy and
opaque texture of the world can be so easily transcended towards its
infinite foundations. How reliable is the transcendental logic which
engineers the transition? Much of it seems to rely on simple oppositions of "finite" and "infinite," on arguments of the sort Augustine

Shutte invokes against the viewpoint of Kerr above: "unless we have a natural orientation beyond the world of finite things to something infinite there is no possibility of our sharing in the divine life."[20] If we reason to God on so shaky a basis as the presumption that the words "finite" and "infinite" have a clear meaning then the facility of our talk about God is no sign of a breakthrough, but rather bespeaks a lack of rigor. Without examining these weaknesses further, I observe that they are neither corrected nor compensated for by the appeal to experiential data, for the phenomenological fleshing out of the transcendental deduction in Rahner always comes after the speculative fact, a varnish on its bareness, as when he speaks of

> the subjective, unthematic, necessary and unfailing consciousness of the knowing subject that is co-present in every spiritual act of knowledge, and the subject's openness to the unlimited expanse of all possible reality.[21]

This portrait of human consciousness is a metaphysics of self-presence derived from Hegel and Aquinas, serenely innocent of the "wounded cogito" revealed by psychoanalysis and structuralism. It is by the appeal of his metaphysical convictions that Rahner persuades, not by a concord between these convictions and the phenomenality of human existence. In every such regrounding of his thought in the immediacy of a (transcendental) experience, Rahner fails to take quite seriously his own principle that the transcendental events of freedom, self-presence, and the like are grasped only through their categoreal mediations. The events are focused by means of a double metaphysical myth. On the one hand the idea that they can in some way be objects of immediate experience is never relinquished, though it is admitted that such experience must ever elude reflective, categoreal articulation. On the other hand, these events are posited and structured as the transcendental *foundations* of everyday experience and concepts. The pathos of immediacy and the pathos of founding blend to give a prestigious mythic presence to these transcendental foundational events within Rahner's system. Haunted by the inaccessible immediacy of the soul's self-presence and presence to God, and convinced that the foundations which make revelation intelligible are to be found nowhere else, Rahner succeeds in visualizing these empty transcendental reaches and opaque originary events more vividly and with more imaginative power than is possible for him in the case of the "surface" data of experience of revelation.

Rahner's distinctions between origins and mediations, transcendental and categoreal, immediacy and thematization, take shape under the control of a metaphysical viewpoint which allows no obscurity in these distinctions, no possibility that the factors distinguished might blend into one another. Yet in practice their functioning in his discourse, under pressure of the double pathos just mentioned, can be somewhat inconsistent. Movement within this system of distinctions is more often than not presented as a step back from a theoretical construction to the experience founding it. Thus the reflective articulation of the structures of knowledge and freedom is referred back to the concrete, finally ineffable, fact of their immediate self-presence of the free, knowing human spirit. But this unthematized original fact never becomes the focus of an autonomous phenomenological inquiry. It is approached from within the metaphysical perspective and articulated solely in terms of that perspective. "We think of a concrete object *within* the *infinite* and apparently empty horizon of thinking itself . . . thinking is conscious of itself"[22]—this is not phenomenology but metaphysical construction; it has nothing to do, for example, with Heidegger's reflections on "thinking" and it is even too global and general to have much in common with what might be its nearer inspiration, the analyses of the activities of the mind in Hegel's *Phenomenology of Mind*. Matters are not improved when this picture of thinking is equated with an "original, unthematic and unreflexive knowledge of God" and when it is claimed that "that thematic knowledge of God . . . which we have in explicitly religious activity and philosophical reflection" is merely an articulation of "what we already know implicitly about ourselves in the depths of our personal self-realization."[23] Neither the thematic nor the unthematic poles are focused here with phenomenological precision, and the account of the relation between them overlooks the complexity of the formations of both religious and philosophical language, and the sharpness of the phenomenological contrast between the thematizations of

God in prayer and philosophy. Both are grasped in terms of the governing model of thematization, a model which seems to place the analyst outside the process of language as if he had some means of independent access to its unthematized foundations.

The chronic ineffectiveness of Rahner's gestures towards phenomenology can only be explained by a reluctance to relinquish the mastery over experience which his categories promise. His loss of contact with *die Sache selbst* can be illustrated from the very passage in which he tries to flesh out his theory by imitating a celebrated paragraph from Heidegger's *Introduction to Metaphysics*. I quote both passages, giving the German words in Rahner which have a Heideggerian resonance.

Rahner:

> The individual person, of course, experiences this fundamental and inescapable structure (*Grundverfassung*) best in that basic situation of his own existence (*Grundbefindlichkeit seines Daseins*) which occurs with special intensity for him as an individual. If, therefore, he is really to understand this reflection on "proofs" for God's existence, the individual person must reflect precisely upon whatever is the clearest experience *for him*: on the luminous and incomprehensible (*unumgreifbar*) light of his spirit; on the capacity for absolute questioning (*Ermöglichung der absoluten Fraglichkeit*) which a person directs against himself and which seemingly reduces him to nothing (*nichtigend*), but in which he reaches radically beyond himself (*sich . . . übergreift*); on annihilating anxiety (*die nichtigende Angst*), which is something quite different from fear of a definite object (*gegenständliche Furcht*) and is prior to the latter as the condition of its possibility; on that joy which surpasses all understanding (lit. which no longer has a name); on the absolute moral obligation in which a person really goes beyond himself (*von sich abspringt*); on the experience of death in which he faces himself in his absolute powerlessness. Man reflects on these and on many other modes of the basic and transcendental experience of human existence (*transzendentale Grunderfahrung des Daseins*). Because he

experiences himself as finite in his self-questioning (*in seiner Fraglichkeit als Endlicher*), he is not able to identify himself with the ground (*Grund*) which discloses itself (*sich gibt*) in this experience as what is innermost and at the same time what is absolutely different. The explicit proofs for God's existence only make thematic this fundamental structure and its term.[24]

Heidegger:

> Everyone at some time, or perhaps even from time to time, is brushed by the hidden might of this question, without quite grasping what is happening to him. In a great despondency for example, when all weight and importance is ebbing away from things and every significance is obscured, the question arises. Perhaps struck only once like the muted stroke of a bell, which sounds into one's existence and gradually dies away again. In a great rejoicing of heart the question is there, because here all things are transformed and seem to be about us for the first time, so that it is just as if we could rather grasp that they are not, then that they are, and are in the way they are. When time lies heavy on our hands the question is there, when we are equally removed from despondency and rejoicing, when however, the stubborn routineness of what is spreads out a wilderness in which it seems to us indifferent whether what is is or whether it is not, wherewith the question again awakens in a peculiar form: Why is there in general anything and not rather nothing?[25]

There is a curious historical irony in Rahner's use of this lecture of Heidegger's (which he may have attended while a student at Freiburg in 1935). *An Introduction to Metaphysics* marks an ambivalent watershed in Heidegger's thinking. It is still nominally governed by the project of the earlier writings, the project of metaphysics as "inquiry beyond or over beings which aims to recover them as such and as a whole for our grasp."[26] This project is implicit in the "fundamental question" of the passage quoted. In 1936 Heidegger first calls this project "ontotheology" and embarks on the radical critique of metaphysics found in the Nietzsche lectures and the associated essays.[27] In 1935 Heidegger is still uncertain and anxious about the ultimate character of Being, which may be gracious or threatening. Medard Boss relates that Heidegger was only conscious of one of his dreams, an anxiety dream in which, interrogated by three professors, he could not find the answer to their question. After the discovery of *Ereignis,* Heidegger dreamed no more. This too should probably be located in 1936. It is commemorated in the unpublished *Beiträge zur Philosophie* of 1936-38.[28] Heidegger's fundamental attitude now becomes one of *Gelassenheit* and the voluntaristic emphasis still evident in *An Introduction to Metaphysics* is overcome (especially in the deconstruction of Nietzsche's Will to Power). The turning to the language of the poets at this time further signals the impossibility for Heidegger to remain any longer within the frames of reference of the metaphysical tradition. When he finally published the transitional *Introduction* in 1953, Heidegger inserted passages between square brackets which correct the metaphysical tenor of the main text. Jean Wahl correctly observed that this *Einführung* to metaphysics might better be described as an *Ausführung.* The irony of Rahner's reading is that he uses Heidegger's text not as a pointer beyond metaphysics but as a way back into it. He thus misses the most precious and original elements in Heidegger's thinking and uses his phenomenology to cement and enrich the metaphysics it was designed to overcome. As Kerr remarks, "to go on saying the kind of thing outlined above, after having studied with Heidegger, shows very considerable powers of resistance to the master's main thoughts."[29]

Rahner's six examples of basic existential situations are far less convincing than Heidegger's three, lacking the poetic precision of what Heidegger evokes. The joy Heidegger describes—a *Jubel des Herzens*—may be enigmatic to the reader, but that some very precise experience (perhaps of being in love) is designated can scarcely be doubted. Rahner's nameless joy in contrast remains incurably nebulous. Whether the light of the intellect or the capacity for absolute questioning really deserve the titles of *Grundbefindlichkeiten* is doubtful. These are the epistemological foundations of the Rahnerian and Corethian varieties of transcendental Thomism respectively, but it is only with some solicitation that they can be

presented as bedrock phenomenological events. Nor is it clear that
our basic experiences of our existence are immediately experiences
of the "inescapable structure" of our finite relatedness to an infinite
ground. Heidegger's basic experiences produce a question, a question which need not necessarily demand a metaphysical answer, but
can issue in a contemplative letting be of beings. Rahner's experiences, in contrast, rather suddenly present us with a metaphysics
of finite and infinite. What makes this less than convincing is the
suspicion that the experiences themselves have already been stylized
in function of the metaphysical scheme. Rahner is content to use
Heidegger's terminology, and makes no effort at an originary naming of the experiences he evokes. This too suggests that he has no
access to an originary experience which is more than a verification
and illustration of his metaphysical anthropology. Generally it may
be observed that the derivative character of theological language—
whether derived from Scripture, metaphysics or existentialism—
testifies to a lack of engagement with the texture of experience.
Metaphysics makes such engagement impossible, subjecting even
the scriptural and existential vocabulary to its frames of understanding, so that it is heard as "jargon" and "padding" and no longer as
the bearer of the phenomenological truth which the metaphysical
system cannot freely welcome. Thus in its language theology does
continual violence to the texture of experience.

But if this is the degree of Rahner's fidelity to the data of human
existence, what can we expect his apprehension of the data of revelation to be? Alas, these are subjected to a process of transcendental
volatilization whose effect is to make impossible any detailed attention to the Word of Scripture. "Revelation in the proper, although
transcendental sense"[30] happens somewhere in the depths of the
human spirit in its transcendent openness to mystery, and God's
saving deeds in history are no more than the exteriorization of this
inner happening. "The self-communication of God to man in grace
as the transcendental constitution of man"[31] similarly anticipates
the external events of the Incarnation and the outpouring of the
Spirit. It is not particularly reassuring to be told that the transcendental "event of God's self-communication" "precisely *as transcendental* . . . is a real history"[32] so that we may therefore speak of

the "transcendental history of revelation."[33] This transcendental
doubling of history is intended to provide the data of revelation with
foundations and conditions of possibility which will enable us to
make sense of them. The result is that the transcendental system
steals the show from the data and robs them of their intrinsic meaning. A clear instance of this may be found in Rahner's handling of
christology.

He writes:

> At an age in the history of the human spirit when there is a
> transcendental anthropology over and beyond a purely empiri-
> cal, a posteriori and descriptive anthropology, and when it can
> no longer be overlooked, an explicit transcendental Christology
> is also necessary, a Christology which asks about the a priori
> conditions in man which make the coming of the message of
> Christ possible. Its absence in the traditional theology runs the
> risk that the assertions of the traditional theology will be
> deemed simply a mythological (in the pejorative sense) overlay
> on historical events, or that we shall have no criterion by means
> of which we are able to distinguish in the traditional Christol-
> ogy between a genuine reality of faith and an interpretation of
> it which is no longer capable of mediating the content of faith
> to us today.[34]

It seems to me clear that Rahner is mistaken about the historical
status and the ineluctability of his transcendental anthropology.
Whether the alternatives to such an anthropology are exhausted by
the rubrics of "empirical, a posteriori and descriptive" is also doubtful. A philosophical and poetic questioning about human being is
surely conceivable which need not fit into the structures of Rahner's
transcendental thinking. Indeed Rahner's transcendental sketch of
human being appears obsolete from the point of view of the principal
movements of art, science, and thought in this century and can only
be a target for dismantling when exposed to their critique. Conversely, Rahner appears to have no means of entering into dialogue
with contemporary literature or philosophy or with the human sciences. His claims for the comprehensiveness of his anthropology
thus function in a void. "The a priori conditions in man which make

the coming of the message of Christ possible" do not seem to me to be an important, or even a possible, object of investigation. Can any generalizing discourse about human being do justice to the pluralism of its manifestations? And have we so clearly grasped "the message of Christ" as to be ready to go on to examine its conditions of possibility? If our thought is engaged by the foreground phenomena of human existence and the Gospel message we quickly find that these claim our thought so completely that there is no room to proceed beyond them to their transcendental background. Transcendental theorizing is possible only at the cost of an extreme simplification and stylization of that about which one wishes to theorize. Even to take the first step of ensconcing oneself in the transcendental horizon one must consign the phenomena to the status of mere appearance, in the classical Platonic gesture. Rahner has not feared to pay the cost of transcendental theory. The only lesson to be derived from the results is Goethe's one: "Look for nothing behind phenomena: they themselves are what is to be learned." "A mythological overlay on historical events" is exactly what Rahner's transcendentalism produces, no less so than Chalcedon, uninterpreted, could do. In no sense does it provide a criterion for eliciting from traditional discourse the buried "genuine reality of faith." Instead faith is abducted into the recesses of transcendental consciousness and becomes disengaged from the historical contexts in which alone Christ is to be encountered. Devotionalism gives life to the resultant phantasmal abstractions. Faith finds an inward liberation in rendering itself immune to the concrete texture of contemporary life with its burdens and questions, hopes and visions. This faith declares itself open to the future, open to the world, when all that it is really open to is an abstract infinite. It is a faith which has returned to fundamentals and redeemed itself from the alienation of the older Neo-Scholasticism. But these fundamentals turn out on examination to consist only in a mystified inward sense of freedom, luminous self-presence, loving acceptance of finitude. Here one has to raise the ideological question: is the immense influence of Rahner's theology as innocent an affair as it seems? For decades his works have circulated throughout the Catholic Church as representing the *ne plus ultra* of theological enlightenment.

Enthusiasm for Rahner has helped to keep "dogmatic theology" alive as the central discipline in theological curricula. He continued to produce answers when everyone else seemed to bring only questions. Rahner's universal acceptability is associated with the immense importance the classical dogmatic formulae have for his thought. In fact the prominence given to these formulae goes hand in hand with the ahistorical mystification of his transcendentalism. Was this mystification somehow attractive to the Catholic mind, providing a shelter for a while against more radical questioning? Was the questioning Rahner served to keep at bay feared as simply destructive, a hemorrhage of faith (so much had faith become identified with its metaphysical embodiment)?

> Anyone who cannot understand what the hypostatic union and the interchange of predicates mean . . . in any other concepts except those of this classical ideology of Incarnation will judge this classical Christology to be in a direct sense *the only* way of expressing our faith in the true relationship between Jesus and God, and our faith in our relationship to him, and hence he will retain it. . . . Anyone who thinks he is able to express what is meant in the classical Christology of the Incarnation in another way without doing violence to what is meant, he may express it differently. This presupposes that he respects the official teaching of the church as a critical norm for his own way of expressing it.[35]

This disjunction is not complete, for it overlooks the common case of those who are convinced that the classical formula is inadequate yet have no new formula to propose. Though they respect Chalcedon as a valid decision in the history of faith, and do not contradict it, they know that true respect for this norm can be shown only in enacting the contemporary equivalent of the intention of faith it originally expressed (and which of course cannot itself be independently reconstructed). They may not have found this equivalent, which is unlikely to take the form of another quasi-metaphysical account of the matter, but neither can they retain the old formula without misgivings, still less regard it as the only way of expressing the truth intended. If a formula dies on one (because the metaphysical horizon has died) one is simply not free to retain it, though one remembers it with respect. The emergence of an adequate witnessing to the humanity and divinity of Jesus in our language of faith cannot be effected simply by wishing it. Like Chalcedon it may be the work of centuries. Nor is it likely ever again to take the totally direct form Chalcedon attempted to implement. Meanwhile our christological thinking takes the form of an ongoing quest. Rahner's disjunction seems to divide his own consciousness curiously, for he approves those who see the classical formula as the only way to express the truth, on the one hand, while at the same time not foreclosing the possibility of another way. To which side of the disjunction does he himself then belong? It almost sounds as if he is resolving the crisis of Chalcedonian theology by a political settlement. Chalcedon either is or is not adequate. If not adequate its deficiencies can be supplemented by a speculative treatment continuous with its own metaphysical texture, which is the solution of most Catholic theologians, or these deficiencies can prompt us to a rerooting of the doctrine in the originary act of faith which is its matrix, which in practice means a deconstruction of the Chalcedonian language with a view of forging a new language more attuned to contemporary awareness of the limits of language and more open than Chalcedon could be, or at least open in a different way, to the phenomenality of biblical revelation. Of the three alternatives I suggest that only the third has any chance of communicating the biblical revelation honestly and effectively in our "postmetaphysical" horizon.

I fear these remarks on Rahner will seem very harsh to those who venerate him, rightly, as one who restored to faith its freedom of speech in a language better matched to the spiritual and intellectual aspirations of the modern world than that of any previous professional Catholic theologian. But Troy did not fall in one night; and an excessive adulation of Rahner could well now serve only to thwart the liberative intentions of his work, which others must continue. This is even more the case with Barth, whose true revolutionary potential lies buried beneath the monuments he and his disciples built over it.

Barth's Partial Overcoming

Barth's quest for the integral phenomenality of revelation is the nearest theological equivalent of the thirst for bedrock reality which sustains the philosophy of Husserl and Heidegger. But this revolutionary quest was increasingly engulfed in what seems in retrospect a misguided restoration of ecclesiastical biblicism,[36] so much so that his name is now more likely to be invoked by those who wish to bolster up some cumbersome neo-orthodoxy, than by those who seek an ally in their protest against the ever-renascent unreality of religious speech on the lips of preacher or professor. Yet these protestors might be the true continuators of Barth's path of overcoming, if they could retrieve his No to metaphysicizing of Christianity and extend it to the uncriticized metaphysics which pervaded the texture of his own affirmations. One metaphysical assumption underlying Barth's and other contemporary theologies[37] is that of an absolute quantity called "Revelation" which functions as a foundation of epistemological certitude. The rigidity of this principle must be shattered if the biblical radicality of Barth's thought is to be retrieved. The Word of God unfolds in our history in a much subtler way than the traditional mystificatory notions of the authority of Scripture can recognize. Biblicism pits Scripture against metaphysics, but in the process structures Scripture as an alternative set of (metaphysical) principles. But Scripture effectively overcomes metaphysical theology only in the constant opening up and unfolding of the questions it sows; this prolonged echo of the scriptural word through history puts the letter of Scripture itself constantly in question, for that letter cannot foreclose the future of the tradition of questioning after God which it initiates. If we keep the questions of Scripture open we can overcome all idolatrous encroachments on them; if we close these questions our biblicism itself becomes idolatrous. Insofar as he built uncritically on Scripture Barth's theology is a theology of Logos rather than Pneuma, an edifice of assertions which paralyzes the movement of questioning faith.

Barth worked on the tradition with a view to recalling all its elements to the originary event of faith's encounter with Revelation:

The content of the Word of God . . . will always be an
authentic and definite encounter with the Lord of man, a revelation which man cannot achieve himself, the revelation of
something new which can only be told him. It will also be the
limitation of his existence by the absolute "out there" of his
Creator, a limitation on the basis of which he can understand
himself only as created out of nothing and upheld over nothing.
It will also be a radical renewal and therewith an obviously
radical criticism of the whole of his present existence, a
renewal and a criticism on the basis of which he can understand himself only as a sinner living by grace and therefore as a
lost sinner closed up against God on his side. Finally it will be
the presence of God as the One who comes . . . a presence on
the basis of which he can understand himself only as hastening
toward this future of the Lord and expecting Him.[38]

The density of the dialectical writing here attempts to catch the
specific force of the biblical Word, undiluted by speculative comprehension, though it may be that the patterning of the situation of
faith as here described is still a little too schematic and prone to
become the vehicle of a speculative play itself.

In his rewriting of Christian dogmatics, Barth constantly tries to
reduce metaphysical statements about God to their biblical
equivalents. God's "being," for example, is apprehended as event
and act, as his loving in freedom. The Trinity is envisioned as
"revealer, revelation, and revealedness" in the event of revelation.
He returns to the biblical narratives underlying the themes of creation, providence, grace, and reconciliation and reduces dogmatic
theology to an elaborate orchestration of these narratives. Dogma
and dogmatics, the usual bearers of metaphysics within theology,
are subordinated to faith's hearing of the Word proclaimed. It would
not be untrue to say that Barth's entire enterprise proceeds under
the sign of the phenomenality of God—which includes the notes of
his hiddenness and "aseity." But Barth's language often falls short
of this project, and the name of God, which occurs in it so regularly,
can seem a convenient abstraction, invoked too often, too assuredly,
so that we remain in doubt if the majestic presence sweeping

through his voluminous pages is one of which we can genuinely say:
"That is God."

Barth saw himself as fighting metaphysics on two fronts, in the
form of Protestant modernism on the one hand and Roman Catholic
natural theology on the other:

> We stand before the fact of heresy. Concretely, we stand before
> the fact of Roman Catholicism in the form which it gave itself
> in the 16th century in the battle against the Reformation.
> Again, within the organized unities of the Evangelical
> Churches themselves, we stand before the fact of pietistic and
> rationalistic Modernism as rooted in mediaeval mysticism and
> humanistic Renaissance. The fact of the modern denial of
> revelation, etc., is quite irrelevant compared with this twofold
> fact.[39]

It seems to me that Barth focuses the opposition in an unsatisfactory
manner here, and especially that the notion of "heresy" is inapposite
to describe the threat to the integrity of faith which he has sighted,
causing him to mislocate his battle in an archaic ecclesiastical perspective. I should say that the "modernist" tradition would be better
characterized as a theological form of what Heidegger calls the
metaphysics of subjectivity, while the Catholic tradition of natural
theology in its post-Tridentine variants belongs to the same mental
world as modern rationalism. Barth's search for the roots of these
traditions in human pride and sinfulness is a mystification which
prevents him from seeing that both traditions belong to the history
of metaphysics and have roots in the medieval and patristic periods,
in Augustine for example. Neglecting to trace the genealogy of these
modern inadequate representations of Christianity back to their
ancient roots, he himself builds uncritically on patristic and medieval ontology. One might also ask if Barth's openness to Scripture
levers him out of the orbit of the same metaphysical provenance,
whether for instance his reliance on it as a source of certitude does
not savor of rationalism and whether the abstract, ahistorical character of his biblical world does not mask a subjective stance.

In the case of the first of the two "heresies," it may have been the
oppressive presence of Roman Catholic scholasticism at the time he

wrote which distracted Barth from a more fundamental target. A deconstructor of Barth would have the task of retrieving all the critical energy he devoted to his tireless attacks on natural theology and reinvesting them in the critique of metaphysical theology as a whole. Barth traces natural theology to a permanent temptation of humanity to be its own master.[40] Had he focused his theme more precisely he might have worked out a concrete historical critique of the sway of metaphysics within Christian discourse, which is not at all due to some permanent structure of human pride, but to determinate historical causes, namely the fact that Christian faith early found itself forced to articulate its message within a metaphysical culture. The so mysterious "vitality" of natural theology is thus nothing more and also nothing less than the vitality of metaphysical reason. Barth, less radical than Luther here perhaps, fails to see that his reproaches might be more tellingly directed against the Logos of Western reason itself insofar as it can induce a blindness and deafness to the specific claim of the biblical revelation. This would lend bite to his assertion that natural theology is "not grateful but grasping, not obedient but self-autonomous"[41] which as it stands sounds too much like an over-emphatic chiding. To subject the Western Logos to attitudes of gratefulness and obedience, to the obedience of faith, is what theology has always struggled to do, with mixed success. But this cannot be brought about by the simple methods of "self-denial" and "self-abnegation" Barth proposes;[42] the preacher here underestimates the intrinsic force of metaphysics, and the difficulty of winning from it the freedom of the language of faith. In attempting to judge the historical formation of natural theology from an aprioristic vantage point supplied by revelation Barth takes a hermeneutical shortcut which makes him unsteady and inconsistent in his reactions. For instance, he throws at natural theology the accusation that it represents an attempt to make Christianity "natural" and respectable, to domesticate it in bourgeois style.[43] But this ideological critique does not emerge from a concrete analysis of the dominance of the metaphysical over the biblical in the discourse of metaphysical theology, e.g., the prevalence in the too numerous Catholic tracts on the "problem of analogy" of metaphysical theorizing about the divine names to the exclusion of any confrontation with the texture of actual religious language. Barth remains at a moralistic level, and so his ideological critique dissolves into *obiter dicta*. The efforts of F. W. Marquart and H. Gollwitzer to see him as the master of a liberative dialogue between the Gospel and politics fail to convince, because politics figure in Barth only as a local palliation of the intrinsic abstraction of his system. Had he been able to focus precisely the inner contradiction of a metaphysical theology, it might have helped him identify more acutely the concrete threats of the integrity of faith in our culture, including the metaphysical causes of its abstractedness from the socio-political. His almost melodramatic use of notions like "heresy" and "pride" makes his sense of what is wrong and his prescription of remedies random and unsystematic, and does not save him from falling into the traps of metaphysical theologizing just as much as the modernists and natural theologians had done.

An example of this unsteady attitude to metaphysics can be found in his treatment of Anselm of Canterbury. Anselm, in Barth's reading, thought entirely and exclusively within the horizon of faith; his proofs of God were no more than explicitations of the proof God himself gives of himself in revelation. Yet it is clear that Anselm, just as much as Aquinas later, formulates metaphysical proofs of God's existence which can be understood by believer and unbeliever alike. It can be argued that Aquinas no less than Anselm integrates these proofs into a general project of *fides quaerens intellectum*. If these proofs have autonomous rational validity, as Anselm claims, then it is hard to see why Barth's rejection of Vatican I's teaching that God can be known by the natural light of human reason does not affect Anselm equally. Barth is sensitive to the language of faith in Anselm's text, especially to such "Barthian" turns as "if some intelligence could think of something better than you, the creature would be above its creator and would judge its creator—and that is completely absurd" (*Proslogion* 3),[44] but he does not recognize the necessity of metaphysical language equally inscribed in Anselm's text. This metaphysical language is often amalgamated confusingly with the language of faith in Anselm, as in the quotation just given, and this may be symptomatic of basic tensions in his thought, which a deconstructive reading could bring to light. But Barth is inattentive to these and imposes instead a consistent reading in terms of faith and revelation. Thus "something than which nothing greater can be thought" (*Prosl.* 2) is interpreted as a revealed divine name,[45] without regard for the fact that Anselm also regards it as an idea which any "fool" can understand. In thus forcibly overruling the metaphysical dimensions of Anselm's thought Barth underestimates the intrinsic consistency and power of metaphysical language. He commits the same mistake in reverse when he brands other forms of natural theology as simple expressions of human willfulness, presuming that their rational force is a mere delusion.

Again, in his critique of Vatican I he uses the curious argument that the Council "intends to make a provisional division or partition in regard to the knowability of God, and this will inevitably lead to a partitioning of the one God as well."[46] Reason can know God as "*rerum omnium principium et finis*" while faith adds knowledge of him as Reconciler and Redeemer. Barth himself is quite happy to think of God as "*rerum omnium principium et finis*" as long as this knowledge is derived exclusively from revelation; otherwise it represents a human image of God, of the sort Feuerbach demolished, an idol. Here Barth again refuses to look closely at the historical texture of the language he is discussing. Do the words "*principium et finis*" not carry the weight of 2500 years of metaphysical speculation on God as first cause and last end, and in taking over the words as part of the language of revelation is not Barth himself accepting notions of causality and teleology which are not part of its content? Can the question of natural theology be abstracted from the history of metaphysics? All great metaphysicians have seen rational theology as intrinsic to the structure of metaphysical thinking and all great Christian theologians have identified the God thus sighted with the God of revelation. This is the tradition Barth seeks to overcome. If the teaching of Vatican I is accepted one will be reluctant to dismiss this tradition as simply untrue. But there are more refined ways of overcoming metaphysics, which do not instantly concentrate on questions of truth and falsehood, but rather on the possibilities of thought and language. A Kantian or Wittgensteinian critique of the metaphysical approach to God might render natural theology profoundly problematic, but need not entirely disqualify its underlying hunches. Barth's onslaught on natural theology, however, eschews any such critical methods on principle, since his rejection is based on the authority of revelation alone.

It seems that the opposition of revelation and natural theology is an ahistorical misapprehension of the tension between faith and metaphysics characteristic of Christian theology, that natural theology is the tip of the metaphysical iceberg and can only be overcome through a critique of the metaphysical thought-forms which inevitably produce it, and of the very texture of our language insofar as it is metaphysical. Barth may be able to purify Scripture of its apparent touches of natural theology, as in his exegesis of Acts 17,[47] but he has not purified his own diction of uncriticized metaphysical elements, e.g., his adoption of the phrase "modes of being" to describe the Trinity from the Cappadocian Fathers, and generally tends to assume the unproblematic concord of dogmatic and biblical, often taking the same hermeneutical shortcuts as in his reading of Anselm, imperfectly reducing the dogmatic to a biblical function without facing squarely the disturbing resistance of its metaphysical component to this reduction. When Barth writes of natural theology that "it is even able to change the theology of revelation, which it tolerates and acknowledges alongside itself, and even consciously superordinates to itself, into an image which is only too like itself, and which at bottom is itself nothing but natural theology"[48] and that "it is the one heresy which is necessary by its very nature,"[49] we can demystify this picture of a serpent of pride lodged in the Church's bosom by translating it as an analysis of the necessity of metaphysical reason and its inbuilt imperialism (which quite swallows up faith in Hegel) against which faith has always struggled. But traditionally faith struggles to retain its identity against the threat of metaphysical absorption while at the same time respecting metaphysics as the force of reason itself. Far from indulging in natural theology as a concession to unbelief, a deceptive form of apologetics, a "masked faith,"[50] Christian theologians have been obliged by rational necessity to explore the questions of "natural theology" inbuilt into the claim of metaphysics to speak of God as first cause and last end of things. Barth rightly seeks to dislodge metaphysical reason from the primacy it again and again reasserts within theology. But a rejection based on the biblical Word alone, uncoupled with systematic or historical insight into what is rejected, cannot be sufficiently clear-sighted to prevent it from slipping in again unnoticed. Historical differentiation of the various elements of his diction (supported by close literary analysis of the texts he quotes) is not systematically attempted in Barthian hermeneutics. Hence his language tends to become rather monochrome, turning in on itself, from want of exposure to the hermeneutical struggle with other languages. The biblical horizon is idealized and unified in function of his own ecclesiastical horizon to generate a *theologia perennis* constructed about concepts of "God" and the "Word of God" which seem foreign to the pluralism of the historical meanings associated with these expressions. If there is an "inflation of revelation" in Barth's theology (P. Althaus) there is a similar inflation of his other key notions (including "God") because they are still to some degree abstracted from the history of their usage.

A clear example of the inadequacy of Barth's critical measures is found in Barth's dealings with the notion of being. The "analogy of being," which Barth denounced as an "invention of Antichrist,"[51] was for Aquinas a critical theory of theological language, allied with negative theology, and its claim was that while we can properly use certain concepts in referring to God, they cannot represent or define God's being as it is in itself. "We cannot grasp what God is, but only what he is not, and what relation (sc. of dependence) all else has to him" (*Contra Gentiles* I 30). Analogy here is not calculable. Its purpose is to keep God from being absorbed and explained by the metaphysical terms used to speak of him. It does not constitute an overcoming of metaphysics, but within the tradition of metaphysical theology its basic thrust could be interpreted as counter-metaphysical. Barth's attacks on the analogy of being do not seem to engage satisfactorily with the depth of the Thomistic viewpoint. Perhaps he would have done better to examine critically the very use of the word "being" in reference to the God of revelation, a word which, perhaps already in the Septuagint's *ego eimi ho ōn*, carries with it the weight of the metaphysical tradition. Unfortunately, instead of pursuing his question back to this level, Barth develops his own theory of analogy which claims that "our words about God can stand in analogy to God's being because, as the Creator of all things, God is the first and last truth of all our words as well. . . . This ability becomes reality . . . as God disposes concerning them in His revelation, giving Himself to them as object and thus giving them veracity."[52] Thus the true sense of "father" and "son" is not their human but their trinitarian sense and the true sense of "space" is the spatiality of God.[53] Such a formula obviously forbids a clear-headed examination of the human and historical roots of religious language. Barth is endlessly versatile in giving a powerful, phenomenologically convincing sense to every biblical and traditional expression, as when the "being" of God becomes the act of his loving in freedom. This versatility excuses him from the task of examining the original birth certificates of these expressions and bringing their questionable or problematic aspects to clear consciousness. Had he done so the result would have been a far less eloquent theology, but one more helpfully in tune with the modern crisis of theological language.

Perhaps the most important metaphysical presupposition shared by Barth and his Roman Catholic critics (especially von Balthasar and Bouillard) is the notion that theology must take the form of a systematic dogmatics. This too prevents them from recognizing the need for theology to take a critical turn, to examine the basic elements of its own language. It also leads them to conflate diverse historical and linguistic data into a unified pattern in which the precise contours of the original language of faith are lost. A major example of this is the conflation of the Genesis accounts of creation with a high christology in CD III i, where Jesus' miracles are paralleled with Elohim's creative fiat.[54] For von Balthasar: "All creation is grounded in the Logos, more precisely, in Jesus Christ. The possibility of creation being distant from God derives ultimately from the Son's readiness to empty himself, to stand over against his father in a relationship of obedience and service."[55] This logical reconstruction of the original grounds of creation and salvation soon begins to spin a gnosis with little biblical warrant: "In the same freedom and love in which God is not alone in Himself but is the eternal begetter of the Son. . . . He also turns as Creator *ad extra* in order that absolutely and outwardly He may not be alone but the One who loves in freedom. . . . He created (the world) because He loved it in His Son who because of its transgressions stood before Him eternally as the Rejected and Crucified."[56] Barth here appeals to New Testament doxologies, the Johannine prologue, and the hymn in Colossians I, but he has elevated the suggestive indications of these hymns to the status of an explanatory metaphysical scheme, using freely such problematic concepts as "eternity." Here the historical horizon of revelation is supplemented by an overarching metaphysical pre-history. Thus Barth's "positivism of revelation" (Bonhoeffer) paradoxically gives rise to what might be called a biblical idealism.

That Barth should be retrieved from the present eclipse of his influence I do not question: his *Dogmatics* is the great book of twentieth century theology, and if it remains a book with seven seals we are bereft of one of the finest guides to a contemporary apprehension of the true bearing of the Christian faith. I can well understand that many people would be happy to keep the evil genie of Barthianism locked forever in its bottle. To give the Bible unrestricted and autonomous authority is a formula for freedom only in exceptional circumstances; in others it can license fanaticism and tyranny, just as much as the "magisterial fundamentalism" of some Roman Catholics can. Yet the basic intention of Barth's biblicism is still valid for the agenda of theology today, if we can wrest from his use of Scripture as dogmatic foundation a different function of the authority of Scripture as opening up a field of questions. Thus deconstructed, Barthian biblicism would have a new lease on life in a more radical form, in defense not of past monuments but of the present actuality of God's Word. Barth also needs to be retrieved from a certain denominational isolation that hangs about him insofar as he sees other churches as heretical, other religions as unbelieving and idolatrous. His work is still a resource for meeting the crisis of metaphysical versions of Christian identity, a crisis which transcends denominational differences and prescribes new conditions binding on all Christian churches in their search for a contemporary language of faith. That language will be born from a critical reappropriation of the tradition grasped in its concreteness, its finitude, its all too human poverty. Sometimes this critical grasp of tradition may look like a reductive positivism or historicism (and even that might be a salutary corrective to the inflated, ghostly status acquired by traditional language when insufficiently criticized). But if the theologian dwells on the Barthian paradox that this tradition, in all its human, historical poverty, nonetheless carries the reality of faith and revelation (a constantly reinterpreted story of salvation, calling for a constantly reinvented praxis), then the struggle with tradition will become the struggle to continue it by venturing a word of faith in today's language and trusting to the grace of the revealing God to make that word ring true.

NOTES

1. Gerhard Ebeling, in Hans Norbert Janowski and Eberhard Stanimler, *Was ist los mit der deutschen Theologie?* (Stuttgart: Kreuz Verlag, 1978), 11.

2. HQD, 49; Maria Villela-Petit objects that idolatry is a moral term, not to be applied indiscriminately to any deficient representation of God (Ibid., 75-80). Marion can elude this critique and justify his moral ire (even against the moral God of Kant!) by admitting that any representation of God is potentially idolatrous, for at some point it may cease to keep faith open to God; conversely, it might be admitted that many idols were not originally idolatrous, and that in particular the work of Christian metaphysics has constantly freed the thought of God from idolatrous appropriation, though this work has now been overtaken by the realization that it must in the end subject God to the principle of sufficient reason, a realization which makes further reliance on metaphysics impossible for faith. To admit such relativity in the differentiation of "idols" from "icons" is to open up very radical questions— Christ is the "icon of the invisible God" (Colossians 1:15) but has Christianity not often made an idol of Christ? The representation of God as Father may equally become idolatrous when its original anti-idolatrous function (in opposition to the God of Law?) is forgotten, or when it is stubbornly sustained against other approaches to God in tension with it: the personal, devotional language goes to seed unless tempered by the alternative impersonal one. When a representation

becomes routine or conventional or psychologically oppressive or ideo-
logically retrograde or sexist then as one clings to it in a willful blindness to its defectiveness the dynamics of idolatry come into play.
Questioning is a perpetually necessary safeguard against this temptation. This is not to deny that some representations are products of
idolatry from the start (for instance the God conveniently drafted by
our Western warlords) while others have an iconic power which can
always be revivified to subvert idolatrous appropriations (Christ
crucified).

3. G.A., Vol. 13, 154.
4. Cf. Eugene T. Gendlin, "Dwelling," Seventeenth Annual Conference
   of the Heidegger Circle, Durham, New Hampshire, May 1983.
5. David Tracy, *Blessed Rage for Order* (New York: Cross-
   road/Seabury, 1975), 155.
6. Schubert Ogden, *Faith and Freedom* (Nashville: Abingdon, 1979), 83;
   cf. Tracy, op. cit., 181: "God alone synthesizes in each new moment all
   the actuality already achieved with all the true possibilities as yet
   unrealized."
7. Tracy, *Blessed Rage*, 183.
8. Ibid., 188.
9. Ibid., 183.
10. Ibid., 189. Luther's "anti-philosophical agape insistence" failed to do
    so!
11. "Perhaps it need not always be the case that the God of the scriptures
    and the God of the philosophers are irreconcilable. In that revolution in
    theological reflection called process thought, perhaps that chasm has
    at last been bridged" (Ibid., 184).
12. Ibid., 189.
13. Edward Schillebeeckx, *Jezus, het vertaal van een levende*
    (Bloemendaal: H. Nelissen, 1974), 543 (ET: *Jesus: An Experiment in
    Christology* (New York: Seabury, 1979), 667).
14. P. Schoonenberg, *Theology Digest*, 29 (1981), p. 105.
15. J. Galot, *Vers une nouvelle christologie* (Gembloux: Duculot-
    Lethielleux, 1971), 44.
16. "The two questions 'who is it?' and 'what is it?' belong to everyday life
    as well as to intellectual speculation," Ibid., 42. Yes, but it is specifi-
    cally Greek to seek a *definition* as answer to these questions and to
    forge words which locate the abstracted essence the questioner is pre-
    sumed to be seeking. That the word *"hypostasis"* or "person" would
    have had a different history without the influence of Christianity does

not erase this character of its functioning in dogmatic discourse. Even if the word "*hypostasis*" as used at Chalcedon is "not associated with any particular philosophy" (Ibid., 42) this does not spell its independence from the metaphysical Logos.

17. Dennis McCann, *Christian Realism and Liberation Theology* (Maryknoll, New York: Orbis, 1981).

18. Jürgen Moltmann's *Der gekreuzigte Gott* (Munich: Kaiser, 1972) is a masterpiece of this kind of edification: "Jesus suffers dying in abandonment, not however death itself, for death can no longer be 'suffered,' because suffering presupposes life. But the Father, who abandons and gives up the Son, suffers the death of the Son in the infinite pain of love—the fatherlessness of the Son corresponds to the sonlessness of the Father, and if God has constituted himself as Father of Jesus Christ, then in the death of his Son he suffers also the death of his fatherhood" (230). (ET: *The Crucified God* [New York: Harper and Row, 1974], 243). Translate this into the language of prayer and its excesses, inspired by speculative zeal, become apparent: "O God, who suffered the death of your fatherhood. . . ."

19. Fergus Kerr, "Rahner Retrospective: III Transcendence or Finitude," *New Blackfriars*, 62 (1981), 370-379 (378).

20. Augustine Shutte, "Human Beings are Transcendent," *New Blackfriars*, 63 (1982), 476-487 (486). Shutte takes Kerr to be denying human transcendence, but that is to simplify the argument. When one queries the very possibility of a certain style of speculation, calling in question its very grammar, then a straightforward denial of what that speculation affirms is open to the same objections as the speculation itself. Kerr's claim that "we cannot get outside our world" would be meaningless as a direct contradiction of Rahner, since it would share the very horizon it challenges. As a methodological corrective, however, it borders on the tautological, and has force in this context only because Rahner's positing of transcendent and transcendental grounds is so lacking in linguistic or phenomenological restraint.

21. Karl Rahner, *Foundations of Christian Faith* (New York: Seabury, 1978), 20.

22. Ibid., 52.

23. Ibid., 52-53.

24. Ibid., 69-70 (=*Grundkurs des Glaubens* [Freiburg: Herder, 1976], 78).

25. "Einführung in die Metaphysik," *G.A.* 40, 3-4 (ET, 1-2).

26. *Basic Writings*, 109; cf. Ch. I, n. 7.

27. Cf. Michael Zimmerman, *Eclipse of the Self*; cf. *G.A.* 40, "Anhang," 217-219. For Heidegger's dream see *Erinnerung an Martin Heidegger* (Pfullingen: Neske, 1977), 39.

28. Summarized by Otto Pöggeler in *Verantwortungen: Festschrift Gerhard Ebeling* (Tübingen: Mohr, 1982).

29. Kerr, "Rahner Retrospective," 376.

30. Rahner, *Foundations*, 57.

31. Ibid., 73.

32. Ibid., 143.

33. Ibid., 161.

34. Ibid., 207.

35. Ibid., 289.

36. For a stirring account of Barth and Rahner as restoration theologians, see Alfredo Fierro, *La imposible ortodoxía* (Salamanca, 1974).

37. Cf. Peter Eicher, *Offenbarung. Prinzip neuzeitlicher Theologie* (Mainz: Kosel, 1977).

38. Karl Barth, *Church Dogmatics*, I i (Edinburgh: Clark, 1975²) (=CD).

39. Ibid., 34.

40. Cf. *CD* II i (Edinburgh, 1957), 135, 165.

41. Ibid., 63.

42. Ibid., 136.

43. Ibid., 141-142.

44. *St. Anselm's Proslogion*, trans. M. J. Charlesworth (Oxford: Clarendon, 1965), 119.

45. Barth, *Anselm: Fides quaerens intellectum* (Richmond, Virginia: John Knox Press, 1960), 75.

46. *CD* II i, 79.

47. Ibid., 121-123.

48. Ibid., 140.

49. Ibid., 141.

50. Ibid., 93.

51. *CD* I i, xiii.

52. *CD* II i, 233.

53. Ibid., 229, 470.

54. *CD* III i (Edinburgh, 1958), 35-38.

55. Hans Urs von Balthasar, *The Theology of Karl Barth* (New York: Holt, Rinehart and Winston, 1971), 231.

56. *CD* III i, 50-51.

III: THE HISTORIC FLAW

One might continue forever the soundings of the previous chapter, showing over and over again how Christian thinking is still unsuspectingly entangled in speculation and estranged from its proper theme. But it is time to widen our lens. Unless we bring the sweep of history into view, even an "eternal" vigilance against the pitfalls of language will never take us beyond local corrections of the distortions we attribute to metaphysics, and these will be taken as random interferences, uninterpretable static, for only history fully reveals their systematic—Heidegger would say destinal—character. Unless they emerge from a thorough involvement with the whole story of the fusion between the worlds of biblical faith and Greek philosophy, even our positive proposals for the renewal of religious language will remain piecemeal and uncoordinated and their underlying laws cannot be clearly defined. Only when the critique of current language is enlarged to become a full-scale historical hermeneutic can we grasp the extent of the sway of metaphysics within this language and at the same time discern its counter-metaphysical potential, insofar as it continues the movement of resistance to Greek reason which has always been stirring in the texture of Christian discourse. This can be retrieved, or rejoined, when the great texts of the past are so read that their explicit metaphysical meaning is overthrown in light of their deeper, partly repressed, character as confessions of faith. Without this deconstructive confrontation with its past, faith must continue to be haunted by metaphysical ways of talking and thinking which it is unable to contest and must remain cut off from the genuinely quickening resources of its tradition, springs of eloquence too well reined in by the canons of classical reason.

Even the surest instincts of faith cannot fill in for the informed suspicion which history teaches. To use any piece of Christian terminology without knowledge of the historical conditions of its production is to be a blind participant in the semantic play of tradition, powerless to operate strategic innovations. Nor can poetic intuition in handling the language of faith do the work of a historical critique of its elements; even Hopkins, Claudel and Eliot become baroque and cumbersome when they use such words as "Incarnation." The critique and renewal of religious language is inevitably short-circuited unless it takes the form of a historical hermeneutic. A reconstruction of the origins of dogma in the usual style would not meet this requirement. It is not the battles of Cyril and Nestorius which produced the Chalcedonian formula, but forces lying beneath what appears on the surface of ecclesiastical history. Chalcedon is historically understood only when grasped as the result of the convergence and conflict between the Gospel kerygma and the Greek ontotheological project. If the Christian tradition is read at this depth it becomes possible to subject the language of faith to a historical differentiation carrying real critical force. Replaced in its historical context the current language is lit up as a battlefield on which faith and metaphysics are engaged in the most recent and perhaps the decisive phase of their bimillennial skirmishings. Speaking the language of faith and reflecting theologically on it then become activities fraught with historical significance in which one's every move signals either an advance towards that freedom in communicating the biblical revelation after which theology has always secretly aspired, or a retreat into the tried and trusted categories on which faith has often been forced to fall back, exhausted.

There are many other historical threats besetting the language of faith, and of these too it could be said that their systematic character and the resources for resisting them which the tradition secretes can only be discovered by a historical critique. A socio-political, or a feminist, or a psychoanalytic critique of the tradition might well seem more urgent than the abstract and delicate theme we have chosen. Our theme, however, engages us with what is most directly at issue in the classical texts, the metaphysical articulation of the faith, whereas the other critiques come at these texts from unexpected quarters. Their questions are equally applicable to the Bible or to other religious traditions, whereas the question of metaphysics focuses a problem specific to Western theology. Thus it is not surprising that within Western theology the topic of metaphysics has long since become explicitly problematical and that a whole tradition of denouncing the hellenizing of the Gospel and seeking out the lost "essence" of Christianity provides our contemporary questioning with a rich, complex background. In comparison with the other critical approaches just mentioned the critique of metaphysics could be described as a critique from inside, and as such perhaps enjoys a central and indispensable position, guiding the other critiques to their proper targets and correcting the short-circuits to which they might be prone if left to their own devices.

But is it really necessary, it may be objected, to organize the theological overcoming of metaphysics as a historical hermeneutic? Did not Wittgenstein carry out his linguistic therapy of philosophical language by choosing his examples from contemporary discourse? Even if some of his examples came from historical sources, he made no effort to reinsert them in their historical context or to provide their genealogy. Nor did he situate his own critical project in relation to a tradition of criticism of philosophical language. He was as content with a few samples of "language on a holiday" as Cezanne was with his bowl of withered apples. But whatever the methodological virtues of Wittgenstein's bracketing of history it is not a helpful model for the critic of the language of faith. Even the simplest element in this language is the product of a complex history from which it cannot be abstracted. When philosophers of religion sketch what they take to be an elementary, universally acceptable concept or representation of "God," for example, their discourse carries many historical overtones of which they are unaware. To say that God is "all-powerful" or "infinite" is to commemorate some distinct and datable breakthrough in humanity's understanding of God, and to summon up the shade of Second Isaiah or Gregory of Nyssa or whoever first articulated the attribute in question. Nor can these attributes be dehistoricized as the redness or fragrance of a rose may be. Their meaning depends on the history of their usage and cannot be independently established, either by reduction to empirical perception or by an a priori conceptual analysis. A purely conceptual construction of the notions of "omnipotence" or "infinity" would carry none of the resonance these terms have acquired in the course of their usage by believing communities. Furthermore, the basic referents of Christian language are not communicated to us in perception or conception, but in the more puzzling form of historical traditions. We latch on to these, ruminate on them, and wrestle with them in a search for some secure understanding of the gracious mystery they attest. Sometimes the traditions communicate clearly and powerfully, but then a cloud passes and they become blurred, opaque, and inaccessible again. We receive, for example, the message that "God is a loving Father," and this for a while is illuminating and liberating, and may found a general entente about the upshot of the entire tradition. But then doubts set in. Is this language sexist, anthropomorphic, psychoanalytically unsound? Is it an image from another time for a reality which can no longer be thus expressed? Because tradition never becomes totally transparent, we can maintain contact with the gracious revelation it communicates only across a constant activity of questioning and rethinking its messages. Tradition imprisons and blinds if we take at face value its surface clarities and dogmatic certitudes, and liberates its charge of light only when we question back to the challenge of mystery which these clarities and certitudes neither explicate nor dispel. The momentous decisions of the past which have determined the sense of the terminology we use, the religious thinkers who have left their imprint on the texture of our speech, are the ghosts with which one must wrestle in undergoing a therapy of the current language of faith. Thus no discipline, other than historiography, is as necessarily and as thoroughly historical in its concerns and procedures as theology must be. The exorcism of the ghosts which haunt our language is impossible unless we track them down in their historical lair. Conversely, appreciation of the vital elements this language still manages to mediate is impossible without awareness of the historical depth of the words we use. The word "faith" itself, for example, would be very depleted if one forgot that contemporary faith is received from a long line of historical witnesses stretching back to Abraham, so that the word unavoidably names not a purely inward, but a historical achievement.

The Tradition of the Question

Even the project of overcoming metaphysics in theology has a historical depth peculiarly its own, for it is implicated in the tradition of protest, originating with Luther, which consciously and explicitly opposed faith to metaphysics, the original Gospel to its hellenization in dogma and Patristic Platonism, the God of Abraham to the God of the philosophers. It is fueled by the pathos of these oppositions, though aware of their hermeneutical limitations as they have become apparent over the centuries. It retrieves and enriches this critical tradition by deploying the passion of faith which sustained it in a more sophisticated way, engaging the texture of metaphysical theology from within, lodging subversively in its text, instead of wasting time on external strictures. It is true that many theologians have tended to view the contrasts between Hebraism and Hellenism, revelation and reason, the "essence of Christianity" and its dogmatic overlay, as tendentious simplifications and see the quest for a dehellenization of Christianity as a romantic tilting at windmills. Nevertheless the problematic explored by the dehellenizing tradition has not gone away. On the contrary, it has continued to ferment and thicken, bursting the simple frameworks in which it was first apprehended, and in more subtle guise it can continue to serve as the chief topic of a hermeneutics of Christian tradition. The old slogans of opposition have lost validity only as fixed theses, but they may still serve as signposts for *directions* of critical thinking, for lines of inquiry which can be kept sufficiently flexible, inventive and open-ended to match the complexity of the bimillennial interplay between faith and metaphysics. No simple thesis, pro- or anti-metaphysical, can be adequate to the endless questions this history suggests. Instead a method of historical reflection is required which can articulate and develop each of the hunches, misgivings, or queries that come to the surface as we live through the crisis of the tradition and prompt us to reassess and reinterpret it. If a hermeneutical method

of adequate complexity is developed, the crisis of metaphysical theology will no longer be experienced as a situation of disarray or an
occasion for pseudo-prophetic polemic, but as the matrix of a constantly increasing lucidity.

Psychoanalysts compare the psyche to a black box emitting frag-
mentary messages from one corner. What goes on inside that box
remains impenetrably obscure. History too can never be reconstructed; its opacity far outweighs the partial insights it suggests.
Yet each major turning of the road opens up intriguing new vistas in
the landscape behind us. The turning which the closure of metaphysics brings about in the history of faith implies an overturning of rigid
models of what that history has been, a discovery of the questionability of the past. The first two millennia of Christianity come to
appear as a great experiment whose failures are as significant and as
instructive as its successes. At a religious level this has been translated as a realization of the "sinfulness" of the Church, but at the level
of concrete historical self-understanding it is better to use the
Heideggerian term "errance" to describe the fateful and unavoidable limitations which the consignment of the Gospel to the cultural
milieu of Western metaphysics imposed. The Christian tradition is
coming to terms with its mistakes, insofar as time has made them
visible, and this unprecedented reflexive process, though experienced as painful and rather devastating, also returns to us our past
as a richer source of instruction than it was ever allowed to be
previously. The past is no longer an impediment to new thinking, but
a practice ground for the endless task of discerning what is authentically Christian from what turns out to be a deviation or a dead end.
Methods of probing analysis must be developed to discover deeper
levels of the sense of the messages the black box of history emits.
Surface chronicles are rightly regarded as of little theological interest, since only rare fragments of the past discourse of Christianity
can engage directly the questions of contemporary faith. The mar-
keting of past luminaries as "relevant" is generally an inept enterprise, and the idea that one can read the answer to present problems
in the pages of Gregory of Nyssa or Maximus the Confessor is a

willful mystification. But a depth-reading of these authors, as exemplifying both the promise and the failure of metaphysical Christianity, can indeed help contemporary faith find a more adequate
articulation of its identity.

I say that the explicitly counter-metaphysical tradition within
Christianity originates with Luther, because, despite his precedents
in the anti-Aristotelean Augustinian theologians of the preceding
centuries and in the German mystics, Luther's opposition of the
Bible and Aristotle has an implicit historical depth that makes it a
qualitative leap beyond Medieval critiques of metaphysics. His
sense of the radical alterity of the Word of God pitted him implicitly
against the whole Western tradition in a sharp collision which has no
precedent and which does not seem to have been experienced at the
same depth by any theologian since. In this century the influence of
dialectical theology has caused Lutheran theologians to rediscover
the *theologia crucis* of the Reformer, but very often their interpretation of it has run contrary to his intentions, and they have presented
him as proposing a subtler "metaphysics of the cross" to replace
faded Aristotelean notions. Moltmann, for instance, attempts to
sublate Luther's utterances into his own speculative kenoticism.
This metaphysical complacency is scarcely the key to a deeper
understanding of the greatest theological opponent of metaphysics.[1]
Instead we should, it seems to me, be ready to substitute the words
"Western reason" wherever Luther writes "Aristotle." Thus we
might translate Thesis 29 of the *Heidelberg Disputation* (1518) as
saying, "If one wishes to think in terms of Western reason without
danger, it is necessary that one first become fully foolish in Christ."[2]
The radical implications of Luther's thought are even clearer if we
translate in these terms Thesis 44 of the *Disputation against Scholastic Theology* of 1516: "One does not become a theologian unless
one does so without Western reason,"[3] unless one steps outside the
historical limitations of metaphysics.

Luther had a fine ear for the incompatibility of philosophical and
biblical diction. In order to bring out the originality and specificity
of the Word of God he sometimes toys with a biblical text, telling us
first what a scholastic philosophizing theologian would make of it,
and then allowing the biblical word to show up this interpretation as

"folly."[4] His best argument against metaphysical theology was to replace it with a deeply felt biblical dialectic, a *sapientia crucis* derived from the prophets and St. Paul. Insofar as he addresses metaphysics directly it is rarely in order to argue with it. Instead he practices a prophetic discernment of the relative unreality and frivolity of metaphysical language when measured against the elemental concerns of the struggle of faith. Metaphysics, for Luther, is not confined to scholasticism. In 1521 he could write "If my soul hates the *homoousion* and refuses to make use of it, this does not make me a heretic."[5] His distaste for metaphysics might have carried him very far in the direction of radicalism. But as in many other areas it was tempered by a retreat to more conservative positions as the years advanced. Luther's vast biblical culture provided him with a rich and secure basis for developing a language of faith independent of metaphysics. After him theologians either fell back into scholastic methods of ordering Christian truth, or protested against metaphysics in the name of other forms of metaphysics rather than on the strength of a comparable encounter with the Word of God. Thus one may suspect that Pascal's focus on the God of Abraham is a narrow one, shaped by a metaphysics of subjectivity, and his opposition to Descartes implies only a change of texture, from the rational lucidity of the *cogito* to the existential lucidity of the heart. Both thinkers order the cosmos around the subject. The biblical material which Pascal marshals is rather thin, and is arranged more often than not within the structures of a rationalistic apologetics. Similarly, the pietism and enthusiasm of the eighteenth century produced critiques of metaphysical theology which lack a primarily biblical basis. Here the opposition is between an enlightenment of the reason and an illuminism of the emotions. This, too, is an intra-metaphysical opposition. Whatever independent biblical or pneumatic inspiration lies behind it is so shaped by the metaphysical topos of emotion versus reason, intuition versus concept, that its original character is effaced. Thus it appears that Luther was able to recover the authentic language of faith and to free it from metaphysics far more effectively than was possible within the narrow horizons of the following centuries, when the struggle between faith and metaphysics was whittled down to the narrow dimensions of the debate between fideism and rationalism.[6] Indeed it may be that the vision of Luther was too vast and too original to be fully received by those who came after him, and that even we today are too much prisoners of metaphysical criteria of rationalism and irrationalism to be able to make his language our own. The matter is complicated by the fact that Luther's own polemical stances only imperfectly express the upheaval that is afoot in his texts, and which only a deconstructive reading can fully retrieve. A theology able to listen to Luther and catch these significant overtones in his writing would need to be just as free from metaphysics as Luther was, just as sensitively immersed in the texture of scriptural thinking, and just as honestly and eloquently in touch with those resources of language and life experience which can give the Gospel a contemporary tongue. Such a theology could claim to understand Luther better than he understood himself, clearing away the residual confusion noted by Kierkegaard when he opined that Luther was not a doctor of Christianity, but a patient.[7] The Lutheran volcano is not extinct. Might we not hope that its next eruption will unite the Church, where it first divided it? This volcano is nothing other than the latent power of the biblical word within the texture of Christian discourse. The glib biblicism of our preaching and teaching nowadays is no proof that we have been shaken by the power of that word, may indeed be the most effective of defenses against such a happening. That is why Luther is so important, as the chief of the very few historical figures who were so shaken, who represent breaches in our culture through which the biblical word has been able to penetrate. Such figures are irreplaceable sources for the renovation of our language of faith, which takes place as a continuation of the history they inaugurate, building on their success, and learning from their failures. They facilitate that "jolt from outside" without which no deconstructive strategy can get underway.

Church history was born amid the controversies of the Counter-Reformation as the Centuriators of Magdeburg and Cardinal Baronius tried to colonize the past for their respective denominations. The widening of the historical debate to include a questioning of the basic value for faith of the dogmatic work of the early Church seems at first to have occurred only in a marginal and sporadic way.

The researches of the Jesuit Denis Petau inspired the Unitarian Souverain to denounce the Platonism of the Fathers as the source of all the errors enshrined in the doctrines of the Trinity and the Incarnation, but his evidence of subordinationism in the Ante Nicene Fathers was stolidly "refuted" by the Anglican Bishop George Bull, and whatever discussions it helped to stimulate on the development of doctrine were on the whole, as Owen Chadwick's entertaining chronicle reveals,[8] rather timid and academic. Only in the nineteenth century did these critical questions about the dogmatic achievements of the early Church leap into life as major theological issues. On the one hand the Romantic cult of interiority and the return to immediate feeling lent a new depth of significance to the quest for the "essence of Christianity"[9] and in the work of Schleiermacher in particular an effort is made to see the dogmatic language of the Church as the formalization of a basic religious experience (the feeling of utter dependence, the sense of being redeemed), and to formulate a critique of that language insofar as it objectifies and externalizes the meaning of that experience in an inappropriate way.[10] On the other hand the sense of historicity which emerged after the French Revolution and found consummate expression in Hegel conferred new speculative interest on the data of Church history. F.C. Baur presented the early history of dogma as reflecting the dialectical interplay of the Petrine and Pauline (Hebraic and Hellenic) principles, and concepts of an organic development of Christian truth began to take shape on the Catholic side in the work of J.A. Möhler. Clearly what took place in this period was less an overcoming than a rejuvenation of metaphysics, the importation of the grandiose speculative perspectives of idealism into the presentation of the Christian faith and its history. Yet in theology as in poetry, Romanticism cannot be reduced to its metaphysical dimensions. The Romantic movement was also one of return to phenomenality, however much that return was waylaid by the fascinating cosmic abstractions of Love, Life, Beauty, the Absolute, or Nature. In comparison with the eighteenth century theologians, those of the early nineteenth century can be seen as recapturing the mysterious and unique character of faith and revelation. If these thinkers tend to add Faith and Revelation to the list of capitalized abstractions mentioned above, if they do not yet have the more precise sense of their existentiality found in Kierkegaard and Newman, or the critical philosophical and historical grasp of their relationships with Greek metaphysics which A. Ritschl and A. Harnack first attained, still it is from the new impulse Romanticism gave to theology that the quest for the basic message of Christianity has drawn much of its vitality ever since. Here is another promising terrain for a deconstructive reading, which would also be a salutary deconstruction of whatever Romantic instincts are still lodged in the bosom of theologians today.

If the quest for the essence of Christianity has a fatal attraction for the Romantic "beautiful soul," one against which the present project must be on guard, nonetheless it may be possible to focus the residue of validity which the quest for the essence of Christianity still retains, despite the realization which became increasingly unavoidable in the subsequent history of the tradition we are examining, namely that there is no such thing as an essence of Christianity which is historically identifiable. Harnack's attempt to locate it in Jesus' teaching of the fatherhood of God and the brotherhood of humanity ran aground on the rediscovery of the eschatological character of Jesus' preaching, and this seemed much too foreign to modern ears to be presented as the essence of Christianity. Nor has Ernst Käsemann's effort to establish a Pauline "canon within the canon" any better chances of success,[11] for Paul cannot be ripped out of the historical context of the debate between him and his predecessors and successors. The claim that any historical individual can incarnate the essence of Christianity, or of anything else, is bound to be an arbitrary imposition. From the start Judaism and Christianity are caught up in a complex self-critique, which is why some see the Bible as "a handbook of religious pathology." The authentic form of the faith has always been something to be constructed, though the work of construction often proceeded under the sign of recovery. Judaism and Christianity have constantly been reinventing themselves and every effort to establish an eternal essence of either has resulted in a form of idolatry—the idolatry of Law diagnosed by Paul, the idolatry of the "dogmatic system" from which Roman Catholicism is beginning to recover, the possible idolatry of an

abstract and disembodied Word of God in dialectical theology. We
never securely possess the essence of Christianity, not even as a
regulative idea guiding efforts at renewal. Instead of an essence
there is the historical sequence of Christian ways of life, bearing a
"family resemblance" to one another. When the vitality of Christian
faith is low the Church continues to practice obsolete forms of
religious life which are no longer a convincing embodiment of the
Gospel. Perhaps idolatry is usually nothing more than a clutching at
gods in which we no longer really believe, the worship of stale gods
rather than false ones, a failure in imagination, a fidelity which has
lost its original motive. If so it may perhaps have been as a perpetual
antidote against it that we were given an unfinished Gospel, a sketch
to be redrawn again and again rather than the complete and authoritative exposition dogmatic Christianity so long attempted to provide. In contesting metaphysical theology, then, we should not set up
one essence against another, as Schleiermacher and Harnack tended
to do. Instead we should rather see the metaphysical epoch of Christianity as taking its place in the series of historical inventions of
Christianity, as the epoch in which it tried to have an essence, and
eventually conducted crusades, pogroms, inquisitions, and religious
wars in the effort to establish that essence. The Christianity which
interpreted itself as essence we can retrospectively interpret as
invention, and thus be freed for our own invention of Christianity.
Liberation theology, for instance, is such an invention, though
tempted to mistake itself for an essence. There is strong biblical
warrant for this theology, but it is not necessary for it to claim to
have tapped the essence of the biblical message. Instead it is the
strongest interpretation of Scripture for this time, and like all such
interpretations it does not hesitate implicitly or explicitly to correct
many of the emphases in the biblical text. To correct the letter by the
spirit is an essential task of any vital scriptural hermeneutic. In the
epoch of metaphysical theology this process was cast in metaphysical form, as the provision of Scripture with its rational foundations,
or the elicitation of hints of spiritual reality from its material indications. Now retrospectively we can see this metaphysical hermeneutics too as a form of the reinvention of the biblical message. The
sensus plenior of Scripture is not a hidden Platonic essence, but the

semantic play it generates when reinterpreted in the Spirit in light of successive historical conjunctures.

Harnack's *History of Dogma* is the most mature and richly documented expression of nineteenth century misgivings about the dogmatic tradition, and it still provides the framework for discussion of the problem of hellenization today. We chronicle previous discussions of the topic towards Harnack as their term and trace present discussions back to him as their origin. Newman's *Essay on Development* holds an analogous position in regard to the narrower topic of the development of dogma. It is because they combine constant sobriety of judgment with an overall tendentiousness that both works have exerted a stimulating influence for so long. Newman might be counted as a counter-metaphysical thinker, since his principal concern was to sight certain basic elements of the world of faith, and he systematically avoided a speculative approach in favor of empirical observation and rhetorical argumentation. He had, however, no conception of the critical work to be done on the metaphysical fabric of patristic theology, and whenever he broaches central dogmas, such as that of the Incarnation, the metaphysical texture of his statements about them clashes with the usual suppleness of his prose and cannot be integrated with his usual themes.

Harnack, less conditioned by specifically ecclesiastical concerns, is extremely clearsighted in his grasp of the historical texture of dogma, and surely the most illuminating remark ever made on the subject is that "Dogma, in its conception and development, is a product of the Greek mind on the soil of the Gospel."[12] Unfortunately his proposals for the overcoming of dogma sound like counsels of defeat, tinged with the positivism and skepticism of the period. Similar sentiments, allied with a Schleiermacherian cult of religious experience and an evolutionist ideology, also vitiated the Modernists' valiant struggle with dogma. A due sense of the rational force of metaphysics and the necessity of the decisions made by the early Church in articulating the Gospel within a metaphysical framework, and a sharper focusing of the texture of biblical faith insofar as one can oppose it to its hellenization, would enrich and correct Harnack's project more than any new increment of historical information can. It may also be the case that the biblical roots of dogma are deeper than Harnack thought, and that dogma can largely be interpreted as the Church's defense of the Gospel against its radical hellenization at the hands of Modalists, Subordinationists, Monophysites, and others who sought to impose a tighter systematic unity on the Christian message.

Catholic apologists have seized on this idea in order to refute Harnack, but to my mind this is to miss deeper bearing of Harnack's thesis, namely the realization that the categories used by the Church in its battle with heresy would be impossible and incomprehensible in any other than a Greek culture, and that these categories became fused with the Gospel truths they were used to defend, with the result that Christianity henceforth presented a new visage to the world, acquiring the character of a dogmatic edifice. Catholic theologians continue to claim, with Pope Leo I, that the great Councils used technical terms not in a philosophical way, but, like the Apostles, *piscatorie*—as fishermen—and some would claim that these terms are immediately transparent expressions of the faith, which cannot become obsolete or inaccessible. This view fails to account for the immense difference between the horizon of biblical faith, even that of the Fourth Gospel, so important for patristic and conciliar theology, and the horizon in which divine being is explicated with the aid of the categories of substance and *hypostasis*. The Bible never defines. Its apparent definitions, e.g., "God is light" (I John 1:5), have nothing to do with the Platonic or Aristotelean notions of *logos* or *horismos*, but articulate contemplative or prophetic breakthroughs to a new level of understanding. The Councils in contrast, which took place in an Empire for which definition was not only theoretically but practically important, attempt very earnestly to define the contours of Christian orthodoxy, at first as a practical measure (to exclude heresy and canonize sound teaching) but increasingly as a speculative one too, as the intrinsic dynamics of the language they used forced them on to further clarifications. Here is only one of the many ways in which Harnack's hellenization-thesis continues to point towards the historical differentiations which must be elaborated if one is to make sense of Christian tradition. Efforts to spell out the differences between the Greek and Hebrew mentalities may often have been jejune and over-schematic. But critics of these efforts should seek subtler differentiations, instead of dismissing the differences as illusory or unimportant. The direction in which Harnack's analyses were moving is one which theologians do ill to neglect. Much of the stagnancy of patristic scholarship is due to a harmonious reading of the Fathers which glides over the tensions between their biblical and their Hellenic heritages, tensions which the questioning of contemporary faith enables us to perceive more clearly than ever before. Subsequent scholarship has not gone beyond Harnack in any essential way. It has refuted details, neglecting the main argument. A major contribution like Aloys Grillmeier's *Christ in Christian Tradition,* for example, basks in the contemplation of the development of the patristic categories, never querying their philosophical provenance or formulating any fundamental critical questions about their adequacy to the biblical revelation, though admitting that "the demand for a complete reappraisal of the Church's belief in Christ right up to the present day is an urgent one."[13] Of course, the complexity of the historical material to be disentangled makes it difficult for a scholar to sustain at the same time a critical question to the tradition. The gap this leaves is filled by unscholarly generalizations on the part of the systematic theologians, both those who use Chalcedon as a launching pad for speculation and those who treat it as a disposable christological "model." Thus the trail that Harnack blazed remains to this day untrodden.

Much of twentieth century theology has been a reaction against liberalism (Barth) or modernism (Neo-Scholasticism) and this has implied a blindness to Harnackian insights in the field of history of dogma and a refusal to face up to the critical historical questions to which dogma is exposed. Theories of the development of dogma or of its function in attesting to the Word of God continued to envision dogma as part of the essential structure of the Church rather than as the product of a certain historical epoch, and one which, within that epoch, assumed a pluralistic variety of forms. Where Harnack came close to seeing the finite, human, historical contours of the dogmatic achievement of the Church, twentieth century theologians regressed to an ahistorical viewpoint, thinking away from Harnack's disturbing questions in the direction of a speculative elaboration of the dogmatic *données.* That speculative quest was built on foundations of sand, and its failure forces us to think back to the historical questions posed by Harnack and to think deeper into them than he himself was able to do. After the speculative trinitarian theologies of Barth, Rahner, Lonergan, Mühlen, Moltmann, Jüngel and Bourassa, it is a relief and a refreshment to return to the basic questions none of them confront, to a shifting of the very elements of classical trinitarian language with a view to reducing those elements to their experiential foundation. Experiential? Yes, for insofar as the original language of Father, Son, and Spirit was an articulation of the community's experience of the Risen Christ (and not a set of revealed propositions), it must be possible to recall the later dogmatic language to this foundation in experience, to a language in immediate interplay with experience, a language of naming rather than one of definition. It is at this level that the sense of the terms "Father," "Son," and "Spirit" is lodged and every effort at ulterior definitions will lose that sense unless constantly checked against the original biblical naming. Without the historical insights of Harnack there is no possibility of carrying out this checking. Dogma has established so powerfully its claim to be nothing more and nothing less than the rational foundation of the biblical data that it can be surmounted only by the most searching examination of its birth certificate, one which keeps in mind the Hellenic origin of the very idea of a "rational foundation." It is only as the bankruptcy of the above-named theologians' efforts to shore up the rational foundations of revelation becomes apparent that the views of Harnack begin to resume some of their former influence and resonance and the flight from the painful task of a genealogical critique of dogma is once again brought to a halt. Why should the return to elements be so painful and speculation so soothing? For the same reason, no doubt, that revolution is painful, or thinking, or prayer, a fear of vulnerability to the other or to the unknown, a fear of living.

The fear just mentioned has in our metaphysical Christian culture taken the form of a fear of Judaism and Jews. The step back out of metaphysical theology is a step towards the Jewish matrix of all our theology. Even a radically biblical theologian of the stature of Barth shows little openness to this repressed Jewish dimension of Christian theology. That is why his biblicism never escapes the mustiness of an ecclesiastical and academic stylization to recover the *Hebraica veritas,* and why from this stilted vantage point he can propound such theses as that it was the monotheism of Israel which crucified Jesus and that "like the monotheism of Islam (its later caricature), it is simply the supreme example, the culmination and completion of the disobedience which from the beginning constituted the human side of the dealings of the one and only God with his chosen people."[14] Many such doctrinaire posturings would have been eliminated automatically had Barth kept his thought in subjection to a respectful dialogue with Judaism (and Islam). Ecclesiastical biblicism does not provide the "jolt from outside" which is needed to spark off a radical rereading of Christian tradition. The diction in which Luther and Calvin articulated their experience of being struck by the Word of God becomes a screen against any such experience when it is imitated by the ecclesiastical biblicist. The encounter with Judaism, on the other hand, exposes one to the biblical message as carried by a tradition which is independent of all the structures of ecclesiastical culture, and which, negated by them for so long, calls all these structures in question. It is thus perhaps in the renewal of Jewish-Christian dialogue that the counter-metaphysical protest of the last four or five centuries is carried forward most radically today. As long as the Word of God remains merely a text we are unlikely to allow it to unsettle our metaphysical identity in any basic way. But when we open to the call of the other in the give and take of dialogue the defensive character of our metaphysical self-definitions may become apparent and we may see, far more clearly than any text could make us see, what transformation of thinking is needed for us to shed our metaphysical identities and "discern the way" of biblical faith in a more elementary and authentic form.[15]

Faith as Deconstructive Principle

What conclusions can we draw from these centuries of unease with the hellenistic metaphysical form Christianity has taken? It is evident, I think, that the questions raised by this tradition of protest cannot be dismissed, and that it would be a mistake for the Church to confuse the defense of faith with the defense of its metaphysical embodiment. But neither can the questions raised be easily resolved, either through some higher speculative conciliation of biblical and philosophical, or through some simple dismissal of metaphysics. Instead one must raise these questions to a new level of methodological clarity and complexity. This can be done, on the one hand, through drawing on the critical resources of such thinkers as Kant, Wittgenstein, and Heidegger in order to focus more clearly the intrinsic limits and perils of metaphysical language and thus provide a firmer theoretical basis for one's sense of its inadequation to faith. On the other hand, one can pursue the historical trail backward to the very first appearance of metaphysical Christianity, in order to discover there in a latent form the same discontent with metaphysics which becomes explicit in Luther. Of course that discontent remained at an incubatory stage for many centuries. Only when the full power of metaphysics to rob Christian discourse of its reality had become apparent in late scholasticism could Luther form his clear diagnosis of metaphysics as an alienation. Nonetheless there is from the start a certain conscious or unconscious tension between the language of faith and that of metaphysics; it is by working along the fault lines this tension leaves in the classical Christian texts that we can hope to split the tradition open, allowing its repressed counter-metaphysical potential to emerge. The protest against metaphysical theology comes to fruition in a new way when a subtler philosophical grasp of the functioning of metaphysical language permits this more intimate deconstruction of the tradition, in which faith seeks out its own authentic voice in the texts of the past, overcoming the language of metaphysical reason which forever threatens to stifle it. In short, both the critique of metaphysical theology stemming from Luther and the crisis of metaphysical reason articulated by philosophers since Kant light up retrospectively a historic flaw running right through the theological tradition, a tug of war between the Greek Logos and the faith of Abraham. That Logos has not become inwardly questionable for the Fathers of the Church as it has for us, nor did they feel, as Luther did, its foreignness to the world of biblical faith. So confident were they in building up their metaphysical account of the faith that their first step was to identify

Christ himself with the Logos of philosophy. Despite this optimism, however, the inner difficulties of the project of conquering the empire of metaphysics for the Gospel began to emerge in the form of threatening heresies, and in subtler forms, which our vantage point allows us to interpret more searchingly than was possible for the Fathers themselves.

The history of theology is not a series of contingent failures to articulate faith adequately. Criticism of tradition cannot be satisfied with a series of local corrections—of Justin's subordinationist Christology, Augustine's pessimism, Origen's spiritual elitism, and so on —but must systematically confront the pattern underlying the inadequacy of the language of Christian theology to its theme. This pattern is the predominance of metaphysics in the mental world of the Fathers and their successors, a pattern reinforced by the breakdown of relations between Judaism and Christianity in the early centuries. A deconstructive view of the history of Christian theology need only take as its theme the constant, ever-varying, tension between faith and the metaphysical horizons of thought in which it was forced to find expression, in order to reveal the secret splendor of this history as the history of faith maintaining its identity in exile. If one attends to the thread of faith running through its tapestry one finds that the history of Christian theology witnesses against itself. Tensions and contradictions in the text between the explicit statements and its implicit attitude of faith are what the deconstructionist looks for, *failles* or clefts which allow the apparently monolithic discourse of the classical theologian to be prized open so that two orientations may be differentiated in the text, one tending to construct a metaphysical edifice in which elements of faith lose their original contours under the mightly spell of the Greek Logos, the other representing a biblically inspired resistance to this development. Any Christian theologian who deserves to be called a classic may be expected to show this ancient tension between Athens and Jerusalem in some form, and to show it textually, allowing wide scope for deconstructionist detective work.

The deconstructionist theologian must beware of received interpretations of the classic Christian texts, which invariably mask the original tension of faith seeking expression in a treacherous medium, and petrify the troubled life of the text into a set of stable opinions. Just as the sense of a Platonic dialogue is lost when one reads it in relation to "the philosophy of Plato," the set of opinions attributed to him, rather than an enactment of philosophical questioning as a living process, so the sense of a theological work is lost when one focuses on the doctrines and theologoumena it contains (even neglecting the fact that these doctrines, later fixed, may have been in the process of formation at the time of composition) rather than on the movement of faith seeking expression which provides the motivating intention of the text. It is not that the theologian has access to any homogeneous entity called "the intention of faith," for the component that might be so designated has a different form in each of the great texts, a form which has to be discerned anew in every case. It takes the flair of the philosopher to discern the basic movement of philosophical questioning in the texts of Plato and it takes the flair of a believer to uncover the movement of faith behind the complex procedures of a great theological text. The tension of a contemporary faith which wrestles with the received forms of tradition provides the necessary pre-understanding for grasping an analogous tension of faith in the ancient text and for building a deconstructive interpretation on that tension. The theologian's ongoing interrogation of the language of his or her own faith is what enables insight into the latent questions in the ancient texts. It is disappointing when scholars undiscriminatingly repeat the questions of the texts they study instead of penetrating the texture of those texts to uncover in them more radical questions which the ancient authors themselves were not able to formulate.

Of course this ambition of understanding the ancient authors better than they understood themselves will encounter objections like that of Paul de Man, who claims that a critic who thinks he or she is demystifying a literary text is in reality being demystified by the text itself.[16] There is some truth in this view, although it underestimates the degree to which the explicitation of the unconscious meaning of the classical texts can be wrested from them only by a violent jolt such as the crises of metaphysics provide. When we cease to treat hallowed theological texts with the devotional or aesthetic complacency of the unquestioning scholar we find that the text itself contains elements of a self-critical awareness which goes half way to meet its critic. The deconstruction of tradition is thus a continuation in more radical style of the critical activity of faith already operative in the tradition itself. The texts of tradition collude with the contemporary believer who would overcome their metaphysical dimension, just as the texts of Scripture collude with the contemporary demythologizer. The theologian's ally in each case is the specificity of faith insofar as it is beyond both myth and metaphysics. The wound that contemporary crises of understanding inflict on tradition, making it seem remote and useless, is thus convertible into a process of healing wherein tradition comes into its own in a new way, bearing witness in its newly recognized brokenness and finitude to the same spirit of faith which underlies our own more complicated questioning. As the monolith is shattered, the human history behind us emerges in its true contours and allows us to place ourselves as continuators of our quest. The critic of tradition is the true friend of tradition, freeing it from forgetfulness (whether its own or that imposed by its interpreters) of its true theme, revealing again, as its defensive embalmers cannot, that it is at heart a tradition of faith.

A quality of faith which both inspires and is made more clearly manifest by the deconstructive hermeneutics of tradition is its *finitude*. Faith is always the faith of a mortal human being at a particular time and place in a determinate relation to a concrete historical tradition. The metaphysical structuration of faith causes it to forget its finitude, giving it a discourse for all times and places, rendered autonomous in regard to the community and its praxis. The reduction of dogmatic metaphysical propositions about God to their true status as context-dependent confessions of faith, which have concrete meaning only in relation to the historical tradition which forms and continually reinterprets them, is an important move in the overcoming of metaphysical theology, one which contradicts the apparent intention of dogmatic formulae to express truth in a purely objective manner. Of course, this metaphysical myth of pure objectivity is partly something retrospectively projected on the formulae of the early Church by scholastic theology in the Middle Ages and still more so in the post-Cartesian period. The dogmas of Nicea and Chalcedon are far more "confessional" in texture and intention than

ever appears from their use in manuals of theology, gestures of faith
born of the tensions of a given historical situation, whose meaning is
quite unabstractable from that concrete context. The sense of Nicea
and Chalcedon today is the pertinence of the memory of that former
finite context to our own finite context. There is no transfinite
context in which we can abstract a sense in these Councils which
history cannot touch. To realize this is to inject an incalculable
element of irony into our dealings with these and other canonized
expressions of faith. Massive exercises in an effort at direct communication about an infinite object, these expressions in reality communicate to the contemporary believer only indirectly, opaquely,
eliciting a subterranean complicity of faith rather than a straightforward repetition. The formulae are tripped up by the finitude and
historicity of their texture, and they can continue to remain effective
vehicles of faith, and to refer to the object of faith, only when used
by the contemporary community with an ironic awareness that what
they intend to say cannot be said in the way they attempt. We have
the same ironic relationship to all our inherited religious language,
including that of the Psalms. Whether we say "There is a river
whose streams make glad the city of God" (Ps. 46:9) or "begotten,
not made, consubstantial with the Father" we know that we are
dealing with limited historical gestures from the past which serve
only obscurely as icons of our present reaching out in faith. To
cultivate such ironic awareness might seem subversive of faith and
of the objectivity of the reference of the language of faith. But a
realistic examination of the conditions of that language forces one to
the opposite conclusion: suppress irony and you have suppressed the
true referentiality of the language of faith; enforce the old-style
directness of utterance and you have struck faith dumb.

How clearly Christians are able to see the human limits of the
religious language of the Koran and the Talmud, or even, when the
veil of an allegorical vision is lifted, that of the Hebrew Bible! How
readily they will admit that the sense of this language can be fully
grasped only from its social context, that the faith it expresses is
mediated by a contingent historical system of representations which
it would take the skills of an anthropologist to reconstruct! The
irreducible pluralism and difference of religious cultures must bring

with it an ineluctable deferral of the directness of reference each of these cultures has naively claimed for its language of faith. Christians too are caught in this maze of indirectness, though they are often as slow to see this in their own case as they are quick to see it in the case of others. Without full realization of the severe historical limits imposed on every religious discourse and a constant humbling awareness of the finite, broken, imperfect, sinful, stumbling, and provisional texture of all religious expression past or present, theology is in danger of becoming bloated and unwholesome, forgetting that it rests on faith and that even the most sacrosanct dogmas and scriptures are no more in their concrete texture than groping, finite, human articulations of that faith. Claims to inspiration and infallibility ring quite false when they mask this. When theologians think back into the finitude of the tradition of faith, instead of thinking away from it, there occurs a renewal similar to that which is achieved when philosophy reroots itself in its basic attitude of questioning. The true grandeur of tradition as a history of faith comes to light, the grandeur of the struggle of sinful and erring believers for the authenticity of their faith. This battle for fidelity takes a new form in every epoch and is never won by a passive retention of the deposit of faith. Orthodoxy, like art, exists only as a struggle to realize vision. The vision is always revision and lives only as born of struggle. When the struggle ceases the deadness of the museum descends on its products, until an equally energetic interpretative response brings them to a new kind of life in the context of a later struggle. Theological tradition lives only as stirred from within or from without by the essential concerns and questions of faith. If the Spirit moves in tradition, to inspire or to preserve from error, it is plausible to believe that his movement is mediated through these concerns and questions. An indiscriminate hallowing of all the elements of tradition blinds us to the pneumatic stirrings in its texture. These are detected only in the ironic and irreverent play of faith with the languages it has received.

Faith as a critical principle, then, subverts everything in the past that is no longer a viable embodiment of faith. In doing so it may liberate treasures of faith hidden in the past but which had become inaccessible to us because of the screening effect of the metaphysical systems in which these treasures were deposed. If we follow the critical hunches of our contemporary faith with confidence, despite the fact that these hunches often come in the negative form of doubts, we can link up with the hidden theme of the tradition, the secret history of faith, which gives vivid human contours to what otherwise seems a history of alienation. Of course, our faith must itself be sustained by the tradition, and our critique of tradition must always be translatable into the terms of the tradition's own critique of itself. Otherwise the prophetic hermeneutic of faith degenerates into mere iconoclastic violence. But if faith is the critical agent we need not fear to "theologize with a hammer," delicately sounding all the hollow spots in the walls of traditional edifices, and occasionally shattering sacred monuments which block the access of faith to its theme.

Conditions of a Hermeneutic "from Faith to Faith"

The method I have been recommending could be called a hermeneutic "from faith to faith" (Rom. 1:17). It presumes that the classical texts, despite the hold of ontotheology, can best be interpreted as witnesses of faith and that faith is never utterly alienated in its metaphysical form, so that there is always something for the believer to read when he approaches the texts of metaphysical theology with an eye to their meaning for faith. It presumes also that it is the reader's own faith which lights up the contemporary sense of the ancient texts. All of this may well be regarded as an idealistic simplification of the problems of hermeneutics today, so we shall attempt to test it here by reflecting on the conditions it must meet.

First of all, is it linguistically viable to speak of "faith" in the way we have? Are we appealing to some supernatural principle superior to and untouched by the range of historical languages in which the word "faith" occurs? Yet theology clearly has no access to any identification of faith not already couched in one of these languages, nor can it abstract a univocal definition of faith from the plurality of the historical senses of the word. It is a multi-storied word, in the sense that the many narratives to which it belongs (and even scholastic theology can be counted as a narrative in this context) are sedimented one on another to produce a semantic saturation. This makes the word so rich that it must seem to lack the clinical sharpness needed if it is to be used in the task of critical hermeneutics.

Much the same objection could be made against Heidegger's hermeneutics of the metaphysical tradition in light of the question of being. Heidegger would answer the objection by claiming that the question of being is the central concern which unifies the history of metaphysics. In some sense it should be possible to claim that faith too is a central theme which unifies the history of theology. Why faith? Why not "love" or "Spirit" or "the Word of God" or "the Church"? Could not these have served equally well as leading themes for a deconstruction of theology? But it is Western theology itself which has conferred a special status on the notion of faith as defining its character, as in the best known definition of theology: "faith seeking understanding." This is because the metaphysical culture in which theology developed emphasized so strongly the noetic aspect of things, that it was necessary for theology to insist on its own unique noetic principle of faith. The importance of orthodoxy and dogma is of a piece with this. Faith in the noetic sense, orthodoxy and dogma are of little importance in the Hebrew scriptures and even in the New Testament it is not the noetic aspect of faith which predominates. The theme of faith unifies the history of Christian theology because it is the badge of Christian identity over against the metaphysical structures which threatened to absorb it. Thus in taking faith as our theme we are espousing the critical, counter-metaphysical resources of classical theology itself insofar as it became increasingly committed to faith as the key to its essential concerns. In the process, however, the notion of faith itself was grasped in narrowly noetic terms, showing once again how deeply Christianity was influenced by metaphysics even in the methods chosen to oppose it. Faith, orthodoxy and dogma, as traditionally understood, are the bulwarks of biblical revelation against its absorption by the Western Logos. Yet these very bulwarks are constantly mined from within by the degree to which they themselves

are shaped by the demands of that Logos. Faith becomes an epistemological principle; orthodoxy tends to equate faith excessively with
correctness of opinion; dogma formulates faith in sets of propositions resembling the sets of theses a philosopher might enunciate.
The theme of faith has organized a strategy of resistance to metaphysics within classical and modern theology, despite the plurality
of senses in which faith was concretely understood and despite the
changeable character of the metaphysical opponent as well. There is
only a family resemblance between the "faith" for which Athanasius stands against Arianism or Gregory of Nyssa against Eunomius
in the fourth century and the "faith" which Kirkegaard defends
against Hegel in the nineteenth, just as there is only a family resemblance between the metaphysical opponents in each case. Nonetheless the sequence of such situations forms a coherent history, the
unfolding of the dilemma of Western theology, caught between Jew
and Greek. Hence the schema of faith versus metaphysics, if broken
down into the sequence of these concrete struggles, can still provide
a deconstructive key to the history of theology.

But if the opposition of faith and metaphysics is itself a metaphysical one, as my remarks about the noetic emphasis in classical theology imply, then how can it serve to deconstruct metaphysical
theology? Will a hermeneutic from faith to faith do any more than
confirm the noetic emphasis and the oppositions it has classically
generated? What strategic innovation can the theme of faith bring
about at this late stage? None, it seems, without the aid of a Derridean turn of the screw, which perhaps might take the following
form: Our inherited use of the idea of "faith" is shaped by the
classical oppositions of faith and reason, orthodoxy and heresy,
submission to dogma and speculative understanding. But there is
beginning to prevail in our language another sense of the word
"faith" which runs counter to this traditional noetic emphasis.
"Faith" in this emergent sense resonates more strongly with the
biblical models of trust in God and openness to God's saving intervention than with any of the classical accounts of faith. The latter
seem confining, while the biblical confessions of faith are now heard
less as dogmatic claims than as events of recognition and trustful
commitment, e.g., Peter's "Thou art the Christ, the Son of the

Living God" (Matt. 16:16). If the spearhead of resistance to metaphysics in classical theology is the emphasis on faith, then the stick-
ing point for a deconstructive reading would seem to be the tension
between the two directions in which the notion of faith is pulled,
back to its biblical origins and forward into a noetic system of
metaphysically shaped dogmas. If we espouse the theme of faith in
classical theology, and so dwell in it that its opposition to metaphysics is radicalized through a shifting of emphasis from its noetic to its
more fundamental biblical character of trust and engagement, then
we can rehandle the tensions between faith and metaphysics in the
classical texts in a more differentiated way. We turn the classical
opposition of faith and metaphysics against the classical notion of
faith insofar as this is itself metaphysical. Thus the classical language is caught in a permanent contradiction with itself, as its every
counter-metaphysical gesture is discovered to be inwardly in partial
collusion with what it opposes. The thrust of that language is against
the gravitational pull of metaphysical reason, yet it scarcely avoids
surrendering to it entirely. Now with the weakening of the force of
gravity of metaphysics as far as faith is concerned, we can perhaps
carry the counter-metaphysical thrust of the classical languages of
faith further in the direction they indicate, perhaps to the point of
leaving the solar system of metaphysics altogether behind. Then it
will no longer be the sun of the Western Logos which provides the
primary illumination and control to theological discourse, but faith
will become more autonomously *sui ipsius interpres,* its own interpreter, and its dialogue with other religious traditions and the
human sciences will be governed by the dynamics of its own quest
rather than by an overarching metaphysics.

However, in this hermeneutic from faith to faith, from faith
imprisoned in metaphysics to faith at last free to find its own articulation, the *from* and the *to* are ideal points of departure and arrival.
For faith is never totally alienated from itself in the language it uses,
however encumbered with myth or metaphysics, nor is it ever totally
present to itself in some at last perfectly essential language. Even the
language of Scripture is not a perfect vehicle of faith. It had a
relative adequacy in its day and continues to enjoy a relative adequacy as long as we struggle to find the spirit the letter conceals. The

theological critique of metaphysical language seeks to move from relative oppression of faith to its relative liberation, in full awareness that its attainments can be only provisional. The overcoming of metaphysics is only the current move or set of moves in the perpetual game of renewing the language of faith. The clarification of the specificity and autonomy of faith over against metaphysics is by no means the final answer to the question about faith's true identity; it merely frees us to pose that question more radically than was hitherto possible. After the solar system come the vacant interstellar spaces, after the assurance of metaphysics the nakedness of faith left to itself, "as dark as night to the understanding."[17] Faith is always embodied in a language, and we can never simply oppose it to its "expression." But one can oppose to the apparent noetic wealth of past languages a new linguistic exercise which insists on articulating the most elemental realities of faith, cutting through all forms of language which do not contribute to this task and treating them as screens against real insight. This quest for the elements will send faith back to the simplest, apparently poorest words of its language and even these will no longer be the carriers of systematic metaphysical insight, for an effort will be made to confine their usage to what befits a pure vocabulary of faith. One can never, of course, establish a pure set of essential names, but this quest for the original poverty of the language of faith can set up a critical ferment which produces a language of faith which in all its utterances is distinctly and consciously counter-metaphysical, a style of speaking which gains its thrust and point from going against the grain of the established ways of articulating faith. There is no simple movement from a metaphysical to a post-metaphysical language of faith, but a change of direction can be brought about if we treat the metaphysical heritage as something of which we must despoil ourselves, rather than build it up further. If we still use metaphysical terms it will be in such a way as to contradict their traditional function of accumulating systematic insight and to show up instead their poverty as words of faith. Any such usage will imply an artful wrench, displacing the word from its metaphysical context and opening it to the articulation of faith. For instance, the "very peripatetic" definition, "God: a noise in the street," which occurs in Ulysses, wrenches the

word "God" out of its habitual metaphysical contexts. Many lines in
Blake achieve similar displacements: "Hold Infinity in the palm of
your hand." The language of Luther or Karl Barth also occasionally
throws up such counter-metaphysical flashes, inspired by Scripture.
But until such displacements infiltrate the entire texture of the
theological usage of traditional jargon progress on the liberation of
theology from metaphysical habit will be slight.

In setting deconstruction at the service of faith in this way are we
not robbing deconstruction of its radical adventurousness, allowing
it to be controlled by a single, fixed ideological orientation? But is
this a correct account of "faith" as we have sighted it (in opposition
to its domesticated presentation in classical theology)? In following
this search for the originary language of faith perhaps we may
discover that the reference and meaning of that language are every
bit as enigmatic as the reference and meaning of the poems of
Mallarmé, on which deconstruction thrives. Could the complexities
latent in our language of faith be brought to light in any other way?
Could any merely literary deconstruction of the language of faith,
playing fast and loose with the rhetorical tropes which constitute it,
match the much more interesting unstitching of that language
which occurs when we contest the habitual rhetoric of faith in the
name of faith itself? Could a deconstruction not guided by faith in
this sense ever successfully engage with the riddlesome and almost
self-contradictory enterprise of the language which can continue to
communicate only by overthrowing all its previous forms. Poetic
creation is subject to a similar law, of course, but its dynamics are
adequately traceable by a literary deconstruction, since its verbal
achievements are an end in themselves. The language of faith, however, always has as its context the struggle to maintain or achieve a
practical, spiritual way of life, and it is this context which gives that
language its peculiar force. The overcoming of former languages of
faith could never be fruitful if it did not proceed from the practical
effort to live the faith in a more radical way, or from a change in the
way of living the faith forced on one by a changing cultural situation. A deconstruction of the language of faith not guided by faith
itself would thus not deal with the language as one of *faith*, but only
with the husk which remains when it is considered as a merely

literary product. Conversely such a deconstruction might teach us much about the possibilities of language in general, but it could not indicate any concrete possibilities for a contemporary language of faith as such.

These remarks bring us to consider another major condition of the hermeneutic from faith to faith, an unavoidable law which is likely to be discomforting to many academic theologians, namely, that this hermeneutic cannot be carried out except by people who are rooted in a community and praxis of faith. A literary deconstructionist might analyze the texture of classical theological discourse and discover that faith was never quite at home in its metaphysical language, and that many elements in that classical discourse point to a more originary language of faith, which would break with the constraints of metaphysics. But without a practical engagement in the contemporary struggle of faith the deconstructionist would be unable to solicit those more originary elements in a strategic way, for want of a strong position of faith *from* which to approach the texts. Such a position cannot be found in a theory of faith but only in the fresh discourse born of engagement. Without these existential moorings a hermeneutic of tradition degenerates into a fastidious sifting of words, unable to articulate the "unthought" of the tradition which only a lively contemporary faith can recognize.

The theologian who is connected by no channels of constant communication with the community whose faith is the sole material of theology has undoubtedly developed a perverse relation to the subject matter, one which makes it very difficult to focus the data of faith in the horizon of faith. In the horizon of the isolated individual these data tend to become objects of doubt and bewilderment and faith in them, a paradoxical exercise. The academic tone is obviously a safer one for a theologian in this situation, for it need never betray the uneasy relation of the believer to the data of faith. The greatness of Kierkegaard is that he masked nothing of his isolation and unease and risked a stance of faith even in the unpropitious conditions that were bound to have, and did have, a distorting effect. A theologian can understand such contemporary forms of alienation from the communal language of faith, but they need not be allowed to define the horizon of the theological hermeneutic. The sureness of touch that marks the theology of Irenaeus or Athanasius shows their thought to be firmly rooted in an ecclesial existence, and sureness of touch in interpreting them demands an analogous rootedness. When the little faith of the theologian is reinforced by and representative of the faith of the community, then its investment in an intellectual quest becomes part of the Church's struggle to reform its own language. The weight of centuries of university theology can make it hard for theologians to find the ecclesial context of their work, so that the quest for that context must be resumed again, yet it is just this step from Athens to Jerusalem which has always given Western theology its peculiar tension and vitality. The following paragraph might be rewritten as the program of a church theologian engaged in overcoming the metaphysical elements in church discourse:

> If it is not to disown the promise and in that way cease to be the Church, the Church is committed to a struggle against the acute chronic diseases from which its proclamation must constantly suffer. But this being the case, its only resource is to seize the weapon of continually listening. But it must listen in such a way that its whole life is put in question. It must listen in such a way that its whole life should be assailed, convulsed, revolutionised and reshaped. . . . the word to which it listens must always be the Word of God. It actually has to go back to its starting-point. It has to show the self-denial and determination to start all over again from that point. Of course, it has to do this as the Church which is marked by all that has existed and occurred in the interval, not in unfaithfulness but in faithfulness, not in ingratitude but in gratitude, not with violence but with regard for the various forms of teaching which have so far been granted to it with more or less human clarity or obscurity, in which and with which it has lived up to the present —yet radically prepared for the fact that today, tomorrow and the day after the whole of its treasure will again have to be enlightened and illuminated, assessed and weighed by the Word of God. . . . This is the necessity which dogmatics has to represent. Its task is to summon to an active consideration of this necessity.[18]

While theologians shun this demanding role they cannot discover the hermeneutic potential of faith.

Yet having said this, I feel it must be added that the overcoming of metaphysics from the horizon of faith, though it is the only approach that can lead back from the classical formations of Christianity to their hidden theme, is in practice usually preceded or sparked off by a disenchantment with metaphysics born of doubt. There are religious thinkers who cannot make securely their own the vast communal and traditional horizons of ecclesial faith, but are constantly balloted by the misgivings which assail their contemporaries in regard to the Church. Such thinkers practice a theology at degree zero, a "wintry" theology (Rahner), so resolute in its noncompliance with the usual complacencies of theological diction that it almost consigns itself to silence. Such thinkers may be hypersensitive to the "bad faith" palpable in certain too vocal manifestations of faith, in whatever speculative or fideistic style, and may feel that faith is better expressed in a patient confrontation with the problems of its language and in an ever-deeper sense of the provisionality and feebleness of all languages of faith. The wintry theologian's faith thus takes the form of methodical doubt directed at any and every expression of faith and shows itself in a modesty and restraint in the use of such words as "God," "grace," "salvation" which come near to utter invisibility. As the conventional languages of faith die away, the wintry theologian becomes more and more oblique in his allusions to the themes of faith, preferring to communicate by a *neti, neti* (not this, not that) of doubtful mystical intent, so that even the language of prayer becomes a lamentation for vanished languages of prayer.

This wintry figure is a type who surfaces throughout the history of Judaism and Christianity, and even has a minor, but honorable, place in Scripture itself in the person of Qohelet. For all its indirectness, such a theology of suspicion may still be listening for the Word of God as the something that is communicated by the language of scripture and tradition even after it has been tested in the crucible of a Beckettian desolation, or as that which is subtly incarnate in secular contexts, the indices of the kingdom to be gleaned in novels, films, or political happenings. This emaciated theology cannot provide the governing perspective for a critical hermeneutic of tradition, which would demand a warmer sympathy with the older languages of faith as well as a more comprehensive vision of what it is given to the Church to live, think, and speak today. But the negative sensitivity it develops should be integrated as a critical factor into all contemporary theology, so that the convincingness of any received language of faith for this age of doubt can be soberly assessed.

In the last analysis the deconstruction of tradition is the effect of a change in the consciousness of the Christian community, a change which it articulates and confirms. It is the reappropriation of the tradition in light of a change in the Church's self-understanding. This theological enterprise is sustained by a movement afoot in the Church at large and thus has everything to gain from remaining in close contact and dialogue with that movement. The damaging marginality which was the lot of Pascal, Kierkegaard, and the Modernists need not be that of the contemporary theological deconstructionist, for the crisis of metaphysical theology has now become a public one and the Church as a whole is thrown back on the necessity of adopting a prophetic style of teaching and acting. Hence the need to reappropriate the tradition as what in a hidden way it is, a tradition of prophetic witness. Thus as theology busies itself with the emendation of its language—like that ship which must undertake repairs in mid-ocean, with no possibility of a return to dry dock—it is enacting the Church's growth "from faith to faith" insofar as *ecclesia semper reformanda* includes the task of *lingua semper reformanda*. I shall now sketch an outline of how the early stages of the tradition might appear when thus viewed.

Hellenization

The dehellenization of Christianity is a task which can never be accomplished. The cultural symbiosis of the biblical and Hellenistic worlds from the fourth century B.C.E. to the fourth century C.E. (when the classical dogmatic shape of Christianity was securely established) brought about so complex a fusion of Greek and

Hebrew elements, at the most fundamental levels of speech, thought, and imagination that, while we may embark on a counter-metaphysical effort to play off the original biblical elements against their later Greek transformation, this direction of thinking, strategically chosen in view of the current needs of faith and opposed to the ascendancy of metaphysical thinking in the past, can never be followed through with complete consequence and transparency. A complete dehellenization of Christianity would have to unwrite the New Testament. Even if we confine our attention to the explicitly metaphysical dimension of hellenistic culture, it is doubtful that the point can ever be reached at which the pure demetaphysicized "essence" of Christianity could be distilled from its original hellenistic articulation.

One of the carriers of metaphysical thinking in the hellenistic world is the imagery of light, which is elaborated at an imaginative, preconceptual level and seems part of the "ordinary language" of religion in the Greek-speaking world. In the fourth century Christianity becomes more logical, conceptual, and dogmatic than before, and the imaginative dynamics of religious discourse are subordinated to this firm logical order. But in the incubatory period of metaphysical theology it is imagination that is dominant; Justin, Clement, and Origen sketch metaphysical systems, but do not treat them as intrinsically more serious than the narrative and symbolic dimensions of their discourse; there is free commerce between the conceptual and the imaginative. The insistence at Nicea on a word which defied imagination, the word *homoousion,* as the anchor of orthodoxy represents a new seriousness in assuming the rigor of metaphysical logic in Christian discourse. Thus, while the metaphysical shape of the thinking of the post-Nicene authors is relatively easy to identify, there is a greater fluidity and mobility in the dealings of the second and third century Fathers with metaphysics, and our diagnosis must take into account subtle virtualities of language and imagery as well as the bold speculative strokes. Philo's metaphysical imagination loved to contemplate "the Absolute, connected with phenomena by His Light-Stream, the Logos or Sophia,"[19] "a Light which was discerned by the Light-Rays that he

shot forth.''[20] In his case this imagery of light is clearly consubstantial with a metaphysical system, albeit one still encased in mythic
representations and reaching only an inchoate conceptual or logical
autonomy. But the writings of Gnosticism and the New Testament
are also full of this light-imagery, which, while it is not explicitly
metaphysical in their case, lends itself easily to the unifying and
grounding habits of thought characteristic of metaphysics. In each
case the contemporary deconstructionist will attempt to interpret
this imagery in a counter-metaphysical direction, thinking back to
the underlying phenomenological realities which the image of light
threatens to mask by intellectualizing and idealizing them.

In the case of the Gospel of John one might begin by overcoming
intellectualizing interpretations of the Gospel, which have held sway
in Christian theology from the start, in order to recover the mystical,
contemplative texture of the Evangelist's thought.[21] But a second
step is also required. The Johannine notions of Logos or Light may
not have been intended in a metaphysical sense by their author, but
they lend themselves to metaphysical interpretation because of their
place in the hellenistic language and imagination. The Johannine
notions themselves must be overcome insofar as they lend themselves to this misinterpretation. The recovery of their counter-metaphysical bearing will be complete only when the stability of these
notions themselves is called in question by the phenomenality of that
to which they witness, through a deconstructive solicitation of the
tensions in John between the system of symbolic themes which
structure the vision of the work and the elements which cannot be
perfectly integrated into that system. Such an extension of the overcoming of metaphysics in the deconstruction of pre-metaphysical
biblical thinking builds a specifically Western road back into the
world of biblical theology, one diametrically opposed to the Western
metaphysical colonization of Scripture in the past.

In Justin, Clement, and Origen, too, there is a developed imagination of light and Logos (to name only two of many similar themes)
which, while it is in collusion with explicitly philosophical methods
of thinking, as the New Testament treatment of such themes is not,
nevertheless also has a side which cannot be simply and directly
classified as metaphysical. Could one, for example, treat Justin's

language about baptism as "illumination" as simply metaphysical? Yet even without speculative intent or conceptual content such religious images can cohere to form an imaginative system which already reveals the lineaments of what will later be precipitated as a full-fledged ontotheology. For instance, a supreme light may be envisioned as the source and foundation of lesser lights, as lighting up the whole cosmos in a universal, unifying way, so that all lives and moves and has its being in this light. A systematic enchainment between the inaccessible light of God, the revealing light of the Logos, the light of truth manifest in the words of Scripture, the light of grace illuminating the *pneumatikoi,* and the light of reason whereby pagans and heretics are overcome is thus first envisioned imaginatively, and only later hammered out in conceptual terms. Surely the elements of this metaphysical imagination can be used by a Christian preacher with a certain suspension of their metaphysical dynamic; we cannot say that the tendency of such imagery in an early Christian writing is always metaphysical, for it may quite well be counter-metaphysical, retrieving perhaps some of the Hebrew overtones of the images of light and Logos, as in "He covers himself with light as with a garment" (cf. Ps 104:2) or in the prophets' accounts of the power of God's creative word. In discerning the drift of the Christian imagination in the early centuries we cannot simply judge in advance that such and such a word or image is "hellenistic" and therefore proto-metaphysical, for faith can always insist unexpectedly on its own irreducible identity by breaking with the prevailing habits of thought of hellenistic culture. The points at which such resistance to the implications of hellenistic diction occurs within that diction itself are perhaps the most instructive feature of Ante-Nicene writing in regard to our problematic.

The period extending from the Wisdom literature of the Hebrew Bible to Augustine and Pseudo-Dionysius offers scholars and theologians countless occasions to pursue a controversy centered on such questions as the following: To what extent is the thought of Philo, Paul, Justin, Origen based on biblical faith, and to what extent is it a product of hellenistic thinking? Is the hellenistic element used apologetically or does it intrinsically determine the thinking of the author? Has authentic faith been swallowed up in quasi-philosophical speculations? Is the God of this author still the God of Abraham, or has Abraham's God been replaced by a metaphysical *arché?* Usually these controversial questions are never satisfactorily resolved. The reason is that the fusion of Greek and Hebrew in these authors is so deep that it often undercuts the authors' own explicit declarations that they intend to adopt a purely biblical or a broadly metaphysical approach. To a large extent they are unconscious of the dimensions of the fusion of Greek and Hebrew that is afoot in their language. Furthermore, such authors as Justin and Origen express a complex ambivalence in their statements about the relations of faith and philosophy, and this is increased when we take into account the unconscious ambivalence to which the texture of their writing testifies. More scholars aim at a positivist accuracy in determining the extent of the biblical and philosophical contributions to the resulting amalgam. But this does not yield insight into the dynamics of the interplay between the two strands in the texts, the complex coming and going between faith and philosophy which in a creative and resourceful writer always reserves surprises for the student. Positivist scholarship cannot enter into the play of the text, seeing it as a mobile interaction of forces, a fermentation set up by the ineluctable convergence of two traditions which could never be perfectly reconciled.

The "hellenistic" and "biblical/ecclesial" readings of Origen, those of Hal Koch, Endre von Ivanka and Franz Heinrich Kettler on the one hand, and those of Henri de Lubac and Henri Crouzel on the other, do become involved in the play of the text, but when they succumb to one-sidedness, either seeing Origen as a philosopher insensitive to the specific concerns of biblical faith, or as a churchman who kept a pure distance from the world of hellenistic philosophical wisdom, they fall victim to the subtlety of Origen's mind, in which faith and philosophy grow together in a mutual accommodation full of ambivalence. Like the Origenist controversies of the past, the present debate among scholars reenacts the tensions in Origen's writing; a reading of Origen which would consciously assume these tensions has yet to be practiced. Each of the opposing tendencies in the present debate provides a refreshing corrective to the other and

from the tug of war between them a creative deconstructive hermeneutics may be born.

Whether they proclaim the superiority of the Gospel to the folly
of philosophy or whether they present Christianity as the true philosophy and the culmination of the partial wisdom of Greece (or
whether with significant inconsistency they do both, as Justin seems
to do), the Fathers of the Church are united in regarding the Word
of Scripture (and the teaching of the Church) as possessing supreme
authority, while the findings of philosophy can have a merely auxiliary status in comparison. This simple fact guarantees to patristic
theology a powerful counter-metaphysical thrust. But it does not
justify the apologetics of those who claim the issue of hellenization is
a pseudo-problem. For despite their conviction of the superiority of
the biblical revelation the Fathers unavoidably understood that revelation in a metaphysical way. When metaphysics encroached on the
integrity of that revelation in a tangible way, they could repel it by a
counter-metaphysical appeal to the authority of God's Word. But
many intangible encroachments they scarcely notice at all, and even
when they do resist metaphysics it is with the aid of alternative
metaphysical models (such as Justin's personalized and transcendent "sowing Word" opposed to the pantheistic Logos of Stoicism;
Origen's substitution of the Trinity for the supreme principles of
Platonism), the metaphysical horizon is the governing horizon of
their thought, and the biblical content is fitted into it, with whatever
local corrections of metaphysics are required. In this battle of languages metaphysics is a winner just as much as the biblical revelation, and it constantly threatens to colonize the latter, making
renewed insistence on the specific character of the biblical revelation
necessary.

How thoroughly Origen made his home in the world of Scripture,
finding that as he preached from the sacred text, sharing his
trouvailles with the community as soon as they were born, "discerning spiritual things for the spiritual," a more life-size wisdom
unfolded than could ever be reached in the technical disputations of
the academy. Yet the very texture of the allegorizing mind Origen
brought to Scripture is Platonic and philosophical through and
through. It is that his christological or ecclesiological exegesis of the

Song of Songs brings the philosophical, spiritualizing method of Philo back to a rich salvation-historical concreteness, nearer to the typology practiced by Paul or the author of Hebrews. Yet that biblical typology itself is one of the elements in the New Testament which most lend themselves to metaphysical misinterpretation, and so need to be overcome in light of the concrete perception of the links between the Hebrew Scriptures and the Christ-event to which they rather clumsily witness. Origen's use of even such typology is inspired by the speculative desire to crack open the hard places of Scripture and make them transparent to spiritual vision. In his capacious and versatile way he is still a system builder as he woos the text this way and that in order to uncover its spiritual meaning. He accommodates his metaphysical aspirations to the great diversity of the biblical data, postponing the satisfaction of the ultimate integration of all these data into a system, but building assiduously towards that ultimate integration through all the relaxed and digressive commentaries he accumulates. This intention is foreign to Paul and to the author of the Letter to the Hebrews. Typology serves in their case to bring home with force a vision of the salvation wrought by Christ. It does not have the discreetly theoretical bearing Origen never tires of trying to confer on it. Typology in Origen is never merely a spiritual exercise, but always a speculative exercise of faith seeking understanding. This can lead him to indulge in typology for typology's sake, on the principle that any increment of theoretical insight is to be valued, however feeble its moral or spiritual impact. Thus the metaphysical horizon of thought was too deeply implanted in Origen's mind, too thoroughly inscribed in his language, for him to be able to overcome it even in constant and exclusive exposure to the biblical text. If this is true in the case of the most ardently biblical of the Fathers, it is clear that there could be no effective defense against the pervasive presence of metaphysics in the early Church. It lodged in every corner of the Christian mind. Fidelity to the Gospel could not be achieved in independence from metaphysics, but only in a lucid struggle to maintain the essentials of Christian identity in and through an adroit handling of the terms and categories of metaphysics. In the Ante-Nicene period this struggle proceeds in a largely nonreflexive way, for the terms and categories of metaphysical theology had not yet acquired strong definition and tensions between the structure of metaphysical thinking and biblical faith were masked by the free communication of their softened idioms. The Nicene showdown changed all this, and raised the struggle between faith and metaphysics to new levels of lucidity in the discourse of precise dogmatic definition and in negative theology. Neither of these, of course, represents a simple triumph of faith over metaphysics, but they both show a sudden conscious alertness to the dangers of metaphysics among the fourth century theologians.

The Origin of Dogma

In identifying the biblical God with the God of metaphysics and Jesus Christ (the Johannine Logos) with the Logos of Greek philosophy, *mutatis mutandis,* the Greek Fathers assumed a homology between Christian and philosophical truth whereby the whole of Greek intellectuality could be taken captive to the truth revealed in Christ. But there is perhaps no such thing as a one-way conquest, and it can be said as well that the Gospel of Christ was taken captive by Greek intellectuality, though not necessarily in a sense implying a real falsification of the Christian faith in those centuries. The threat of such a falsification was, however, a real one, as heresy after heresy tried to push the homology between faith and philosophy too far. To counter this threat the orthodox Church had recourse to increasingly emphatic methods of stressing the specific elements of the message of faith over against efforts to reduce them to philosophical schemes of understanding; hence the emergence of that peculiar type of utterance we call dogmatic. The alliance of faith and philosophy triumphed gloriously over pagan myth and superstition and over the deviations of Gnosticism, and its advantages far outweighed whatever perils it might bring. As the basic principles of philosophy were increasingly redefined in Christian terms—so that cosmology was founded in the biblical doctrine of creation, theology, and theodicy in the doctrine of the Father and his Logos, ethics, and psychology in the doctrines of sin and grace—a process of intellectual transfusion occurred whereby Christianity was enabled to replace metaphysics as the supreme intellectual system of the West.

Was this an entirely unambiguous realization of the biblical command: "Go, teach all nations . . ."? or was it, like Constantinism, an experiment which can teach us as much by its failures as by its successes? The creeds and dogmas which were originally forged to defend Christian identity against absorption by Hellenistic currents of thought and religiosity, became after Nicea the instruments of the exclusive establishment of Christianity as the true philosophy abrogating all others. A deconstruction of this development could begin by recovering the defensive sense of dogma and overcoming its constructive aspirations to build a total systematic explication of the real in which the dogmas play the role of first principles. But even defensive dogma insofar as it lends itself to this constructive misuse must itself be overcome in light of the phenomenality of revelation to which it is answerable. Dogma may have been counter-metaphysical insofar as it preserved the identity of faith against metaphysical absorption; but by its emphasis on definition and certitude and its claim to be treated as a first principle dogma betrayed its own purpose and became the instrument of the strongest assumption of a metaphysical identity by the Christian faith.

The first really severe crisis of the alliance between faith and metaphysics is that signaled by the Arian heresy, which, building on the thought of the earlier Fathers, attempted to push the homology between the Christian doctrines of God, the Logos, and creation and the structures of Platonic theology and cosmology to the point of confounding the ontological status of the eternal Son with that of the demiurge who mediates between God and the world in Middle Platonic theory. As a systematic intensification of the subordinationism latent in previous theology, Arianism had both a progressivist and a traditionalist appeal. The metaphysical streamlining of the Christian message which it proposed must have seemed in harmony with the spirit of that Constantinian period in which a hitherto unprecedented harmony between Church and culture had been attained. Had Arianism prevailed the tensions between Christian faith and its metaphysical environment might have ceased forever; but faith itself would then also have ceased.

Much has been written in recent years on the Nicene *homoousion* as an instance of the Church's resistance to hellenization in the early centuries. The Fathers of Nicea used this word, it is claimed, as simple pastors warding off a clear and present danger to the integrity of the faith and with a certain suspension of whatever subtle metaphysical overtones might attach to the word *ousia* (nature, substance, stuff, being) in this context. Though the word sounds philosophical its introduction into the Creed has nothing to do with philosophy but directly expresses a necessity of faith. Athanasius, the great defender of Nicea, is, indeed, one of the least speculative of the Fathers, excelling in the rebuttal of unsound argument and the marshalling of scriptural support for the basic elements of doctrine. He has the strength of an elemental thinker, and as such might serve as a model for anyone wishing to return to the biblical bedrock of the Christian tradition. His task was to lay the foundations of a new period in theology by clearing the ground of every philosophical futility and setting forth in strong relief the set of basic truths in which the Christian message consists.

But in thus limiting the authority and the activities of metaphysical reason, Nicea and Athanasius paradoxically launched the greatest period of metaphysical theology. The refutation of Arianism demanded a new vigilance and logical rigor of theologians. To enter into and dismantle the arguments of the Arians, and still more so of the logic-chopping Neo-Arians (Eunomians), was a task that demanded an unprecedented linguistic and conceptual precision. It also widened the gap between the increasingly rarefied arguments of theology and the scriptural texture of preaching. The extreme concentration of attention on the Son's eternal procession "from the *ousia* of the Father," though sustained by a constant supply of scriptural and soteriological argument, habituated theologians to discussions of the divine essence in abstraction from the horizon of revelation. But it is the more rigorously logical texture of their argumentation which most testifies to the triumph of metaphysics in the Nicene theologians. Athanasius frequently shows that Arian claims would rob the economy of salvation of its necessary grounds, and presents the orthodox teaching as a set of fundamental logical principles undergirding the language of Scripture and worship and far surpassing the alternative Arian hermeneutic in coherence and

salvific impact. Chief among these principles is the sharpened differentiation between the being of God and the being of creatures, and
the correlative precision in defining the divine and human natures of
Christ and their different functions. The connections between cause
and effect, ground and grounded, in the system of Christian truth
are spelled out with a new insistence—especially the dependence of
our salvation and "divinization" on the gracing of human nature
through its assumption by one who is truly God. (Even in the conventional apologetic of the *De Incarnatione* Athanasius justifies the
Christian message far more radically than Origen in the *Contra
Celsum* by showing the causes underlying every aspect of the incarnation, death, and resurrection of Christ and conferring logical
rationality on what at first seems a far-fetched tale.) Athanasius can
never be content with the verbal surface of the Christian revelation,
for this surface has become treacherous, due to the Arian claim that
such titles as "Lord" and "God" are only honorifically conferred on
Christ. He defends the reference of these titles by tracing them back
to their ground in the ontological structures they reflect. Thus
despite the elemental nature of his concerns, his exclusive desire to
uphold the integrity of the biblical message and to prevent its words
from being robbed of their reality, Athanasius follows the methods
of metaphysical reasoning more tenaciously than any previous
Christian writer, constantly thinking towards the logical ground of
the claims of faith. The fact that this thinking is defensive in its
intent, and that its highest constructive aim is to provide a viable
scriptural hermeneutic, and the fact that it repetitively insists on
essentials to the exclusion of the least speculative digression, certainly indicate a wariness of any metaphysical thinking not regulated by the biblical Word. But Athanasius uses metaphysics to fight
metaphysics, as he hammers out a set of axioms and reinforces a
system of logical connections which will provide the groundplan for
a new, more radical metaphysical structuration of the faith. Thus,
the counter-metaphysical thrust of the Council of Nicea is rapidly
integrated into a reorganized system of metaphysical theology, and
what was intended to defend the integrity of biblical revelation in
fact generates a systematic, logical presentation of biblical truth,
whose capacity to lure the mind away from the horizons of biblical

revelation eventually becomes far greater than anything that preceded it.

Negative Theology

The renewal of negative theology among the Nicene Fathers is a
sign of their nascent awareness of the dangers of the new style of
theologizing. Hilary of Poitiers and Gregory of Nyssa in particular
return again and again to the themes of the infinity and incomprehensibility of God, not only in polemic against Arian presumption,
but also in a reflexive critique of the status of their own theological
language. The themes of the divine incomprehensibility and uncon-
tainability were largely devotional rather than methodological in
earlier writers since Philo. Now they are integrated fully into the
texture of theological argumentation, though not yet developed systematically in the manner of Pseudo-Dionysius. This apophatic current is another of the counter-metaphysical thrusts in which
Christian faith reveals its autonomous vitality at each point in its
history at which it is threatened with absorption by metaphysics.
But it too meets the fate of each of these movements of resistance,
and is absorbed into a more capacious metaphysical theology, thus
confirming the sway of metaphysical reason rather than overthrowing it. Yet each of these movements testifies to the final irreducibility of faith to metaphysical comprehension. If we retrieve this
dimension of their significance, through a critique of what allowed
them to be overtaken by the metaphysics they opposed, recovering,
for example, the biblical witness of the Nicene *homoousion* by
subordinating it to the scriptural confession of Christ ("My Lord
and my God"—John 20:28), to which it has nothing to add, and by
dismantling the metaphysical vision the word has carried, then we
can espouse faith's historical resistance to metaphysics with a new
clarity and depth, doing full justice to those dogmatic, apophatic, or
biblicist gestures which a speculative theology would emasculate by
smoothly integrating them into its texture. The ruggedness and
thorniness of the path of Christian thought is no accident, but shows
that biblical faith intrinsically frustrates the ontotheological aspirations of those who subscribe to it. Faith can show its strength at

times in great displays of logical and causal reasoning and in that soundness of intellect which Athanasius and Thomas Aquinas share despite the worlds that separate them. But a point comes in every case at which the pretentions of logic and causality are curbed, are seen to be "all straw," and a return to the inexhaustibility of the biblical confession of faith is prescribed.

The tensions which produce negative theology and which continue to inhabit its texture can be most interestingly studied in Gregory of Nyssa, the first master of a theoretical negative theology in the Christian Church. It is still, indeed, a rather elementary theory (the most systematic articulation is found in the second book of the *Contra Eunomium*[22]), yet by that very fact more illustrative of the motives and bearing of negative theology than the highflown developments of the Pseudo-Dionysius. Negative theology evaluates the inherent tensions of metaphysical theology to a new level, without eliminating or overcoming them. First there is the tension between the explicit, dogmatic formulation of Christian truths and the awareness that these formulations play those truths false—that the words fall short of what the mind can glimpse, and that the mind glimpses how much the incomprehensibility of God exceeds what it may comprehend. The very notion of substance (*ousia*) is inwardly split by this tension in Gregory: on the one hand it is used with all the logical rigor the Arian controversy had made needful; on the other, *ousia* becomes a name for the intrinsic incomprehensibility of God's being, of which Gregory will say that we can know *that* it is, not *what* it is, or that we know its activities (in creation and salvation), its *energeiai,* but not the divine essence itself. Next is the tension between devotional awareness of the *Deus semper maior,* rooted in scriptural meditation, and the coldly theoretical exercise of theological polemic. This tension produces on the one hand the devotion to divine infinity, which draws the mind to constant growth and purification, and whose resonances Gregory explored in the late works on the *Life of Moses* and the *Song of Songs,* works in which the contemplative methods of Philo and Origen are infused with new electricity as they are systematically referred to this more dynamic account of how the soul rests in God; and, on the other hand the dry whittling away of Eunomian claims, through a realistic, almost skeptical, insistence on the impossibility of grasping his essence in any name, not even in a scriptural one much less a philosophical innovation like Eunomius's *ingenerate,* all words being merely human stammerings.

Divine infinity might be a formula for a hypercritical attitude to religious language, a pure negation, on the one hand, or for a visionary creativeness, a freedom for contemplation on the other. Excessive movement in either direction (and Gregory is pulled in both) is checked by the obligation of respecting the language of Scripture and dogma, the obligation of a kataphatic positivity. One may plausibly suspect that this restraining force is weakened in Pseudo-Dionysius, whose vaulting paths of negation plunge too readily into the mystical dark. When Pseudo-Dionysius writes:

> There the simple, absolved and unchanged mysteries of theology
> lie hidden in the darkness beyond light
>   of the hidden mystical silence,
> there, in the greatest darkness,
>   that beyond all that is most evident
>   exceedingly illuminates the sightless intellects,[23]

it is hard to avoid the impression that these "mysteries" have very little to do with the phenomenality of the God of biblical revelation. The delicate equilibrium of an ecclesial theology, like Basil's or Gregory's, has snapped, yielding to the ascendancy of a Neo-Platonic pathos. Negative theology, though originating in a sense of the inadequacy of metaphysical categories, can itself assume a quite imperious ontotheological form, if the ineffability of the One is itself erected into a grounding principle in function of which the language of faith is systematized. Pseudo-Dionysian strategies of cancellation, unlike the modest *oion* of Plotinus, order the various biblical and philosophical names of God towards their suspension in the simplicity of the absolute as mystically apprehended, overriding the elements in the texture of biblical and dogmatic language which resist this schematization. Not a modest sense of the inadequacy of naming, which would preserve all the more jealously the concrete texture of the hard won store of traditional names, but a fluent mastery over names in view of a privileged access to the nameless which grounds them, appears to be the dominant instinct of Pseudo-Dionysian thought, an instinct which signifies the reappropriation of negative theology by the ontotheological habit of mind it was designed to resist. The charade of fictive authorship betrays Pseudo-Dionysius's awareness that his theology could not be that of the real Church, since it practices a stylization of the language of faith which quite unmoors it from concrete ecclesial or biblical contests. To a deconstructive ear at least, the Dionysian text, with its unbroken tone of enthusiasm, will constantly suggest the suspicion that the prefix "Pseudo" has resonances beyond nomenclature.

Gregory's apophaticism is also liable to be governed by metaphysical structures of thought, insofar as he conceives of it as a way of going *beyond* the constituted system of kataphatic utterance to a higher intuition which brings the speculative quest of theology to its fulfillment, rather than as a means of preserving the poverty and modesty of biblical and liturgical language against speculative absorption, that is, as a step *behind* the constituted system to the data of revelation it attests in a broken and inadequate way. To acclaim negative theology as an "overcoming of metaphysics" is to overlook the fact that the imperative of "Beyond!" which dominates much negative theology is itself a continuation of the grounding movement of ontotheology, even when it takes the paradoxical form of grounding ground in the groundless. Speculation first reaches the lofty concept of the *causa sui* and then, without querying this concept phenomenologically or critically, pushes it beyond, fueled by the same desire for absolute ground, to postulate a ground so absolute as to thwart the grasp of all our categories:

> It is not dark nor light,
>   not error, and not truth.
> There is universally
>   neither position nor denial of it.[24]

Gregory's thinking of divine infinity differs from this because it is constantly opposed to the speculative ambition of Eunomius, and functions thus as a counsel of sobriety, and also because it is rooted in a scriptural meditation. At times one fears that "infinity" is going to become another variant of the Platonic absolute, especially when

Gregory proposes a division (*diairēsis*) of reality into sensible and intelligible rather than into created and uncreated. Even the latter, Nicene and biblical, distinction can become the framework for a Platonic *anabasis,* which grasps the infinity of God not as his otherness in the biblical sense, but as a "groundless ground" whose grounding force we discover ever more fully as we advance in contemplation, so that it provides unending satisfaction to the aspirations of ontotheology.

In Gregory or in Pseudo-Dionysius the language of "beyond being," or not-being in a non-privative sense, could be seen as a deepening of this insistence on the primacy of being, not an overcoming of it. Being still serves here as the supreme principle of a metaphysical ordering of reality, although we can only say of this supreme being that it is, not what it is. That very simplification of thought and diction when the summit is attained satisfies metaphysical reason far more than it frustrates it. If negative theology were carried a little farther, if it reacted on its own language (rather than heightening it by further negations of the Pseudo-Dionysian sort), querying even the adequacy of the language of being to form a hedge around the mystery of God, admitting the suspicion that the mystery has already slipped away as soon as this language begins, then negative theology could fulfill its counter-metaphysical vocation. But negative theology could not accept this loss of its hierarchical and ontological bearings, and therefore it is more in the tensions and ambiguities of its project than in its systematic form, more in the unrest it symptomatizes and the critical sensibility it generates than in the stilted theses in which it sums up its claims, that we can find the points at which it opens onto the overcoming of metaphysics.

Negative theology remains metaphysical above all because it initiates a self-critique of theology beginning from above, from the postulate of divine incomprehensibility, a postulate which is constructed by the methods of metaphysical thinking, by an ever more complex play with the structuring oppositions of finite and infinite, created and uncreated, sensible and intelligible, composite and simple. In contrast, the current "dark night" of theology takes the form of a self-critique from below, which instead of waiting until inscrutable mystery emerges in the discourse of theology (in the paradoxes of grace and freedom, Trinity and unity, or in those generated by any of the simple oppositions mentioned above) and then declaring that God transcends our thoughts and speech, undertakes a more radical ascesis (drawing the lessons of classical negative theology to the fullest extent) by realizing from the start the human and historical limits of the words we find to talk about God. This critique from below avoids the logical trap whereby negative theology is absorbed again and again into confident speculative systems, namely, the paradox that to know the limits of language or thinking one must already have access to a higher viewpoint beyond those limits. In contrast, to say that one calls God "Father" only as a human, culturally limited, way of denoting one's sense of his goodness and care for his creatures is to refer one's language back to the phenomenal level or rather to the infinite play of languages in which phenomenality is manifest. As the privileged status religious expressions always claim for themselves is thus put in question, it becomes less and less possible to accept them as stable premises for speculation. Here is a style of negative theology, then, whose dynamic is not homologous with the grounding movement of ontotheology, but opposed to it at every moment, refusing to relinquish the least of the words of faith to its systematizing drive.

*   *   *

This rapid sketch of some of the main avenues of a deconstructive hermeneutic of the tradition of metaphysical theology is, of course, endlessly modifiable as applied in detail, a task quite beyond the resources of the present work. In the next chapter, however, I shall narrow the focus to a single text, not merely for illustrative purposes, but also to reveal some further twists in the tangled relationship of faith and metaphysics.

NOTES

1. Cf. Edgar Thaidigmann, "Kreuz und Wirklichkeit. Zur Aneignung der 'Heidelberger Disputationen' Luthers," *Luther Jahrbuch,* 48 (1981), 80–96, esp. 92–95.
2. "Qui sine periculo volet in Aristotele Philosophari, necesse est ut ante, bene stultificetur in Christo" (W.A. I, 355).
3. "Theologus non fit nisi id fit sine Aristotele" (W.A. I, 226).
4. In discussing Psalm 1.1: "Happy the man . . ." Luther presents not only hedonism, but, *still more,* the philosophical views which root happiness and virtue, as miserable and futile in contrast to the power of the biblical word. (Cf. *Operationes in Psalmos* 1518–1521, *ad loc.,* in *Archiv zur Weimarer Ausgabe,* I).
5. "Quod si odit anima mea vocem homousion, et nolim ea uti, non ero haereticus" (W.A. VIII, 117).
6. The discussion of the rivalry between faith and "insight" in Hegel's *Phenomenology* might be reworked, from a vantage point opposed to Hegel's, in terms of a theological interpretation of the history of faith.
7. Cf. *Søren Kierkegaard's Journals and Papers,* III, ed. Howard V. Hong and Edna H. Hong (Indiana University Press, 1975), 101: "He is an exceedingly important patient for Christendom, but he is not the physician."
8. Owen Chadwick, *From Bossuet to Newman* (Cambridge University Press, 1957).
9. For a historical study of this notion, see H. Wagenhammer, *Das Wesen des Christentums,* Mainz, 1974.
10. Cf. Friedrich Schleiermacher, *The Christian Faith,* ed. H. R. Mackintosh and J. S. Stewart (New York: Harper and Row, 1963), 389: "The ecclesiastical formulae concerning the Person of Christ need to be subjected to continual criticism. The ecclesiastical formulae are, on the one hand, products of controversy, in that, although the original consciousness was the same in all, yet the thought expressive of it took different forms . . ."; 390: "Dogmatic was overloaded with a multitude of definitions, which have absolutely no other relation to the immediate Christian self-consciousness than that indicated by the history of controversy."
11. Cf. Robert L. Wilken, *The Myth of Christian Beginnings* (Garden City, New York: Doubleday, 1971) (repr. University of Notre Dame Press).

12. Harnack, *History of Dogma,* trans. Neil Buchanan (London, 1905), 17.
13. Aloys Grillmeier, *Christ in Christian Tradition* (London: Mowbrays, 1975²), 557.
14. *Church Dogmatics,* II i, 453.
15. Cf. Paul M. Van Buren, *Discerning the Way* (New York: Crossroad, 1980).
16. Cf. Paul Bove, *Destructive Poetics* (New York: Columbia University Press, 1980), Chapter One.
17. St. John of the Cross, *Ascent of Mount Carmel,* trans. E. Allison Peers (Garden City, New York: Doubleday, 1958), 106.
18. *Church Dogmatics,* I ii, 804.
19. Edwin R. Goodenough, *By Light, Light, The Mystic Gospel of Hellenistic Judaism* (New Haven: Yale University Press, 1925), 7.
20. Ibid., 8.
21. Cf. J. S. O'Leary, "Limitations to the Understanding of John in Christian Theology," *Studia Biblica* II, ed. Elizabeth A. Livingstone (Sheffield, 1980), 227–241.
22. *Gregorii Nysseni Opera,* I, ed. W. Jaeger (Leiden: Brill, 1960), 245 ff.
23. Pseudo-Dionysius Areopagite, *Myst. Theol.* 1.1 (trans. John D. Jones, *The Divine Names and the Mystical Theology,* Milwaukee: Marquette University Press, 1980).
24. Ibid., 5.

IV: OVERCOMING AUGUSTINE

The deconstruction of tradition acquires flesh and bones only through close work on individual texts, and no essay on the topic, however programmatic in intent, could be adequate if it eschewed the task of showing how deconstruction might proceed in textual practice. A body of work as disciplined, as thoroughly reflected, as sober and vigilant as that of the great Christian theologians is no easy target for this exercise. Nor can a random deconstruction which merely notes the rhetorical tricks the text plays on itself suffice. The exercise must have a theological intent and a theological upshot, like Paul's deconstruction of Judaism and Luther's deconstruction of Catholicism. It will be prompted "from the outside" by the remembrance of the scriptural word and the questions of contemporary faith, but it must lodge in the texts it chooses for its operations, opening them up from within. Without such critical immanence there can be no engaged reading of the witnesses of faith, and tradition remains a dead weight to be revered or despised. The following suggestions on how to read Augustine's *Confessions* may not yet have attained that strategic point of penetration at which a text yields up a "strong" reading. However, they may prompt others to more effective inroads and they do at least, I hope, raise a question mark against the "respectable" readings of Augustine which continue to abound, one of the best of which is here chosen as a counterfoil.

In an earlier effort at a deconstructive approach to Augustine's *De Trinitate*[1] I opposed Augustine's experience of God as Spirit to his explicitation of that experience in the language of being, substance, essence, and form which is determinative in various guises throughout that deeply self-divided work. Similar language in the *Confessions* seemed to me to remain strictly subordinate to an articulation of contemplative experience in which biblical, narrative, and metaphorical elements served to capture contours of reality which elude the grasp of metaphysical reason. A re-tractation of these thoughts at a more fundamental level leads me to suspect that the substance/spirit tension of the *De Trinitate* is a secondary formation and that it is largely an intra-metaphysical one. It reflects the deeper tension between what I will call the "biblical" and the metaphysical dimensions of Augustine's thought, and this tension too belongs to a metaphysical landscape which the contemporary language of faith tries to leave behind, first playing off the biblical against the metaphysical, but then transcending both for a more autonomous articulation of *die Sache selbst*. The Bible as opposed to metaphysics is quickly enlisted for a series of roles within the discourse of metaphysics—God as "infinite," "other," "Thou" is still represented as a set of principles. Still less does an appeal to contemplative experience provide a foothold for overcoming Augustine, for his own control of every nuance of such an appeal is not to be bettered and, in fact, the language of immediate experience, the language of Spirit, in the *Confessions* powerfully reinforces Platonic ideals of presence, interiority, certitude, and recollection.[2] "In the *Confessions* Augustine uses a metaphorical and descriptive language to evoke his religious experience. Even when he uses terms like 'substance' and 'being' in that work, one feels that they are vehicles of a contemplative intuition which transcends the strictly metaphysical sense of these words."[3] This is characteristic of the pre-critical language which it is so difficult to avoid when trying to overcome metaphysics. A "religious experience" or "contemplative intuition" accessible to "descriptive language" is in need of a double demystification. First, no language is merely descriptive; language always marshals complex interpretative codes. Second, no experience ever comes uncoded, and the *Confessions* is a very complex play of codes from which an "original experience" can scarcely be excavated.

The *Confessions* is Augustine's triumphant reading of his own life, a Proustian lighting up of the palimpsest, which is as much a work of imagination as a literal report. A *novum* comes to pass when Augustine's experiences and reflections, the conflicts he has surmounted and the conflicts that continue, the languages he has outgrown and the languages he still strives to master and reconcile, precipitate the crystallization which brings unprecedented lucidity to bear on his life and the human condition in general. A reading of life, one's own or everyone's, is never a literal x-ray. To be at all illuminating it must be a symbolic fiction, eliciting form from a chaos of contingency which admits of a theoretically infinite number of interpretations. Such form is the product not of unaided individual insight, but also of the culture of the period. Augustine's reading of his life depends heavily, then, on the forms of reading accessible to him, literary, philosophical, and biblical. The textuality of the *Confessions* bears witness to the extraordinary degree to which its author (or one is tempted to say the text itself) is conscious of the conditions of its composition. For the *Confessions* is above all a chronicle of readings: its narrator is always reading, always searching for the right reading, and the *Confessions* itself is that reading which was sought all along. The *Confessions* humbly lodges in the greater text of Scripture, especially Genesis and the Psalms, regarding its reading as only an increment of the process whereby the whole of life is lit up by the Word of God. The *Aeneid,* the *Hortensius,* the *Categories,* the books of the Manicheans and the Neo-Platonists, the signs presented by dreams, encounters, chance, bereavement, or illness, above all the sequence of narrations relayed from one person to another in Book VIII, culminating in the flash of lightning whereby the passage from Saint Paul deciphers the sense of Augustine's life and liberates him by that stroke, all of these keep the narrator incessantly busy with his task of reading. The "thing in itself" behind all these readings, and towards which their genuine or illusory illuminations converge—what is it? What is the truth of Augustine's experience? It turns out to be nothing else than the document he is writing, the reading in which all previous readings are subsumed. Never again will Augustine be able to read his life so convincingly; from his comment on this text in the *Retractations* one is tempted to imagine that he consulted it often himself when he wished to read his life, and that he never found a more interesting reading than the one constructed there. Mallarmé's dictum that everything in the world exists to issue in a book is verified in this case with a vengeance. In producing so powerful a reading of his own life Augustine may have become its prisoner, and made countless others

its prisoners, in providing them, too, with a reading of their experience to which they found nothing to add.

The excess of the truth of textuality over the explicit metaphysical statements in the *Confessions* was grasped in misleading terms
when I suggested that the metaphysical expressions are being used
as metaphors for contemplative experience in that work. The distinction between literal and metaphorical is itself a metaphysical
one. Augustine's own "metaphors"—e.g., the guiding "hand" of
God—can be just as much carriers of the metaphysical orientation
of meaning as his literal metaphysical terms. In fact the texture of
the *Confessions* is richer than that of the *De Trinitate* not because it
is more metaphorical but because both its abstract and figurative
language admit a *double reading* much more readily and reward-
ingly than the *De Trinitate* does. One can interpret the image of the
"hand" of God metaphysically, as a metaphor for "providence"; but
it also invites one to read it "literally" as a biblical naming of the
divine presence which cannot be adequately translated into those
metaphysical terms. One can interpret the word "being" in the
Confessions in a straightforward metaphysical sense, literally, or
one can attend to the biblical resonances of the surrounding discourse and reinterpret it accordingly as a "metaphor" for the reality
or holiness of God. In the richest passages of the *Confessions* the
possibility of a breakdown of the metaphysical distinction between
literal and metaphorical thus begins to emerge. However, Augustine's explicit metaphysical reflection is often itself so complex and
highly reflected that what appears to be an image almost breaking
the bounds of metaphysical reason may turn out to be perfectly well-
behaved figuration of a complex of paradoxical concept fully worked
out elsewhere in the text.[4]

A double reading of Augustine can play off the biblical overtones
of his language against its dominant metaphysical orientation,
stressing for instance the biblical overtones of *caritas* against his
tendency to grasp it in terms reminiscent of philosophical notions of
eros. The Platonic and biblical codes through which Augustine's
experience was mediated, and which he was able to reactivate and
reinterpret in light of his experience, reinforce one another in the
single powerful reading constructed in the *Confessions*. The first

step in a deconstruction must be to subvert the dominance of metaphysics by pitting the latent implications of the biblical code against
the Platonic ideals of experience to which Augustine keeps them
subordinate. But even such oppositions as that of eros and agape are
still intra-metaphysical. Indeed, there is no outside of metaphysics.
What one can do, however, is to resist the metaphysical orientation
of Augustine's chain of signifiers, the magnetism of God as ground,
origin, goal, point of rest, source of certitude and transparent
insight, which inspires so much of his writing, and instead read the
text *backwards,* following the not quite suppressed clues of the
biblical metaphors, in order to reassert the claims of a God who
eludes all metaphysical attempts to fix "his" identity. The rich
biblical content of the *Confessions* thus provides the surest foothold
for a counter-metaphysical reading. The goal of such a reading is
not, however, a reduction of Augustine's experience to purely biblical terms. Instead what is aimed at is an opening of both the dominant metaphysical orientation and the residual irrecuperable
biblical elements of Augustine's text to a language which more
adequately apprehends the matter of faith in contemporary terms.
The biblical elements are used to subvert the metaphysical framework, but the process of deconstruction may react on them in turn,
raising questions larger than that of the overcoming of metaphysics.

For instance, the God of Augustine is recognizably the "Thou" of
biblical revelation, and as such always threatens to burst the bounds
of the metaphysical system wherein Augustine apprehends this
"Thou." Every dimension of the biblical metaphorical and anthropomorphic language about God can be perfectly integrated into a
metaphysical order by means of the Origenian method of interpreting this language in a spiritual sense. It is not that this language in
its original Jewish context needed to be spiritualized, for the Platonic differentiation of sense and spirit is foreign to the world of the
Hebrew Scriptures. In a culture for which the distinction of sense
and spirit is axiomatic the force of the biblical anthropomorphic
language can be retrieved only by the detour of a spiritualization
followed by a metaphorical concretization; the hand of God really
means his providence, but one can speak of his providence graphi-
cally as his hand, using that expression now in a metaphorical sense.

It is to the degree that Augustine's language in its vivid leaps of imagination partly eludes this Origenian grammar that a flaw in its metaphysical texture can be sighted. In the *Confessions* metaphysical awareness raises biblical diction to a higher power, while the step back from metaphysical propriety to daringly direct anthropomorphism suddenly invests metaphysical notions with unexpected existential force. Where Origen is pedestrian, Augustine constantly generates dramatic effects of spiritualization and concretization through the interplay of these registers. Thus the God of Augustine is at once a set of metaphysical attributes—subject and will, omnipotent, omnipresent, omniscient, spirit, being itself, source of all being, and providential orderer of all events—and a "Thou" whose reality is not exhausted in this listing of attributes, but demands dramatic narration. The narration of God's actions is controlled and deanthropomorphized by the securely established metaphysics of God, yet there is a biblical nakedness in Augustine's dealings with God which allows him to show himself baffled, like Job, by the inscrutability of this "Thou," as where Augustine asks "What am I to you, that you command me to love you?" (*Conf.* I 5). When Augustine steps back from calm metaphysical vision to a direct wrestling with the mystery of God in this way he may be indicating a more primordial layer in his apprehension of the phenomenality of God, one which potentially calls in question the adequacy of the controlling metaphysical topology. For the Fathers the spiritual exegesis of biblical anthropomorphism was felt as a progress in the freedom of the language of faith, a freedom Augustine fully appreciated, for Ambrose's Origenian sermons on Genesis had freed him from Manichean literalism, effecting the first major breakthrough in the process of his conversion. A further stage in this freedom was the ability to use these anthropomorphisms freely in a higher spiritual sense; Augustine enjoyed this freedom more than any of his predecessors, reveling in its paradoxes (just but merciful, seeking though in need of nothing, angry but calm) and supplementing them with metaphysical paradox. But a further level of freedom in the language of faith is touched when Augustine reverts to a biblical diction which simply calls out to God in faith, without attempting to situate him metaphysically. This level of language is the one to which we must appeal, for we no longer find the meta-physical regime prevalent in the other levels to be capable of effect-ing progress in the freedom of the language of faith for us. The strategy of our reading is determined by the historical conjuncture, the crisis of metaphysics, which has robbed Augustine's metaphysi-cal assurance of any major significance for our faith and which throws us back instead on the basic grounds of Augustine's convic-tion. To reach these basic grounds we must perform a phenomeno-logical reduction of Augustine's metaphysical projections or constructions to the basic experience of faith which his text articulates.

But, and here the larger question surfaces, might it not be that even this bedrock biblical level in Augustine's faith is also largely experienced as alien by contemporary believers? Augustine's God, even as "Thou," is largely a metaphysical construct, an apotheosis of the Western ego and will. But even in the basic biblical evocation of God as loving agent, personal presence, object of trust and utter dependence, insofar as it can be abstracted from its metaphysical elaboration, one may be inclined to suspect that somehow Augustine protests too much. His metaphysical preoccupations led him to over-accentuate certain aspects of Scripture, centering everything on the claustrophobic drama between the individual sinner and the will of God in judgment or grace. Contemporary faith must first apprehend Augustine's testimony to the reality of this experience (which it can do only by overcoming the metaphysical terms in which it is articu-lated) but then it will be obliged to go a step further and, in dialogue with this Augustinian experience, set about demythologizing these conceptions of God and the self in which the West has invested so heavily. The Bible itself, it may be, provides alternative perspectives which might allow us to take these representations more lightly than the Augustinian tradition does, but a salutary jolt from the outside might also be provided by religious traditions completely indepen-dent of Semitic or Hellenic conceptions of divine personality, sin, individuality, or will. To the Taoist seeking a bedrock awareness of reality as an "uncarved block,"[5] Augustine's assertion of God as supreme will, dominant over all things, must appear as a crude overleaping of the phenomenality of world; to a Buddhist the sharp distinctions of self, world, creation, and Creator would illustrate a fixated attachment to relative notions.[6] Indeed, the narrative and doxological texture of the Bible itself and the nature of the Hebrew tongue never allow any of these notions to become as stabilized as they do when grasped in terms of being by Western thinkers. Thus where a metaphysical mind, even when reaching back to a more primordial biblical language, tends to make the biblical notions more rigid and massive than they need be, a post-metaphysical sensibility recalls all these notions to their experiential foundation and reveals them as the imperfect constructions of a given culture, subject to challenge and questioning in dialogue with other worlds of experience. Thus the overcoming of metaphysics is the first step in the Western journey to an open dialogue with other traditions.

Suffering the Text

Many patristic texts can excite a mild historical sympathy, while their literary conventions and philosophical assumptions prevent the contemporary believer from entering fully into the world of their authors. Augustine's *Confessions* still largely escapes this cultural obsolescence, continuing to speak "from faith to faith" and to challenge and unsettle its readers. If we wish to come to terms critically with the tradition which has shaped our faith, it is as impossible to avoid a confrontation with this text as with the Councils of Nicea or Chalcedon. Yet, despite its continuing power to question us, the favorite spiritual reading of the West for so many centuries no longer speaks as directly to its contemporary readers. The metaphysical presuppositions Augustine found so satisfying and illuminating, the convictions which strongly girded his universe, now seem the feeblest part of his work, while its power seems to live on in those elements which do not quite fit this metaphysical framework or which strain against it in subtle ways. This paradox makes the *Confessions* an ideal site for a demonstration of the difference our proposed approach makes in practice to the reading of the Christian classics. As we differentiate "faith" and "metaphysics" in the very texture of Augustine's writing the programmatic observations of the preceding chapters will acquire a richer complexion and the positive goal of our inquiry, to be sketched in the concluding chapter, will begin to come into view.

It is not perhaps possible to prove that the contemporary reaction to Augustine's text is what I have stated it to be. For this starting point of a deconstructive reading I must simply appeal to the experience of the reader of Augustine's text. When, for instance, one reads: "I would not be at all, my God, unless you were in me" (I 2.2.), is one not pulled in two directions, on the one hand drawn into a devotional participation in Augustine's sense of utter dependence on God, on the other thrown back by the formalization of that devotional stance through a metaphysics of *esse*? The direct appropriation of Augustine's words is made problematic once it is seen that they are burdened with a fairly elaborate theory of being. To take another of the countless possible examples, when one reads: "Why, o perverse soul, do you follow your flesh? Let it rather be converted to follow you" (IV 11.17), one may find that these words resonate with everyone's awareness of moral alienation and with the thirst for a correct ordering of life, and one may be pleased by their literary elegance, but is it possible to silence the questions so summary an imposition of anthropological dualism on the texture of existence must provoke? At every turn in Augustine's texts the post-Kantian reader will stumble on such occasions for misgiving.

Even passages which at first seem free of metaphysical formalization, and from which one might hope to spin an Augustinianism of the heart, a spiritual language propelled by a play of images and no longer subject to a governing metaphysical scheme, turn out on closer acquaintance to contain a high quotient of implicit metaphysics. For instance when Augustine writes: "Do not be vain, O my soul, nor allow the ear of your heart to be deafened by the tumult of your vanity" (IV 11.16), the imaginative vividness of this is largely the product of a metaphysical scheme. The Origenian notion of the spiritual senses, brilliantly exploited throughout the *Confessions,* allows Augustine to systematically transfer to the realm of the spiritual the language of the sensible. What seems a flash of imagination has Platonic method in it. The underlying distinction between inner and outer in all its fertile variations is inseparably linked with the Platonic dualism of soul and body. Similarly, all Augustine's reflections on the presence or absence of God to the sinner are controlled by a set of carefully formulated quasi-Plotinian theorems about omnipresence. Above all, the nostalgia for rest and certitude in the divine presence and for transparent self-presence, the ruling desire which fuels Augustine's eloquence and imagination is itself the product of metaphysical presuppositions: God envisaged as ultimate ground and ultimate goal, the point of rest in a system of relations; the soul's self-presence seen as a necessary mediation of the return to that ground. Conversion is the basic structure of existence for Augustine and it is grounded in the axiom that "you have made us for yourself, O Lord, and our hearts are restless until they rest in you" (I 1.1). Centuries of readers have made these words too their own in an unproblematic way. But can we? In that phrase "you have made us for yourself" do we not detect a questionable stepping outside the horizon of the given to take a loftier view of God's ontological and causal relation to the creature? Do we not suspect that this somewhat abstract and privatized evocation of resting in the Lord is a construction conditioned by a metaphysics of creation, and that a wider and fuller sense of what such resting in the Lord might mean could be attained if one left behind this metaphysical perspective in order to espouse the "hints and guesses" of a personal divine presence which real-life occasions suggest? Is Augustine not unduly universalizing and formalizing the particularity of this presence, imposing on it the status of a metaphysical origin?

Pursuing these suspicions we find that the questionability of metaphysics haunts every corner of the text, forbidding us to take anything simply at its face value. There is no doubting the reality of Augustine's experience of God's presence and providence; yet metaphysical schemas again and again seem to inhibit his articulation of the concrete modalities of that presence. Augustine's God is a metaphysical God, but also the living God of the biblical revelation, the former at the expense of the latter. If the metaphysics of God's presence in the *Confessions* can nonetheless subserve his witness of biblical faith, it is because this metaphysics is constantly being solicited and inflected by biblical emphases. My claim, therefore, is that we cannot link up with Augustine the witness of faith as long as

we take for granted the apparently seamless mutual complementa-
tion of the languages of faith and metaphysics in his text. Only by
driving a wedge between them, building on indications of tension in
the writing itself, can we recover the clues for faith embedded in the
text, clues which the prevailing metaphysical discourse tends to
misinterpret.

Such a reading demands that we attend to the reactions of dissatisfaction, even the sense of oppression, the text elicits, not writing
them off as a distraction, but recognizing them as hermeneutically
relevant, as clues to the possibility of a subversive and liberative
solicitation of the text. Those who bring an attitude of uniform
admiration to Augustine are not necessarily his best readers. If one
practices a hermeneutics of "suffering the text," consciously registering the malaise it induces and seeking the sources of this malaise,
one is likely to obtain a more precise and more engaging sense of the
contemporary significance of Augustine. Fifteen centuries of
Augustine's influence have made us familiar with the oppressive
potential of his thought and as we apply this consciousness to Augustine's texts we may discover an alternative reading which dismantles
his metaphysical formalization of spiritual experience. Indeed we
have little chance of recovering the truth of the Christian tradition
for today unless we cultivate this consciousness in regard to every
corner of that tradition, questioning after what underlies its possibly
overemphatic claims and counterclaims (seven sacraments or two?),
its rather dogged repetitions (e.g., the resumption of patristic dogmatic language by Luther and Melanchthon despite their initial
resistance), and its networks of moral and doctrinal argument which
might seem to constitute again and again a Law which the Gospel
would again and again abrogate. It is only through this process of
reassessment that the vision these broken instruments defended can
be deciphered anew. Our dealings with Scripture provide precedents
for this approach: in a world mapped out for nuclear extinction we
cannot share the Psalms' cosmic optimism, yet in a paradoxical way
we do cling to their imperative of praise, as a protest against the
nuclear corruption of nature and our hearts;[7] we cannot be awe-
struck by the quaint miracles in the Acts of the Apostles, but we can
take them as betokening the fullness of the Spirit in the early

Church; we wince at the anti-Semitic resonances of passages in Matthew and John, yet this reaction is truer to the spirit of the gospel message than a pious complacency would be. No text written by human beings is without its shadow side, which the passage of time may throw into deeper relief. Theology is largely a struggle with these shadows.

To wrestle with the *Confessions* in this way need not be a purely negative task. Indeed it may be a spiritual exercise in a more authentic sense than a straightforward reading can any longer be, as we continue Augustine's spiritual quest in opposition to the metaphysics which originally sustained it, but now hinder our participation in it. It might be thought that this counter-metaphysical reading is a timid substitute for what the "masters of suspicion" (Marx, Nietzsche and Freud) might find in Augustine. A Marxist might see the *Confessions* as powerfully constraining the Gospel within the limits of individual subjectivity and, through its influence on people like Petrarch and Pascal, giving spiritual legitimation to the culture of bourgeois individualism. Nietzsche thought Augustine "lacked distinction in his desires and gestures to an insulting degree,"[8] suggesting that one might query whether one who lived so much in the light of eternal, unchanging forms could remain fully and authentically human. Freudian approaches to the *Confessions* have not been very illuminating, but it is sure that the powerful affective investments of that work, which have had such an influence on subsequent religious feeling, call for ongoing analysis and assessment. Each of these critiques, however, brings us back to the question of metaphysics. Augustine instituted a thorough metaphysical formalization not only of Christian beliefs, but of Christian experience and language. The doctrinal tenets of the Greek Fathers, translated into the more tightly logical medium of Latin, were assembled in a rather petrified system, in which the margin of vagueness or mystery they retained in Greek was mercilessly lopped away. Dogma became fixed as never before, and henceforth provided the unquestioned basis for every form of "faith seeking understanding" in the Latin West. At the same time, a metaphysical form was imposed on the whole of experience, a systematic geography of love and desire, joy and suffering, sin and virtue. The transmission of that form in the West implied the dominance of a single religious diction, the capacious terminology of Augustine's Latin, capable of integrating and controlling every stirring of the Spirit in its lucid texture. Thus in whichever direction one pursued either religious experience or theological speculation after Augustine one came up against the all-embracing structures of his groundplan, which seemed the definitive institution of the boundaries of Christian truth. Nor could an escape be found through a return to Scripture, since Scripture was automatically read (even by the Reformers) through Augustinian eyes. If the Church today is vulnerable to the critiques of Marx, Freud, and Nietzsche it is largely because of an Augustinianism insufficiently overcome, that is, a metaphysical institutionalization of the Gospel which does not allow it to deploy its liberative challenge in concrete interplay with social and psychological situations, but tries to inscribe its message in a systematic code.

A counter-metaphysical reading is not only a more central approach to the problems of the Augustinian legacy; it is also more practicable than a directly Marxian or Freudian critique. It demands that we read the text *backwards,* undoing the harmony which the centuries-long symbiosis of faith and metaphysics generated, attending instead to the biblical diction of faith insofar as its absorption by metaphysics remains incomplete, soliciting this troublesome, unintegrated residue so as to bring to light in the text a largely repressed biblical witness of faith. In raising biblical faith to the transparency of the concept Augustine may have augmented the danger latent in all credal statements, the danger that faith becomes a theoretical ideology to which one subscribes, rather than a communal vision which is always being reshaped. As we overcome the transparency and systematic character of his vision, recapturing the opaque texture of the underlying biblical confessions of faith, we discern the human and historical contours of Augustine's witness as an accommodation of the Gospel message to the intellectual conditions by which he was bound. The metaphysical lucidity of his articulation of the vision of faith is the explicit surface of his finding and defining of Christian identity under the conditions of that time. But if we look at the back of the mirror, through an examination of the textual embodiment of this metaphysical explication of the faith, we find that Augustine has something more to tell us about Christian identity, for his style betrays the resistance of faith to any metaphysical systematization. Explicitly, the biblical and metaphysical elements coexist in harmonious fusion. But the texture of the writing reveals a constant friction between them, which Augustine himself does not reflexively control. Heidegger, in 1921, saw this tension, somewhat simplistically, as one between experience and its conceptual articulation: "The conceptuality taken up by Augustine falsifies the experience to be expressed in it. . . . While Augustine lives and thinks in the unrest which characterizes factical life, he becomes untrue to himself and misses the factical life-experience of original Christianity through the quietism of the *fruitio Dei* which comes from Neo-Platonism."[9] This opposition of existence and interpretation needs to be substantiated by a textual study tracing the tension between two languages in Augustine. Such a study would absolve us from the futile effort to reconstruct Augustine's experience independently of its linguistic inscription, and from the need to solve the historical puzzles his narration of his conversion creates, allowing us to attend instead to the functioning of the text and the possibilities of a new reading which it allows.

Ontotheology or Theologal Ontology?

Deconstructive insight can sometimes be facilitated by a critique of an exemplary standard reading of the target text, and in this case a recent essay of Dominique Dubarle, in which scholarship is laced with an unusual degree of philosophical alertness, provides an ideal foil. Indeed Dubarle's essay has been recommended by the *Revue des Etudes Augustiniennes* as a wholesome corrective to the dangerous views of Augustine's deconstructors.[10] His study has the warrant of Augustine's own self-understanding, but misses the insights of those who subject Augustine to the Heideggerian critique of ontotheology. Dubarle contrasts Augustine's "theologal ontology" with ontotheology, but seems to understand by the latter a rationalistic natural theology in the manner of Christian Wolff, rather than a project intrinsic in various degrees of explicitness to all metaphysics. It is evident that as early as the *De Vera Religione* (390) and the

De Libero Arbitrio (395) Augustine is intent on projecting a total-izing systematic grasp of being-as-such and beings-as-a-whole. In his basic ontology he depends largely on Porphyry. His own most energetic thinking on the nature of being-as-such is concerned with the axiom that "whatever is, is good, insofar as it is, and evil is not." As for beings-as-a-whole, his universe is a hierarchy of participation in being, of which God, the supreme being and source of being, is the summit. The sense of the intrinsic goodness of being-as-such is supplemented by a notion of the intrinsic order and harmony of the universe. The sense of the hierarchical unity under God of beings-as-a-whole is supplemented by variations on the theme of an ascent from the body (mutable and sensible) to the soul (incorporeal but still mutable) to God (spiritual and immutable). Indeed the entire biblical economy provides further supplementation to this ontotheo-logical structure, as we shall see. Thus what Dubarle calls "theolo-gal" or even "Christic" ontology turns out then to be a major triumph of ontotheology, its colonization of the world of faith.

As ontotheology Autustine's thought falls prey to the Heidegger-ian critique. If a phenomenological insight underlies Augustine's axiom of the convertibility of being and goodness, Augustine did not dwell with that insight, but used it to provide metaphysical explana-tions and grounds for the existence of things. Instead of questioning back to the true phenomenality of being he built speculative accounts of the order and structure of reality. A deconstruction of Augustine along these lines might be possible, building on the ten-sion between his ordering mentality and his inchoate phenomenolog-ical perceptions whose development that quest for speculative order frustrated. But this is not the concern of a theological critique of Augustine. Our task is rather to gauge the degree to which Augus-tine's discourse succeeds in being what it is principally intended to be, a discourse of faith, and to examine how his ontotheological methods of thinking help or hinder that purpose. Since we are dealing with what is perhaps the most perfect expression of the spirit of faith within the culture of Western metaphysics, it is clear that this task, however inadequately we fulfill it, is a matter of epochal import. Dubarle rushes through an open door when he points out that the richness and coherence of Augustine's theologal ontology cannot be reduced to the "platitude of the ontology or 'natural theology' found in manuals,"[11] but the very perfection of Augustine's performance on its own terms calls forth the higher criticism which notes the points at which this system founders on the impossibility of fully capturing—or even correctly placing—the "theologal" or the "Christic" within the structures of a systematic ontology, however modified to accommodate them. Is this merely a question of fashion? Was it natural to explicate the mystery of God and Christ in terms of being and Logos when these were the culturally recognized names for ultimate reality, and do we now drop this language only because the words carry less weight? I think the issue is more basic than this. Augustine obeys the imperative of metaphysical reason in bringing God and Christ into relation with the supreme principles of ontotheology; for him this is a matter of rational necessity, not cultural accommodation. Only with the Reformation did the possible independence, and even the necessary independence, of faith from metaphysics come into view. There is no assured reflexive grasp of such an independence before this, it seems. It is exactly that polyphonic symbiosis of Christian and philosophical culture, so natural and necessary to Augustine, and on which the strength and beauty of his writing depends, which has become basically questionable to us, the heirs of Luther and Kant, so that our entire relationship to Augustine has shifted to another plane.

It is true that Augustine articulates his experiences, or rather the reflexive interpretation of them precipitated in his mind some twenty years after the event, in ontological terms, and that he does this very smoothly and coherently. The metaphysical discourse seems to unfold organically from the contemplative experience he associates with his reading of the books of the Platonists. Previously the narrator had wallowed clumsily in the ontologies of Manicheanism and Stoicism, sensing their inadequacy to the true nature of God and the soul. Now he gains immediate contemplative access to spiritual reality, and begins at once to articulate the content of this vision in ontological terms. Contemplative insight translates into ontotheological coherence without any apparent gap. Augustine knew no better language for the reality he had glimpsed. He quarries from his encounter with the reality of God a vision of being as such: "I saw them neither altogether to be, nor altogether not to be . . ." (VII 11.17); "And it was revealed to me that the things which are corrupted are good . . ." (VII 12.18); "And all things are true insofar as they are . . ." (15.21), and a vision of beings as a whole, grounded and unified in the supreme being, God: "I saw that they owed it to you that they are, and that they are all finite in you, but in another way, not as in a place (as Augustine had previously imagined), but because you are he who holds all things in his hand by truth" (15.21). This contemplative, theologal ontology, like that of Aquinas, appears to be seamless robe, providing the bedrock foundation of the Christian vision of reality, based on the doctrine of creation, incapable of being surpassed or displaced.

A frontal attack on the truth of this theologal ontological vision would of course be misguided, just as a denial of the doctrines of the Trinity or the Incarnation would be. But in each case a lateral critique of the linguistic and conceptual texture in which these doctrinal convictions are embodied is obligatory, not only because of the exigencies of modern philosophy, but also because many contemporary believers find the classical language unpalatable, although unwilling to surrender belief in the divinity of Christ, the trinitarian nature of God and the dependence of all that exists on a loving creator. A phenomenological critique of Augustine's language will differentiate distinct strands in it, revealing it to be an amalgam whose elements are bound by a very high valency, but not an absolute one. One might say that in a metaphysical epoch Augustine's or Aquinas's vision is the finest expression possible of the truth of the doctrine of creation, the light of reason converging irresistibly with the light of faith, but that with the closure of this epoch the conjunction appears in retrospect as dissoluble, through a reduction of both the philosophical and the theological elements to their phenomenological origins.

If we read *Confessions* VII 10.16 ff. with a view to this differentiation of strands and to the laying bare of their contrasting phenomenological foundations, we discover that the text lends itself quite well to this operation, though it is inspired by concerns foreign to the

conscious intention of its author, concerns possible only to those who
have experienced the crises of metaphysics and the correlative crises
of traditional formulations of faith. The text colludes with its critic
as anatomy colludes with the surgeon's knife, despite the violence of
the incision in both cases. For the historical faultline sundering faith
and metaphysics even in their closest embrace is found to appear
whenever biblical language is sensitively used in Christian theology,
even when there is no explicit consciousness of its counter-metaphysical thrust. The contemporary critic will solicit that language,
accentuating its irreducibility to the surrounding metaphysical categories, thus setting up a ferment of self-contradiction in the text.
Metaphysical lucidity is no longer serenely superimposed on the
biblical elements, but is seen as straining against them. Conversely,
where the biblical elements seem to be merely tagged on to the
metaphysical ones, they are no longer seen as innocent appendages
but as irremediably compromising the transparency of the concept.
Even if biblical elements irreducible to metaphysics are marginal-
ized in the text, they can constitute a quintessential instance of the
treacherous margin, calling in question the entire metaphysical
order which seeks in vain to integrate them. Augustine generally
seeks, unlike the scholastics, to saturate his text with biblical allusions, so that if one can speak of marginality here it is only in the
sense that the biblical strand is tightly bound into place by the
governing metaphysical arrangements. The biblical text is massively
present, but in an interpretation which is ninety percent metaphysical; it is the ten percent residue of unintegrated biblical diction
which provides the margin for our solicitation.

For instance, the opening words of VII 10.16 combine biblical
and Plotinian themes in what is almost an exercise in theological
punning. Deeply satisfying as this harmony is, it must be noted that
while the philosophical themes are transformed through being
referred to a personal God and his enabling grace, the biblical
themes undergo the more radical transformation. "And thence
admonished to return to myself": the books of the Platonists are a
providential means whereby God recalls the erring soul, but this idea
is mediated through Platonic conceptions of sensible traces of imma-
terial reality; Augustine returns to himself as the Prodigal Son

comes to his senses, but much more as the Plotinian soul recollects itself, withdrawing from its dispersion in sense fantasy. If there is a ten percent of biblical matter here which resists integration into the metaphysical translation, it must be sought in Augustine's tone of voice, the tone of confession which places the sinner before the God of mercy. The next words, "I entered into my own interiority led by you and I was able to, since you became my helper" (cf. Ps. 56:7), present grace as what mediates the soul's self-presence or self-transparency, and as so often it is the scriptural allusion which most resists integration into the governing metaphysical scheme. Grace as a *principle* has been well integrated into the metaphysical structure of Christian theology, but the concrete biblical presentation of God's favor and saving intervention (the phenomenological origin of all later thematizations of grace) could never satisfactorily be presented as a principle. The trouble is that in trying to do justice to this "unprincipled" character of grace and to the divine freedom, theologians felt obliged to produce auxiliary principles, such as the principle of the gratuity of grace, or the principle of predestination. The metaphysics of grace became the most puzzling corner of theology, and its relation to the revelation of God's saving favor, for whose defense it had been constructed, became impossible to discern. As the narrative particularity of the present passage cedes in Augustine's writing to the prevalence of grace as a metaphysical principle this speculative effort to provide the grounds of grace (in the name of defending its groundlessness) is launched, with the catastrophic consequences already apparent in the Saint's last writings, where the defender of divine freedom in fact appears to be hedging it about with calculations born of a logic of fear.

"I entered and saw with a certain eye of my mind, above that eye of my soul—above my mind—an unchanging light, not the ordinary one all flesh can see, nor anything similar to it though bigger, as if this light were to shine much, much brighter so as to fill all by its size. Not such was that light, but other, quite other, from all these." The contrast of inner and outer light is entirely Platonic—the parable of the cavern (*Republic* VII) and Plotinus's *On Beauty* (*Ennead* I 6)—and even the key of interiority into which Augustine translated the conjunction between the mind's eye and the light above it

cannot be presented as a specifically Christian or Pauline importation, since it merely develops the pathos of recollection already
present in Platonic or Plotinian *anamnēsis, aphairēsis,* and *anabasis.* This spirituality, greatly as it has prevailed in Christian culture,
is not at all biblical. In contrast Augustine's sense of himself as an
individual "I" addressed by the divine "Thou," though it too has
become ninety percent metaphysics (enriching metaphysics with a
new set of themes, refining, and sharpening its concepts of the
particular), does have a distinctively biblical cast which is never
quite submerged in the texture of his metaphysical theology. Note
the stylistic jump in the next sentence as the biblical theme of
creation emerges along with the evocation of the divine "Thou" and
the human "I": "Nor was it above my mind as oil is above water or
the sky above the earth, but it was above me because it made me and
I was below it because I was made by it." The Plotinian texture of
the discourse is almost ripped by the twist the words *ipsa fecit me*
introduce. Augustine first described his experience as one of spiritual self-transparency; now it is a discovery of creaturehood. The
two accounts are welded together almost by force. We are not concerned with what Augustine "really" experienced at Milan; probably no pure kernel could be extracted from the interpretative
schemes which both facilitated and explicated the experience, and it
may be that a combination and partial clash of two schemes presided
over the original experience; or it may be that the creational scheme
was later imposed over the Plotinian one, as seeming to do more
justice to the true import of the experience. In any case there is a
significant slippage here in the text. It recurs in a subtler form in the
next sentences: "Who knows truth, knows this light, and who knows
this light, knows eternity. Charity knows this light. O eternal truth
and true charity and dear eternity! You are my God; to you I sigh
day and night" (cf. Ps. 42:2). In Platonism eros mediates the vision
of the forms, and the forms possess self-identical being. Augustine
replaces eros with charity, the form of beauty with divine truth and
the timelessness of the intelligible world with the eternity of the
biblical heaven. But charity, truth, and eternity are just as much
metaphysical principles as those they replace. Augustine's crypto-
trinitarian invocation of them is a modulation from the exposition of

these metaphysical principles to the undisguised biblical prayer of the final quotation. But that modulation again masks a stylistic leap, and repeated reading confirms the impression that the words "you are my God" almost wrench Augustine's discourse out of its metaphysical course. *Caritas, veritas, aeternitas* are the bearers of ontotheological aspiration after a totalizing apprehension of the being of beings; but the implicit system is almost exploded when Augustine turns to address them as "my God." The God one calls on in prayer and the totalizing principle one constructs in speculation are not as easy to identify as Augustine's simple "you are" suggests. Can a "you" ever be a principle or set of principles?

These subtle tensions are acerbated when Augustine introduces the Porphyrian language of "*esse*" into the interpretation of his illumination at Milan: "And when I knew you for the first time, you lifted me up that I might see that that which I wished to see indeed had being but that I who wished to see had not being as yet. You struck the weakness of my gaze, shining powerfully on me so that I trembled in love and dread, and I found myself to be far from you in a region of dissimilitude, as if I were hearing your voice from on high: 'I am the food of the full-grown: grow and you shall feed on me, nor shall you change me into you as the food of your flesh, but you shall be changed into me.' And I realized that you punished man for wickedness and that you had caused my soul to dry up like a spider's web. And I said: 'Is truth then nothing, since it is not diffused through either finite or infinite space?' And you called from afar: 'I am who I am' (Ex. 3:14) and I heard as one hears in the heart, nor was there further room for doubt: I had more easily doubted myself to live than the existence of truth, which is perceived through the consideration of the things that are made." The quotation of Exodus 3:14 here is the king-pin of the ontological interpretation of the contrast between the reality of God and his own weak state. The "region of dissimilitude" is the Plotinian terminology for the lowest degree of being, verging on non-being (*Ennead* I 8.13). Augustine has not yet being, cannot yet participate in the fullness of being which is God: this ontological reading underlies the food-image. The hierarchical, participational ontology of the following paragraphs is already present here *in nuce,* as the concluding allusion to Romans 1:20 makes clear.

But the quotation from Exodus might also be read as indicating a more primordial level in Augustine's experience, which the prevalent ontological scheme does not perfectly embrace, an encounter, like that of Moses, between the majesty and holiness of God and the sinfulness of the individual. The Platonic imagery of blinding light is yoked together with the biblical "Thou" who "lifts up" Augustine and addresses him in biblical style; the spiritual sense of sight functions Platonically, but the spiritual sense of hearing functions biblically, and is significantly located in the heart rather than in the mind. This presence of a personal and active God dislodges the Platonic elements so that they become illustrative of and subservient to a biblical evocation of God, losing some of their own intrinsic weight. The language of being in this paragraph is no longer an end in itself as it was for Plato or Aristotle. The reality of God is what is of first importance, and the language of being is "used" to express it in what might almost be described as a metaphorical way. The language of illumination in Augustine is a strange hybrid, because of the deflection imposed on its Platonic terms by reference to a biblical image of God as active, vigilant, personal presence. Yet both the language of being and that of illumination continue to have a metaphysical function of locating God (one might almost say keeping God in place) as the supreme ground of being and knowledge. The personal God of Augustine is thus only partly the God of the Bible. Despite the ultimate irreducibility of the divine "Thou" to metaphysics, Augustine's God remains nine-tenths a metaphysical construction. To draw out the more primordial biblical sense of God from the prevailing metaphysical discourse about God great attention to the tone and narrative movement of the text is required, for one can easily mistake Augustine's powerful metaphysical evocations of God's presence and providence as simply biblical, while it is just as easy to miss the irreducibly non-metaphysical touches in his narration of God's dealings with him. Utterances like "Thou hast made us for thyself . . ." or "O true charity and beloved eternity!" might seem utterly in tune with the tenor of biblical language to the unsuspecting reader, who might equally underestimate the degree to which the Platonic substance of "you struck the weakness of my gaze, shining on me violently" is hollowed out and undermined by the presence of the word "you."

I am trying to show that the *Confessions* is an inherently troubled and instable composition, as is every text which attempts an original synthesis of faith and metaphysics. Amplify the resonances of the biblical language in such a text and dissonances begin to be heard between it and the metaphysical elements; the converse is true to a lesser extent (amplify the Platonic resonances and their incompatibility with the language of faith appears). Like the themes thrown together at the high point of the *Mastersingers* overture, faith and metaphysics do not harmonize; it is only the orchestration which keeps them together. Augustine is a master of orchestration, and the attempt to recover the autonomy of faith will take nothing from his art. But in lesser hands the discourse of metaphysical theology abounds in grating dissonances, especially in its contemporary revivals. Augustine resites Porphyrian ontology between the abyssal poles of divine infinity ("Thou") and the nothing whence creatures ("I") are drawn, causing the ontotheological notion of God as supreme cause to rhyme richly with the biblical confession of the Lordship of the Creator. But allow any autonomy to the biblical God over against his ontological characterization and a fatal gap appears. If the supreme cause of ontotheology is retained as a secondary description of God it will continue to interfere and clash with the biblical one despite so many apparent reasons for concord; the worst dissonances are between notes very near in pitch. So we find that the discord between the God of Abraham and the God of metaphysics cannot be resolved by compromises, but only by critical overcoming.

Dubarle's reading of *Confessions* VII 10.16 ff. provides an instructive contrast. "Saint Augustine describes the perception of a radical difference between the being of God and that of his creature. . . . He speaks of God as being and of divine being, not of the unique One of Plotinus."[12] One notes the monochromatically ontological character of this reading. "The 'dissimilitude' caused by sin . . . is discerned . . . only in the light of ontological dissimilitude."[13] Here Dubarle solicits Augustine's text in such a way as to promote the primacy of the ontological framework over the biblical elements. This seems to me the exact opposite of the procedure required for a creative theological hermeneutic. But Dubarle can also solicit the text in the other direction: "Augustine's statements (about the non-being of evil, VII 12.18) presuppose a mind raised to a spiritual and intellectual understanding which makes forcefully present to it that light which is the divine truth of the Word. . . . Espousing in some sense the divine gaze on creation, one who lives this act of understanding knows experientially that evil is nothing which subsists."[14] Here Augustine's metaphysical thinking is quite dissolved into the contemplative experience from which it is quarried; the phenomenological content of his vision of the goodness of being is emphasized at the expense of the ontotheological structure of his argument. But even the contemplative vision here is governed intimately by the structures of Platonic metaphysics. This reading overlooks the biblical elements in the text, e.g., "that truly is, which abides immutably. 'But for me it is good to cling to God' (cf. Ps. 72:34), because if I do not abide in him, neither can I abide in myself" (VII 11.17). The Psalm text is in sharp stylistic contrast with what precedes and the language of "abiding" is capable of a double reading, as meaning either the Plotinian soul's self-presence, dependent on its upward gaze towards the intelligibles, or a biblical trust in God which preserves one in righteousness. Thus Dubarle elevates Augustine's metaphysics to the spiritual level to counter the charge of ontotheology, but does not raise it to the biblical level, for this would cause it to founder.

One cannot accept without question the equation of Augustine's ontology with a participation in the divine view of things, nor does the joyful contemplative certitude attaching to the vision guarantee the adequacy of the categories it employs. In "seeing" the structure of being so transparently, Augustine may in fact already be falling away from the real source of his joy and certitude, exchanging a phenomenological or contemplative apprehension for the projection of an objectifying totalization of beings as a whole, a projection which is a theoretical conclusion, not an immediate given of contemplative experience. We must read the explicitly metaphysical utterances of the text backwards, attending to every trace of a more originary sense which they have already begun to rationalize, and especially to the biblical elements insofar as they partly betray that the metaphysical schemes are not entirely adequate to capture this deeper layer of meaning. In all this one must, however, try to avoid the temptation to posit a transcendental signified in the form of an original pure experience, whether one of Eastern-style contemplative illumination or of biblical encounter with the holiness of God. We have no access to the original experience, which exists for us only in the play of textual possibilities in what Augustine wrote so much later; our difficulty in interpreting that textual play, and the variety of readings it can generate, testify to the complexity of Augustine's own task of articulating and interpreting his experience; all we can do is continue the play, avoiding the danger of replacing the metaphysical interpretation with another claiming the same stability and adequacy. The increasing complication and undecidability of our reading is not gratuitous, but is part of the way the text functions, and a tribute to its power. It is because it involves us in its play and lures us on to investigate its "unthought" implications that this text still claims our attention. Were its meaning utterly straightforward, so that there could be no room for soundings and solicitations which refuse to take it at face value, then we could register Augustine's views, but scarcely dialogue with them, for there would be nothing in his writing which could respond to our questioning.

At least the argumentative parts of this passage of *Confessions* VII must be admitted to have a secondary character in relation to the deliveries of contemplative vision, for the logic-chopping about the goodness of what is corruptible (12.18) and the cosmic harmony which makes what appears evil in one respect good in another (13.19) is surely the product of the everyday reflecting mind, drawing on two traditions of homely philosophical argument as it attempts to tease out the implications of the clue, no more than a clue, which contemplation brought. A false materialist metaphysics yields to a true metaphysics of divine spirituality and the goodness of being. It is a contemplative experience that causes the latter to "click" for Augustine, giving him an essential clue for its acceptance. But while this change of languages is an advance in truth for

Augustine, it is by no means a gift of an absolutely adequate language, and one could even say that it was precisely because he was a contemplative that Augustine continues to betray in his writing the tensions between the biblical and the metaphysical, needing both languages to express the fullness of God and incapable of repressing for the sake of uniformity either of the languages in which his praise found voice.

Augustine also describes his inability to sustain the contemplative vision, due above all to his weakened moral state. He comes back to this more systematically at VII 17.23 where in his ascents from the appreciation of corporeal beauty, through the principles of aesthetic judgment, to the eternal truth enabling this judgment, and from corporeal things, through sensation and the inner sense, to the power of reason and the Light which enlightens it, Augustine clearly locates the divine at the summit of a hierarchy of beings. This hierarchy is not a contemplative datum but a metaphysical scheme used as a launching pad for a contemplative exercise. The exercise reveals explicitly a truth about God which remained implicit in the experience described in VII 10.16, namely "the impossibility of having direct knowledge, assured and penetrating, of that which God properly is,"[15] or the noetic impenetrability of God, which Dubarle correlates with the ontological divine infinity also borne in on Augustine in his contemplative experience. I suspect that Dubarle overemphasizes the noetic-philosophical dimension of this experience of being thrown back by the majesty of God. The "weakness" to which this is ascribed is just as much a concrete condition of sinfulness as an ontological structure of finitude; perhaps here too is an occasion for deconstructive play. It is not only that God is impenetrable because infinite; there is also here a biblical sense of the exalted holiness of God, inspiring a sense of sin now, but admitting a more substantial contemplative enjoyment in the vision at Ostia described in Book IX. Augustine deals with God as both a "Thou" and as the summit of a metaphysical hierarchy and while the two approaches supplement one another they can also leave minor loose ends in the text, loose ends which the deconstructionist can pull on so as to unstitch its fabric. One might solicit Augustine's sense of the elusiveness of God and ask if it does not react on the Platonic topologies whereby he continues to fix the place of God so confidently, as summit of a hierarchy, *summum* and ground of the perfections of being, truth, goodness. Is there a dehiscence between these topologies and the activity of the divine "Thou" who both raises Augustine to himself and withdraws from his grasp? Can God be at once the passive object of contemplation and the active subject of self-revelation and self-concealment? Either the *anabasis* must be taken lightly, as the ladder one throws away having mounted it, or the revelation must be subordinated to its ontotheological structures. Augustine combines *anabasis* and revelation by avoiding ever having to choose between these two possibilities. If he is a theologal ontologist rather than an ontotheologist it is because he sustains so well this delicate equilibrium. But logically his ontology demands to become ontotheology in the fullest sense, and thus exclude an integral account of the God of revelation, while conversely the biblical element in his thinking strains towards its autonomy, which would throw off the language of metaphysics.

A Christic Ontology?

Now we must examine the surprising twist in Dubarle's interpretation, whereby he presents the ontology of *Confessions* VII as displaced or sublated in a richer, more specifically Christian formation of thought, which he calls a "Christic ontology." This I see as a Hegelian, dialectical resolution of the tensions between faith and metaphysics in Augustine's text. I oppose to it a phenomenological reading which takes the *failles* in the text as indications of the unthought, invitations to deeper questioning. One such *faille* (fault/flaw) is the stylistic heterogeneity of *Confessions* VII and VIII. As Dubarle remarks: "At first sight it looks as if once the theologal ontology and the encounter between monotheistic faith and the philosophical conception of God have been posited as preliminaries the specifically Christian dimension of existence is deployed according to the order of a religious faith on which the considerations of philosophical ontology have no hold."[16] However, Dubarle resolves this problem by presenting Augustine's christology

and soteriology as completing and enriching the "virtuality of theologal ontology"[17] Augustine shares with Platonism, in a richly unified thinking which transcends the concern with ontological
construction or even with "the systematic organization of theological material."[18] Undoubtedly this unity exists, and it is more the
unity of a contemplative vision than a system. But the disunities it
embraces, particularly the gaps between the biblical and metaphysical contributions, the former of which constantly frustrates the latter's constantly renewed urge towards system, should be closely
studied. What I have calculated to be the ten percent resistance of
the biblical elements to metaphysical integration effectively prevents the Augustinian world of thought from ever closing in on itself
as a fully constituted system. A literary sign of this state of affairs is
the mosaic texture of Augustine's writing, in which lines of argument derived from Scripture are juxtaposed with others depending
more on philosophical traditions with little attempt at a textural
fusion of the two (e.g., in *De Trinitate* XIII a philosophical argument about the desire for beatitude leads to a biblical exposition of
faith as the means to attain it; as the biblical references enter the
philosophical ones leave). "It is the whole of the teaching of the
Christian faith, the truth of the God of monotheism and the truth of
the incarnate Word, which the ontological understanding (of Book
VII) serves in reality to undergird and outline, at least *de jure*,"[19]
writes Dubarle, the latter phrase being added because this unity of
ontology and soteriology is not explicitly presented in *Confessions*
VII-VIII. The doctrinal unity of Augustine's views hardly needs to
be defended. But the leaps one notices in the text, the leap from the
ontological lessons drawn from the Milan experience (VII 10.16-
16.22) to the account of the moral quandary into which it plunges
Augustine (17.23-21.27) and the narration of his release from this
quandry through "putting on the Lord Jesus Christ" in VIII, reflect
the great distances between the different cultures Augustine reconciled in his person, the worlds of Plotinus and of Paul. His Plotinus is
Christianized, to the point of appearing as a teacher of Christianity
without the incarnation and kenosis of the Word, and his Paul is
metaphysicized, as the treatment of the themes of Romans VII in
Confessions VIII shows. Nonetheless he could not fully weave the

two together in a single texture of argument. The unity of the
Confessions is thus in the end the unity of a narrative. Narrative is
the only medium in which Plotinus can be surpassed by Paul. To
attempt such a surpassing in the medium of metaphysical argument
would be to reduce Paul to metaphysical terms and to miss the
concrete reality of conversion and grace; to attempt it by completely
reducing the Plotinian themes to themes of biblical faith would
constitute the overcoming of metaphysics! This is not a possibility
for Augustine.

It is true that elsewhere Augustine does unify ontology and christology in a single argument. My claim is that as far as Augustine
succeeds in doing this he falls short of the powerful witness of faith
achieved in the *Confessions*. In *Confessions* VII Augustine indicates
the place of Jesus Christ only in relation to the second feature of the
Milan experience, his inability to abide in the contemplation of his
God, and refrains from the attempt to place him in the ontological
framework established in VII 10.16-16.22; in *Confessions* VIII the
ontological background yields to the dramatic foreground of conversion, and it is through a series of concrete narratives, placed one
against another like a series of lenses concentrating light to a single
searing point, that Augustine comes to his supreme, remarkably
non-intellectual, non-noetic moment of truth. When Augustine integrates christology and ontology more explicitly, it is at the expense
of the phenomenological power of *Confessions* VIII. The *volonté de
système* begins to close in on the biblical message. Where Dubarle
finds in the sequence of *Confessions* VII and VIII the announce-
ment and initiation of "an entire intellectual economy of Christian
theology and, in a more hidden way, of ontology itself,"[20] I would
rather say that this is what the sense of these books becomes when
they are interpreted ontotheologically and that the economy thus
established is none other than that of metaphysical theology, that is,
basically, ontotheology. But there is also to be found in the sequence
of these books the possibility of a quite different economy of Christian theology, building on the differentiation of faith from philosophy. Augustine never sought to realize this possibility, yet his texts
as we have them call on us to do it for him.

Dubarle speaks of a Christic displacement of the ontology of *Confessions* VII but in reality he eludes the possibility of a true Christic displacement which, following Augustine himself, would build on the theologal displacement of the God of metaphysics by the biblical "Thou" which we have already glimpsed in *Confessions* VII. Dubarle's displacement is in reality a confirmation and the difference the biblical language he invokes makes to the metaphysical structure of Augustine's thought is minor. In fact any difference it could make is erased in the dialectic of the *nomen essentiae* ("I am who am," "He who is") and the *nomen misericordiae* ("I am the God of Abraham, the God of Isaac and the God of Jacob"—Exodus 3:15), for the second of these names is neatly subordinated to the first, signifying how the infinite, impenetrable God stoops to the limits of human comprehension. Faith is associated with the *nomen misericordiae,* which refers to the economy of historical signs; these are systematically subordinated to the eternal signified, mysteriously indicated in the *nomen essentiae.* To abide in the horizon of faith in God of Abraham is difficult when it is over-arched in advance by the transhistorical naming of God as *ipsum esse.* Dubarle claims that "the two namings of God cause their respective meanings to be continued and as it were reversed one in the other."[21] Jesus is the fullest expression of the *nomen misericordiae,* yet his own fullest self-expression is a return to the *nomen essentiae,* the "I am" of the Fourth Gospel. Conversely, "the ontology of the divine substance" always contains implicitly a moment of "Christological mercy" so that "the essential nexus of Augustine's theology is Christological much rather than ontotheological."[22] The divine name "EST" is not simply ontological in the philosophical sense; for Augustine it includes "a certain connotation of the divine Word . . . coming to implant in this world the reality of divine filiation."[23] Here again I suspect that the unity of the simplicity of the divine substance and the fullness of the biblical revelation in the word "EST" is a matter of orchestration in which the alterity of metaphysical and biblical is smoothed over. Dubarle sees Augustine as "recovering the unity of the two nominations distinguished in Exodus."[24] What is their unity in the original biblical narrative? It is the unity of the holiness and unapproachable mystery of the Lord on

the one hand and his fidelity to Israel on the other, a unity which can
be grasped in contemplation, not in a speculative synthesis but in
constant wonder that the Most High has looked down with compas-
sion on his people. The two divine names can be held together in a
phenomenological way, as both names lay claim on the believer, and
insofar as Augustine holds them together thus his thought moves in
a biblical horizon foreign to metaphysics; but insofar as he attempts
to hold them together with the bonds of speculative logic, in which
"the interior structurations of the divine reality" are united with "an
ontology founded in the reasoned perception of the difference
between the creature and God the Creator" and a "synergy" is
installed between "purely human knowledge and the intelligent
reflection and apperception of faith,"[25] the result is that the duality
of biblical names is replaced by a duality of biblical faith seeking
metaphysical understanding. Thus Augustine accommodates the
truths of faith as best he can to the requirements of metaphysical
reason by expanding the unifying notion of "being" so as to embrace
them comprehensively, locating all the data of Scripture on an
ontotheological map. The enlargement of the language of being to
embrace the procession of the Word, the Incarnation and salvation
history is continuous with the movement within Neo-Platonism
which was generous in using the word "being" to designate the
supreme hypostases and the lesser realities depending on them. Even
if this movement received a new force from the doctrine of creation,
there is nothing in it which intrinsically conflicts with the fundamental orientation of metaphysics. Augustine applies this ontological
grid to scriptural as well as to cosmological or psychological data,
but it is not here that his radical difference from the philosophers is
to be found; for that we must look to the "Thou" to whom the whole
construction is referred. Augustine himself tends to integrate the
divine "Thou" within metaphysics. Faith, instead of being explicated in terms of a calling on or trusting in God, terms irreducible to
any other, becomes an epistemological and ontological principle,
which fits us for "seeing in an ineffable way that ineffable being"
(De Trinitate I 2.3). Yet Augustine's direct language of faith is so
passionately engaged with the "Thou" of the God of Abraham that
the functional and mediating status of faith within the metaphysical

scheme of things is often left behind for a style of confession inspired by the Psalms, in which faith dwells entirely in its relation to its object, renouncing any aspiration to situate speculatively either itself or its object. The faith overflowing in such cries as *Confessions* I 5.5 ("Who shall grant me to rest in thee . . .") and throughout the whole of the *Confessions* insofar as they are regulated by the vivid conviction of the address to the divine "Thou" eludes articulation in the categories of the Platonic *via-patria,* purgation-vision, temporal-eternal, visible-invisible, belief-knowledge schemes. The object of this faith, like the God of the New Testament (who is Spirit, Love), cannot in the last analysis be named by any metaphysical term. Even though ninety percent of what Augustine says about God and faith represents a superb metaphysical apprehension of these ideas, the remaining ten percent, the part that to the contemporary reader seems to witness most powerfully to the reality of faith and to the reality of God, breaks open the framework of metaphysical names and evokes God in the open-ended "Thou" whom we may name as we will (*"Summe, optime, potentissime, omnipotentissime . . .," Confessions* I 4.4) as long as every name is heard as declaring the surpassing greatness of that "Thou" and does not fall back again within the limits of a metaphysical representation. Only in this openness are the divine names "Christic": Christ opens them up to their fullest resonance. The name "EST" sometimes has this status in Augustine; but insofar as it becomes the key-word of an ontological system, bringing Christ into place in an ontological scheme, it can no longer figure as a fitting name for God in our discourse. Like the word "Absolute" it is too burdened with the historical aspirations of ontotheology to name worthily the God of faith.

Augustine the Believer

In any effort to overcome metaphysics in Christian tradition, Augustine is surely "the man to beat." Few historical figures have imposed their authority as uncontestedly. But in what did this authority consist? Can faith today simply accept Augustine's authority unreservedly, or can our faith be nourished by his only across a questioning relationship? No other document exemplifies as convincingly as the *Confessions* what it means to see with the eyes of faith. Augustine's mastery of biblical and metaphysical paradox allows him to focus the phenomenality of God as apprehended by faith; the genre of the confession, both prayer and narration, provided a uniquely effective medium for this focusing. But in addition the wide span of his experience and the intensity of his philosophical, ethical and religious meditation on it enabled him to grasp the contours of his own life, and of human life in general, not only with an existential and psychological insight equal to that of any other writer, but with an unwavering theological and metaphysical lucidity which lights up in uncanny detail the byways of sin and grace, human folly and divine providence, firmly establishing the right order of things at every turn. It is not so much that Augustine assumes a divine view from above on human life; in fact he writes in constant awareness of the defective human status of his insights. Rather, his powerful experience of being known and judged by God is what he is chiefly concerned to articulate, and it quite naturally unfolds into a comprehensive examination of the human conscience.

However, if our analysis of the *Confessions* is correct, it may be that to a contemporary reading they can be seen to suffer the defect of their virtue, namely, an excess of metaphysical lucidity, a too definitive ordering of the world and of life. This defect has two roots: the nature of Augustine's faith and the metaphysical texture of his thinking. As a metaphysical thinker Augustine works towards a comprehensive and exhaustive ordering of the data of experience; his writing is surely in large part inspired by the will to uncover such total order; the inconclusive, the open-ended, the ambiguous emerge as surds on which this ambition stumbles again and again, but they are never delighted in as pointers to another kind of insight; Augustine is never content to let them be, still less to allow them to subversively unravel the dominant metaphysical texture of his thought. Augustine's faith is founded on the authority of the Church, an authority whose providential epistemological function he proved in opposition to Neo-Platonist and Manichean presumption.[26] His conversion spelled a total identification with this authority, to the point that he became its living embodiment. To what extent was this act of faith too a metaphysical principle, a ground of certitude and insight on which he could capitalize in his voluminous writings and in the other activities which served to further define and round out the ideal of the orthodox Christian Church? To what extent has the traditional Western conception of the Church's mode of teaching and acting in the world been a metaphysical construction? Is faith obliged to outgrow this Augustinian model of ecclesial existence, and to find a new one, inspired not only by biblical models (the people of God, the body of Christ), which Augustine's ecclesiology in any case fully subsumed, but, more essentially, by the necessity for the Church to become a questioning, dialogal community in accord with the wider contemporary horizons of its mission and in accord with the critical turn Western consciousness has taken? Is the Church an institution which masters life in a system of metaphysical insight or is it a community of prophetic faith which relinquishes such pretentions in order to discern what the Lord's will is for the here and now? To what extent are the Church's "answers" always subordinate to a deeper life of questioning in faith, of seeking after God? Augustinian faith seeks understanding; but perhaps this dynamic of seeking is best retrieved today if interpreted in terms of a universal human search which is not suspended or even limited by the act of Christian faith (or of any other kind of faith) but continues unceasingly under whatever religious or areligious complexion. Confession of the Church's faith remains an act of obedience, giving a foothold of certitude, but with such a greatly heightened sense of the historicity of the tradition in which it enables one to share and of the fragility and questionability of the categories which it obliges one to assume, that faith is henceforth much less conscious of "having the answers" than of having gained a *locus standi* for pursuing the questions at greater depth.

A differentiated reception of Augustine's faith along these lines would enable us to overcome the oppressive aspect of his legacy, and to overcome it not through skeptical negation but through the affirmation of the deepest implications of that faith. Where Augustine hammers Scripture and metaphysics together in triumphant affirmation, we allow the tensions between them to prompt the formation of a more delicate and questioning language about God. Where

Augustine maps human life in the light of eternity, we pursue the method of Augustinian phenomenology more consequently than Augustine himself did and reduce this mapping more strictly to the phenomenological data to which it testifies. Even as "Thou," Augustine's God is too massive, even oppressive, a presence, so that we are obliged to question even the most basic and biblical stance of Augustinian faith, opening it up to a sense of the relativity of the indications of God found even in the most privileged experience. The reality of Augustine's experience is to be retrieved across a critical consciousness of the inadequacies of his language as these have become apparent. This can be done by reinterpreting Augustine in light of a new set of coordinates, those of contemporary faith, admitting the questionability of the metaphysical and even the biblical coordinates which were entirely determinative in his own discourse. Of course what is thus retrieved is no longer the experience of Augustine; that experience is no longer possible for us. But it is a more authentic communication "from faith to faith" than can be reached by fictitious efforts to repeat that experience, whether in the key of metaphysical enlightenment, biblical piety, or existentialist revamping. This differentiated reception of the *Confessions* should make possible a more decisive overcoming of the later Augustine. As a bishop Augustine enacted on the grandest scale the practical consequences of the excess of metaphysical lucidity and the stylized repertoire of biblical themes which give his faith its peculiar cast. A work like the *City of God* may in part deserve to be celebrated as a triumph of the vision of faith, but it may also represent the rather summary burial of classical humanity. In ordering all reality according to the will of God, Augustine may have increasingly depleted the phenomena of experience of their intrinsic significance, with the result that the will of God too became an increasingly abstract principle. Thus the career of Augustine, by its very consistency, which despite its strong but narrow biblical basis is primarily a metaphysical consistency, may have inflicted a deep wound on Western consciousness, reinforcing the absolutism of the metaphysical principle of ground with the absolutism of a dogmatic certitude of faith which matched it perfectly. In this career we witness the final convergence of Christianity and metaphysics under the unity of a single principle, the God of the West, a principle which would hold sway even over such critics of metaphysics as Luther, Calvin, and Pascal. It is surely this God—and not the moral God of Kant or some other convenient scapegoat—which is in question when thinkers like Nietzsche diagnose "the death of God" (one must presume they were sufficiently familiar with their traditions to know what they meant by "God"). If Augustine's God has died, it may be that the God of the Bible insofar as "he" lends himself to this understanding is also attainted. By exploiting to the full one virtuality of the biblical legacy Augustine may have shown the dangers of that aspect and made a more differentiated reading of Scripture obligatory for us—one which might seek traces there of Nietzsche's "God who dances."

In the study of Augustine we confront in its most characteristic form the religious identity of our Western world, including, it may be suspected, that original sin of our religion, a fanaticism of metaphysical abstraction, to which many subsequent more visible evils might be traced. That study should be a work of healing, a patient dismantling of those decisions, largely determined by the prior developments of metaphysical theology, which continue to block our access to a life of faith today. As this work of healing the Western believing mind proceeds, a transformation of thinking begins to take place, analogous, in the realm of faith, to that which Heidegger and others have mapped elsewhere. The immensity of Augustine's work and influence and the small success of the explicit efforts which have been made to overcome that influence are but one indication of how long the task of transforming tradition must continue. One must linger for a long time with each of its great monuments before their significance for contemporary faith, both their oppressive significance as metaphysical construction and their liberative significance as witness, can be brought into view. It would be premature to claim that this past has been outgrown and put behind us, and that we can go on to state boldly the meaning of Christian faith for today without further ado. On the other hand, the ongoing task of overcoming tradition need not entirely paralyze the present articulation of faith. In fact without such an effort at articulation the task of overcoming would lack the contemporary coordinates which guide it. Thus we now proceed, in the final chapter, to articulate the essence of Christianity in contemporary terms, though conscious that the ghost of Augustine, and the other ghosts of the past, have not been shaken off or adequately pacified, and that our reflections of this theme must therefore be even more provisional and programmatic than those on the topic of overcoming metaphysics.

NOTES

1. "Dieu-Esprit et Dieu-Substance chez saint Augustin," *Recherches de science religieuse,* 69 (1981), 357–391.
2. The vision at Ostia was undoubtedly an immediate experience of great force (*Conf.* IX 10) yet it is narrated as a double Platonic anabasis (the experience itself and its "recollection in tranquillity") culminating each time in the image of "touching" the eternal—the supreme Platonic aspiration, here clad in a sumptuous biblical garb.
3. O'Leary, "Dieu-Esprit et Dieu-Substance," 357–358.
4. This is best illustrated by Robert J. O'Connell's investigations of the Plotinian metaphors in the *Confessions.*
5. Cf. Chang Chung-yuan, *Creativity and Taoism* (New York: Harper and Row, 1963), 19–53.
6. Cf. Jacques Gernet, *Chine et christianisme* (Paris: Gallimard, 1982), 290–299.
7. Cf. Daniel Berrigan, *Uncommon Prayer* (New York: Crossroad, 1978).
8. Nietzsche, *Werke,* ed. Karl Schlechta, II, 614.
9. Summary from Otto Pöggeler, *Der Denkweg Martin Heidegger* (Pfullingen: Neske, 1963), 39. Cf. J. L. Mehta, *Martin Heidegger: The Way and the Vision* (Honolulu: University Press of Hawaii, 1976²), 12: "in the philosophy of Augustine an original and basic religious experience is perverted by being conceptualized in terms of uncritically accepted metaphysical ideas." For a diametrically opposed line of criticism, see Kurt Flasch, *Augustin: Einführung in sein Denken* (Stuttgart: Reclam, 1980).
10. Dominique Dubarle, "Essai sur l'ontologie théologale de saint Augustin," *Recherches augustiniennes,* 16 (1981), 197–288. Cf. Goulven Madec, *Revue des études augustiniennes,* 28 (1982), 345–347 (review of O'Leary, Marion).

11. Dubarle, "Essai," 200. Yet there is a certain flatness if we compare
    Augustine with Plotinus. See Joachim Ritter, *Mundus Intelligibilis*
    (Frankfurt: Klostermann, 1937).
12. Ibid., 209–210.
13. Ibid., 211, no. 21.
14. Ibid., 212.
15. Ibid., 218.
16. Ibid., 221.
17. Ibid., 222.
18. Ibid.
19. Ibid., 202.
20. Ibid., 203.
21. Ibid., 228. (For the two names of God see *En.* in *Ps.* 121:5)
22. Ibid., 229.
23. Ibid., 231.
24. Ibid., 232.
25. Ibid.
26. I have discussed this in "En lisant le *De utilitate credendi* de saint
    Augustin," *La Croyance,* ed. Jean Greisch, coll. *Philosophie,* vol. 6
    (Paris: Beauchesne, 1982), 29–49.

V: THE ESSENCE
OF CHRISTIANITY

Christian identity has been metaphysical for two millennia. It has been founded on a comprehensive dogmatic vision in which all reality was ordered in function of its first origin and final goal. Within a metaphysical culture the essence of Christianity could be satisfactorily expressed in dogmatic formulations, of which the Nicene Creed was the most central. The emergence in recent centuries of an explicit quest for the essence of Christianity stemmed from a sense that this credal definition of Christian identity was no longer sufficient and that it was necessary to step back behind it to some more fundamental and immediate apprehension of Christian truth. But this quest for the essence of Christianity was itself governed by metaphysics, first of all in its point of departure—it tended to envisage "Christianity" as a united whole, a system whose principles might be laid bare like any other "-ism," and thus stepped away from the vantage point of faith itself, supplementing the quest intrinsic to faith with a detached philosophical consideration of its essence; second, in its effort to reduce the Christian message to a single explanatory principle—even such a fine phrase as Harnack's "eternal life in the midst of time" might suggest that Christianity can be explained as the interplay of two abstract principles, the eternal and the temporal, the absolute and the relative; third, in the very ambition to secure an "essence" of Christianity—this implied the desire to step above the stream of the historical manifestations of Christian faith in order to grasp it *sub specie aeternitatis;* the essence once grasped, all the rest could be mastered as inessential manifestation; fourth, in the realm in which the essence was located, the realm of modern metaphysical ideals of subjectivity and immediate experience. These metaphysical emphases were corrected in dialectical theology which showed that one cannot speak adequately of faith from outside the situation of being addressed by the Word of

God; that this Word is "living and active" and refuses to be summarized as a principle or set of principles; that the Word cannot be detached from its historical manifestations—including Scripture, church teaching, and preaching—though it may effect an immanent critique of them, to which theological reflection must be attuned; that the sphere of subjectivity does not ground or regulate the hearing of faith but is rather called in question by it, so that it loses its self-evidence.

However, the quest for the essence of Christianity now survives in a different form, as a concrete question of identity. This question is conditioned by consciousness of several aspects of the historical situation of Christianity which dialectical theology did not sufficiently acknowledge. When the closure of metaphysics and the consequent loss of the traditional Christian metaphysical self-understanding are fully registered; when one is aware of the radical historicity of every aspect of the life of faith, a historicity which can no longer be camouflaged by metaphysical presuppositions; when one traces the reference to a given cultural milieu and to a given praxis or "form of life" inscribed in every discourse of faith; when one realizes that the context-dependent representations of faith are never simply translatable from one historical horizon to another; when one sounds the contingency of the historical forms faith has taken and of the language we have inherited, which is seen to be intrinsically inconclusive, open-ended and infinitely revisable—then the question of the essence of Christianity takes the following shape: "How can Christian identity be expressed realistically and convincingly today, in the clarity of a conscious assumption of its own historicity, and without any uncritical dependence on inherited representations?" The answer cannot take the form of an unending scholarly self-critique, for it must be a declaration of faith, albeit a modest, sober, and questioning one. What are the conditions of a valid contemporary articulation of Christian faith?

The Imperative of Simplicity

Although the quest for essential Christianity has often succumbed to the nostalgia for the primordial simplicity of some immediate experience, and thus fallen under the sway of a metaphysics erecting this primordial ground into a supreme principle of explanation, nevertheless any radical questioning after religious identity is bound to obey an imperative of simplicity, a thirst for firsthand contact with the heart of the matter, such as has been manifest in all the major turning points of the history of religion. On the other hand, a consciousness of historicity indicates the limits by which the realization of this imperative is bound. It is no longer possible, for example, to project the historical myths of recovered origins on which most religious reforms of the past have been based. We see too clearly that in all these efforts the founding figure, Abraham, Jesus, the Buddha, Mahomet, is made the subject of a series of fictions, each intended to free the pure firsthand experience of the faith from secondary accretions of later tradition, but each in fact representing a new creative initiative in the tradition. Nor are these prophetic initiatives ever able to cut through the knots of history as cleanly as they aim to do. The path to the simple is never a simple one. The radical prophetic gesture of a Jeremiah or a Stephen against the temple, of Paul in regard to the law, of Luther in regard to religious externality, is quickly subsumed in a tradition of correction and commentary; it may serve to inspire and guide a complex process of theological and historical unraveling, as theologians "tidy up" after the prophet's passage, but in this subsequent stocktaking the inspiring gesture itself is relativized in an unending critical reassessment. History thus teaches that definitive access to the simple core of faith is a largely illusory goal. Indeed every attempt to define such a simple core becomes the foundation of a complex tradition against which another prophet must in turn raise the cry for simplification. It is true that any articulation of essential Christianity today must depend either on some practical living out of Christian love in relation to the demands of the times or on some great contemplative enlightenment like that of Augustine, and that such prophetic or contemplative happenings in the Christian community provide the supreme *locus theologicus* in which theology must dwell in order to trace the emergent shape of Christian identity. It is here that theology encounters the imperative of simplicity in concrete form. But even charity and contemplation are historically embedded; they are not a recovery of the original, or the perennial, offering an escape from history, but represent the work of the Spirit in this particular moment, a work which will be unrepeatable tomorrow. Critical historical awareness can keep the space clear for this work, preventing it from being haunted by those memories of past forms of Christian experience which every Christian has inherited and which can tempt both individual and community to a somnambulistic repetition of the past, either unconsciously or in some proud movement of restoration. Furthermore, historically conscious theology can draw out the full implications of these realizations of Christianity in praxis and contemplation, interpreting them in function of the historical situation in which Christianity, having lost its metaphysical identity, is forced to question back to its origins in a more radical way.

This questioning back is not an escape from history, but rather the full assumption of historicity. It spells, for instance, not an idealization of the New Testament, but a critical sifting of its discourse in view of the subsequent course of the history it founded. In action, contemplation, and theological reflection Christianity today is defining its identity anew, in a creative reprise of the first self-definition of the Christian community in the New Testament. But why is it necessary to redefine Christian identity? Why not be content, as a Wittgensteinian linguistic therapist would be, to let language take care of itself, that is, having overcome its metaphysical elements, to let the great flood of Christian discourse flow on unimpeded in all its richness? The reason is that even in its biblical dimensions this discourse has become involved in a dangerous inflationary career, using too freely words which have been detached from their historical context, or else invoking these words and their context in forgetfulness of the fact that this context is no longer accessible. Such words as "Father," "Son," and "Spirit" and such contexts as those in the New Testament are subject to this inflationary exploitation in any Sunday homily. The inflation can be corrected only by providing a contemporary objective correlate for every word used and by reevaluating every word in function of its historical significance and its pertinence to the contemporary situation addressed. Such a critique extended to the entire range of

Christian discourse amounts to a review of the historical shape of
Christian tradition from the New Testament on. The Christian faith
must no longer be seen in mystifying terms as something which
dropped from heaven, but as historical through and through. If the
great intellectual adventure of Christianity in this century has been
its exposure to the critical currents of Western thinking (including
Marxism), it is probably that the next adventure, which has scarcely
begun, will be that of a full-scale confrontation with the traditions
and mentalities of the East. The Christian tradition will not be ready
for that adventure unless it enjoys a concrete, demystified historical
self-understanding. This demands not only the overcoming of metaphysics, but also a reinterpretation of the New Testament witness in
a renewed dialogue with Judaism. Christianity carries its "other" in
its bosom, for Judaism is the rock from which it was hewn. In the
metaphysical period the encounter with Judaism was ruled unnecessary; the "Old Testament" was subordinated to the new through the
logic of Platonism building on the Messianic typology of the infant
Church, which is one of the features of the New Testament that
surely demand to be reviewed; the historicity of Israel and of Christianity as deriving from Israel was erased in metaphysical schemata
and the way in which Christianity and Judaism are thrown together
in an unresolved historical problematic was ignored. Unless this
concrete history is now fully accepted Christians will go to meet
other faiths carrying a burden of abstractions which have lost both
their historical and their contemporary context and which can only
generate confusion in dialogue. No doubt the other faiths will have
to face their historicity in a similar way.

A concrete historical self-understanding frees Christians for dialogue with other faiths; it also makes possible the focusing and
application of Christian energies, for it allows one to experience
faith as a specific historical project rather than a set of timeless
velleities. The healing effect of this historical reduction may be
compared to that of psychoanalysis; and just as one embarking on
psychoanalysis expects not total self-knowledge, but a provisional
self-understanding adequate for the business of living here and now,
so a contemporary grasp of Christian identity is sufficient if it gives

the community a critical insight into its tradition and a lucid perspective on the present historical engagements of faith. Insight in both cases is provisional, sufficient for the day. At each turning of the path of faith through history past perspectives are shut off and the stretch of road to be traveled in the present is lit up; this too disappears at the next turning, while the forest itself remains fairly impenetrable. But just as the provisionality of the attainments of psychoanalysis does not lessen the force of the command "Know Thyself," neither does the complexity of history dissolve the imperative of simplicity which urges us towards that provisional breakthrough which makes it possible to live by faith here and now. As theology is conscious both of this imperative and of its provisionality it becomes a functional theology, a therapy of contemporary faith. It relinquishes the aspiration to add speculative gains to faith's small degree of knowledge of its objects; indeed it may even whittle away this knowledge, hastening the process of its attrition insofar as it is illusory or anachronistic. Instead it aims at precise discernment of the present historical context of faith and of the possibilities granted by that context, fully accepting the limitations of what Ricoeur calls *le croyable disponible,* but also ready to welcome the scandalous breakthrough of essential Christianity wherever the Spirit produces it, fully accepting the death of the old, so as to be free to welcome the new. This discernment must also overcome those counter-essences which always spring up alongside prophetic recoveries of the essence (as Gnosticism almost strangled Christianity in the cradle, or as the false prophets simulated the true).

For metaphysical Christianity encounter with other traditions is always a secondary affair, classed under the rubric of mission or ecumenism. But today it is the presence of those other traditions which presses Christianity into shape, revealing to it its precise historical identity. "They know nought of Christianity who only. Christianity know" (Ninian Smart). For a questioning faith mission is less the promulgation of dogma than a sharing of traditions in the context of a larger questioning after truth; as dialogue becomes increasingly inescapable the texture of Christianity becomes dialogal through and through, and its creeds appear as starting points in a quest which cannot be continued without the assistance of the other.

The positivity of the biblical revelation is reinterpreted as that of an incomplete and culturally limited project of faith which depends for its continued realization on the corrections and supplements coming from the religious insight of other cultures (as well as from the secular, "religionless" culture of the West). The scriptural affirmations continue to be fertile and to open the human mind to God only when understood in this open-ended way. The dewesternization of Christianity which the present decentering of the traditional historical role of the West makes necessary goes further than most projects of inculturation (such as those of Joseph Spae), and involves not only the overcoming of metaphysics, but also the relativization of the Semitic and Hellenic cultural forms of Scripture. Thus, the aim of certain Indian theologians to build a bridge directly from the language of Scripture to that of Hinduism, bypassing the metaphysical categories of the West—as well as similar tendencies in Latin American liberation theology—can involve a mystifying, ahistorical appeal to the world of the Bible which also contradicts authentic inculturation.

Viewed in this larger perspective (which in today's world is the only realistic one) the differences between the Christian churches lose much of their importance, and can be seen as serving chiefly for mutual correction. The dialogue with Judaism already unites Protestants and Catholics, focusing their attention on the basic Christian themes, and the dialogue with Eastern religions, in which the very premises of both Judaism and Christianity become problematic, further radicalizes that task of "discerning the way" which both Judaism and Christianity share. In practice the overcoming of metaphysics is closely associated with this new exposure of Christianity to its Jewish matrix (and of both Judaism and Christianity to a wider field of questions) and it cannot be carried out seriously without this breadth of exposure; a narrowly intra-Christian or intra-denominational tinkering with the language of faith cannot achieve the step back from the sphere of metaphysical Christianity to the "original Christianity" it occludes; this step back can be nothing less than a remembrance of the Jewish matrix of Christian faith and of the historical decisions which founded a separate Christian identity. To focus Christian identity it is not enough to think

back from the horizons of the contemporary Christian denominations, all of them shaped by Western metaphysics and culture; one
must also think forward from Judaism, reevaluating the necessity
and legitimacy of the Christian innovations and querying their cultural provenance. This dialogue with Judaism can be fruitfully pursued only in the context of a search for a truth which transcends both
Judaism and Christianity as historically constituted and in partner-
ship with other participants in that search. This spells a relativization of secondary identities and a transgression of denominational
taboos which may indeed bring with it the risk of "religious indiffer-
entism," but that risk is surely preferable to the misunderstandings
and violence generated by the co-existence of mutually contradictory religions which refuse to be questioned and challenged by one
another. If Christianity is made conscious in dialogue of its historical and cultural limits its affirmation of God is tempered by a
greater sense of mystery, a sense that the identity of God is primarily
a theme for questioning, and this emperically induced nescience is
perhaps the characteristic contemporary mark of the authentic simplicity of faith.

The contemporary quest for essential Christianity also involves
the effort to trace the language and the claims of faith back to a
fundamental validating experience. The truth of any religion, it is
assumed, is primarily lodged in such a founding experience, and all
religions are in more intimate dialogue at this level, if only we can
gain access to it, than in their secondary reflexive formulations.
Though the goals which such a quest for firsthand experience
projects are often illusory, and though there is perhaps no pure
religious experience not dependent on the mediation of a tradition of
reflection, still the search for the underlying phenomenality of revelation is a legitimate direction of enquiry, even if it is a direction that
can never be followed through to its ideal destination. To check and
control Christian language it is necessary to attempt to trace it back
to the experience from which it is born, or rather to forcibly convert
that language back to its equivalents at the level of phenomenality.
How this might be done in regard to the christological claims which
are the chief distinguishing marks of Christianity I shall attempt to
show in the following examination of the Nicene Creed and the

Fourth Gospel. Guided by the imperative of recovering the dimension of phenomenality, we may discover that the textuality of tradition opens up approaches to religious truth larger and subtler than the dogmatic, and that through it sounds the question "Who do you say that I am?" in a way that subverts the unity and authority of its explicit doctrinal statements, revealing them as mere pointers to a still outstanding answer. This subversion of the dogmatic letter by the questioning Spirit reveals that the settled truth of dogma is of less importance to faith than the unsettling truth which emerges unpredictably in poem or parable, in the prophetic reading of a situation, in enlightening gestures—Jesus healing on the Sabbath—which transcend every formulable principle or regulated practice. The identity of Christ is constantly being uncovered in such unsettling moments of truth, which show him to be *semper maior,* as elusive in his final identity as God himself. It is only because beneath all formal affirmations the question "Who do you say that I am?" remains an unmasterable question that the notion of the divinity of Christ can be a credible one. As we attempt to trace the import of that notion at the level of phenomenality, in a "loving strife about the matter itself" with the great texts which by their dependence on myth or metaphysics partly occlude this level, we will come to see that the figure of Christ as it has been grasped in traditional horizons is but a partial and provisional sketch of the Christ to be discovered in the great learning process thrust upon us by the opening up of larger horizons of questioning today. As tradition is overcome under the pressure of this vaster future upon it, the cross and resurrection of Jesus come into new focus in the travail of difference. The Christ we have known is only a limited historical manifestation of Christ; the Christ whom faith holds to be universal is not yet manifest. The former is the seed which must fall in the ground again and again and die if the full dimensions of the incarnate phenomenality of God are to become apparent. The entire language of pre-existence, resurrection, and exaltation names this hidden dimension of Christ towards which Christian faith is always underway, losing Christ again and again in order to find him in his fullness. Knowledge of Christ "according to the flesh" (2 Cor. 5:16) is always surpassed and relativized in the quest for the Lord who is Spirit

(3:17-18). To present any defined concept or representation of Christ as the key to world history can only be a form of metaphysical imperialism. But if one lets the figure of Jesus be a divine question to the world, a question whose full implications—"the breadth and length and height and depth" (Eph. 3:18)—are always unfolding, often canceling former understandings, then the universality of such a question is not offensive, since the question is modified by each new group to which it is addressed, and each such modification undoes old answers.

The Nicene Creed

How does the question of Christ to this generation alter or undo the classic Christian understanding of Christ expressed in the Nicene Creed? Can the Creed be recited today as an adequate expression of the question of Christ in its universality, or does it confine that question within the limited cultural horizons of Jewish myth and Greek metaphysics? Some contemporary theologians claim that the divinity of Christ is sufficiently acknowledged if he is accepted as God's word to our Western culture. This view undermines the New Testament claims at a basic level. It stems from a confusion between the authentic Christ of faith, who is *semper maior,* and the figure of Christ which was absolutized in the West and presented as the "concrete universal" (Hegel) in which all other religious traditions found consummation; in reaction to this the "myth of God incarnate" theorists produce an equally metaphysical account of a culturally limited Christ, an account probably originating in nineteenth century Neo-Hegelian circles. The universal status of Christ in the New Testament, on the other hand (cf. Matt. 28:18; John 17:2; Heb. 1:2; Rev. 1:8, etc.), can no longer be adequately grasped in the traditional mythical and metaphysical expression of it, such as those of the Nicene Creed, and demands of us, not only the demythologization and dehellenization which our sense of historicity makes mandatory in any case, but a new style of thinking which will permit the question "Who do you say that I am?" to resound both in Western and in other cultures in a more penetrating way, no longer stifled by the prompt metaphysical or mythical answer.

In addition to asking whether the Creed matches the true universality of the Christ of faith, we must also ask if it effectively poses the question of Christ in its *historicity*. For although the Christ of faith is always greater than the historical manifestations of Christ (including the historical Jesus and all reconstructions or idealizations of him), nonetheless the ongoing revelation of Christ can never be ripped from its historical sheath and can never be apprehended independently of a narration of the story of Jesus of Nazareth. This narration must be raised to a pneumatic level, under pain of idolatry, and this is already accomplished in Paul and John. A contemporary narration would have to take into account the larger history that has opened up for us, enlarging both the "Old Testament" past to which Paul and John referred and the conception of the "Gentiles" which was their measure of the universality of Christ. The concrete historical self-understanding of the Christian community is expressed in such a narrational topography of the revelation of Christ which need not fear to revise and enlarge that of the New Testament. While the Nicene Creed does set the figure of Jesus Christ in a narrational context, within the predominantly metaphysical structure of the Creed that history is frozen and stylized, subordinated to the timeless patterns of the Trinity and of the distinction between Creator and creation. The reciter of the Creed is not drawn into close engagement with the historical texture of the Christ-event; instead such engagement is reduced to anamnesis of Jesus and expectation of his second coming. Just as the Creed confines the universality of Christ within a metaphysical concept of that universality, so it reduces the historicity of Christ to the "essential facts" about the earthly Jesus and the exalted Christ, with no indication that both are being refocused constantly as history unfolds.

As the universality of the question of Christ unfolds, anamnesis of the historical Jesus is correspondingly modified. The historical Jesus may never be erased, but there is truth in the idea that it is the *that* rather than the *what* of his life, teaching, death, and resurrection which matters. If Jesus was a male Jew, the Christ of faith is neither Jew nor Greek, male nor female (Gal. 3:28), though a merely metaphysical notion of this universality has gone hand in hand with anti-

semitism and racism and has not been able to celebrate the Jewish-
ness of "the Christ according to the flesh" (Rom. 9:5). If Jesus was a
celibate, the bridegroom of the Canticle could represent a sexual
fulfillment which accords eminently with spiritual liberation (here
Goethe may correct Augustine or Asia heal Europe). If Jesus died at
one place and time, the Christ recognized in the breaking of bread is
a gift to all places and times (but how our liturgies confine the gift!).
Theological appeals to the humanity of Jesus should always be
conditioned by the full breadth of the present form of the question of
Christ. Contemporary secularity, for example, allows us to project
images of the humanity of Jesus as "the man for others" (Bonhoeffer) or as the one whose existence reveals that life itself is grace
(James Mackey). It does not really matter if these portraits solicit
the exegetical data, for the Christ of faith has always supplemented
and corrected the historical Jesus, and reshaped the memory of
Jesus according to its own requirements, nor does a scholarly reconstruction of the historical Jesus offer a yardstick for measuring these
developments. (The value of such historical research for faith is
indirect, helping to shatter images of the humanity of Jesus which
have become unworthy of the Christ of faith and prompting new
focusings of that humanity, but never itself presenting an image of
Jesus which can be directly assumed by contemporary faith.) Furthermore, the memory of Jesus is never adequately realized unless
he is also grasped as "the human face of God." Any image of Jesus
can become an idol, and the iconic status of Christ crucified has to
be reconquered again and again in an effort to refocus it as divine
revelation. Because the Christ of faith is never definitively apprehended, the figure of Jesus can correspondingly be remembered in
an unending variety of ways. Because the universality of the Christian message is never fully manifest (except in premature or illusory
metaphysical projections), the historicity of Christianity is correspondingly subject to unending reassessment. It appears that the
Nicene Creed forecloses this process of questioning at both ends.

However, the Nicene Creed may still be used as a badge of
Christian identity in a way similar to that in which the *Marseillaise,*
despite the disappearance of its *Sitz im Leben,* serves to express the
historical identity of France. Thus recited, the Creed is not a fully

direct expression of contemporary faith, but an act of commitment to the tradition of faith, mediated by historical memory of a classical moment in the life of that tradition. A historically conscious recitation of the Creed accepts it as binding on faith, but only across a number of transformations which the language of the Creed itself, when critically sifted, is found to prescribe. In the second article of the Creed, for instance, we can differentiate the following layers of language:

(1) The assertive and commissive speech act "I believe in . . ." which governs all the other statements, ensuring that they are neither simple statements of fact, on the one hand, nor merely devotional or affective utterances on the other;

(2) The confessional *naming* of "One Lord, Jesus Christ," which indicates the primary object of this assertion and commitment; the entire second article is an explicitation of what is thus named;

(3) What seems bare statement of fact—"crucified under Pontius Pilate"; the credal context implies a declaration that this fact is religiously significant and not to be forgotten;

(4) More stylized diction in which the credal coloration of fact becomes manifest—"suffered and was buried";

(5) Quasi-historical statements whose texture is permeated by numinous references—"he came down from heaven, took flesh of the Holy Spirit from the Virgin Mary," "he rose on the third day . . . and he ascended into heaven . . . and he will come again in glory." Here the confession regards historical events in light of their heavenly background with the help of representations which are mythical in texture. When one realizes the obsolescence of the cultural matrices from which such representations are drawn and the impossibility of stepping behind history in order to view it from an eternal vantage point, then one finds that the language of the Creed prescribes a recovery of the phenomenological foundations of such statements. The descent/ascent schema is an archaic and cryptic pointer to the mystery of Christ, which challenges our faith to apprehend it in more accessible terms;

(6) Interpretative clauses which give a theological (chiefly soteriological) reason for the events recalled—"for us men and for our

salvation," "for us," "according to the Scriptures," "to judge the living and the dead";

(7) A statement of the ontological significance of the Incarnation —"and became man." Perhaps we can convincingly recapture the force of this affirmation only by translating it into the language of a christology from below;

(8) The historical data are transcended toward their foundations in a more radical way in the narration of a celestial pre-history— "the only-begotten Son of God, born of the Father";

(9) The celestial post-history—"he sits at the right hand of the Father" differs from 5 and is closer to 8 in the boldness of its construction in a mythical space and time quite beyond history. Contemporary faith understands that the ultimate identity of Christ is to be sought in the divine dimensions thus indicated, but cannot make convincing use of the mythical language to point to that dimension. Instead it is challenged to apprehend the phenomenality of the Christ of faith in terms which make it comprehensible why such language was used;

(10)Theological notes appended to ward off heretical misreadings of the mythic narration—"before all ages" (against Arius); "of his kingdom there will be no end" (against Marcellus of Ancyra; without this polemic intent it would be merely a devotional reminiscence of Luke 1:33, in tension with the economy of credal language);

(11) A second set of theological notes imposing a new logical precision on the mythic narration—"God from God . . . true God from true God, begotten not made." This reflexive underlining of the ontological status attaching to the terms of the narrative reveals the emergence of a logically vigilant doctrinal consciousness. One senses that a metaphysical insistence is beginning to overload and distort the narrative texture;

(12) The doxological supplement "light from light" may be an effort to compensate for this distortion, providing a mythical, narrative equivalent for the daunting bareness of "God from God";

(13) A second layer of logical clarification using the notion of "substance"—"that is, of the substance of the Father" (Nicea, 325, only), "of one substance with the Father." These clearly cannot be reintegrated into the narrative context. For the metaphysical culture

from which the Creed comes the reduction of the mythic narrative to its logically defined ontological foundations may have been a liberating demythologization. To a contemporary believer these efforts at precision are likely to seem questionable in themselves (can the logic of *ousia* be at all useful in such a rarefied region of application?) and to increase the questionability of the mythic language they presuppose by revealing the path of increasing abstraction onto which it leads us if we try to sustain it consistently. Again we are referred back to the level of phenomenality, where we must seek the pneumatic Christ who belongs to the same realm as God or the Spirit of God and cannot be thought of in lesser terms;

(14) A phrase from the narrative of creation which serves to define the ontological status of the three divine hypostases in the Creed—"through him all things were made" (cf. "Creator of heaven and earth" and "Lord, giver of live" of Father and Spirit respectively). This location of the being of the triune God in terms of creation is not unproblematic to a contemporary believer either; its perspective is still that of the celestial pre-history and it attempts to grasp the phenomenon of the world from a point outside it. The phenomenological foundation of faith in the creative roles of Father, Son, and Spirit needs to be elucidated, and the process of that elucidation might be an unending one, making it very difficult to summarily project the notion of a Creator and to define the ontological status of Creator and creation.

The Creed offers an exhaustive topology of the being and function of Jesus Christ, within a horizon which embraces Creator and creation, the being and manifestation of God, the origin and destiny of the world, eternity and time, past, present, and future. But it seems that this comprehensive horizon is no longer accessible to us, that we are thrown back on the intra-historical phenomenality of revelation, so that our confession of Christ (or of the Father or the Holy Spirit) can spell an opening up to that phenomenality, but not a leap beyond it. The Creed provides the names "Father," "Son," and "Spirit" with an ontological foundation, referring to a divine substance and tracing the being of Christ to his eternal divine generation; the contemporaneous theology of three "hypostases" of one "substance" completes this ontological underpinning. But it seems that our faith is unable to transcend the naming of Father, Son, and Spirit towards its ontological ground. For us they indicate dimensions of the phenomenality of God in revelation; the terms "substance" and "person," and even the language of the divine "relations," seem an unnecessary redoubling of faith's naming of God, which distracts from the exploration of the phenomenality of which is thus named. The unity of God is not effectively preserved by the declaration that there is one underlying substance behind the three names, but should be sought instead in the interplay of the three dimensions in the experience of revelation. The Creed fixes the trinitarian names as points of departure for their salvation-historical and ontological explication. But it seems that even these names can be desacralized by a linguistic and historical awareness which sees their formation neither as a divine mandate nor a conceptual necessity, but as a human effort to map the phenomenality of revelation, a creative or poetic achievement influenced by many contributory cultural streams (none of the three names are unique to Judaism or Christianity). It is not particularly surprising that our faith should be left in the lurch by its traditional language when one considers not only the general problem of the transmission of meaning through history, but the peculiar fragility attached to religious expressions by reason of their ambitious metaphorical structure. Paradoxically, the intrinsic fragility of religious diction has not lessened its extreme durability in practice. This paradox is probably to be explained by the sacralization of this diction which made it seem adequate even when it wasn't and which ensured that endless efforts of reinterpretation and repristination would be made before any element of the sacral diction was abandoned. But we may be moving into a period in which faith will live with a more humble awareness of the fragility of its language. The saying of faith may turn out to be something qualitatively different from the sonorousness and pathos of religious diction. A faith which constantly sifts and questions its language may become incapable of exerting the hypnotic fascination characteristic of religion. But that too is part of the price to be paid for a future culture of questioning faiths in dialogue.

The fragility of the Creed is chiefly due to the dependence of the referring power of metaphorical expressions on context and intention. The metaphor "smitten by Eros" might have had a serious meaning and a distinct reference for Sappho, but it is impossible to use it except in a facetious sense today. This impossibility is not a question of taste but of necessity. The cultural coordinates of the original metaphor have not been transmitted; in the course of the tradition Eros has degenerated to a rococo Cupid. The change of context makes it impossible to use the metaphor with the same passionate intentionality as Sappho might have invested in it. Analogously, the power of the metaphor "born of the Father before time began" depends on a cultural and religious context in which the representation of an eternal sonship can have a rich significance and also on the speaker's intentionality of faith which can effectively refer to the object of faith by means of this metaphor. At the time of Nicea faith in Christ culminated in the recognition of him as God's eternal Son. It was not realized that this provision of the celestial backdrop to the figure of Jesus was largely a work of imagination rather than a literal and logical definition of the thing in itself. Yet the extension of the word "son" beyond its normal usage clearly betrays the metaphoricity which cannot be ironed out of the credal expressions. Now the use of this image to express faith's apprehension of the ultimate significance of Jesus Christ has become problematic to the degree that the cultural coordinates of the image have not been transmitted. These coordinates include a mythical concern with origins, a metaphysical concern with grounds and an anthropological valorization of paternity, three attitudes which converge to reinforce the image of eternal sonship. But if these attitudes have become obsolete (for reasons no less numerous and complex than those which established them in the first place) then the intention of faith cannot securely ride on their back. Thus the confession of Christ as eternal Son no longer satisfactorily fulfills the intention of faith, no longer effectively refers to the object of faith. No amount of work on the terms "substance," "hypostasis," or "relation" in the theological laboratory can correct this deficiency of the primary metaphor, for theology can only make sense of the biblical metaphor through retrieving the phenomenality it names. If the metaphor of divine sonship no longer opens out onto the ineffable, but reveals cultural limits which make it impossible for faith to rest in it unquestioningly, and if one cannot find the way back to the original context in which that metaphorical name could be meaningfully uttered, then one is obliged to explore the present context of the language of faith and to find those expressions which best express the intention of faith today. If the name "Son" is retained it will be in a sense that allows it to signify a contemporary apprehension of the phenomenality of Christ.

It seems then that as we recite the Creed today we experience the tensions of Christian tradition in a particularly rich way. We affirm the Creed's witness of faith and consciously stand in continuity with it in the one tradition; in this affirmation all Christians stand united. But on the other hand we are aware that the Creed is assailed at every point by questions arising not only from the exposure of its language to general laws of semantic relativity and semantic obsolescence (and meaning and reference are so closely intertwined that these laws threaten even the basic capacity of the Creed to refer to its intended objects) but also from the present concern of faith to do justice to the phenomenality of Christ, which is felt to be occluded by metaphysical universals or mythic origins. In reciting the Creed, then, we assume our history as a uncomplete task, seeing clearly in retrospect the poverty and provisionality of this past language, and realizing that we must seek new words having the same poverty and provisionality. An experience of this historical depth was not available to previous generations of Christians and it is one which is bound to have a transforming effect on Christian language and Christian self-identity. This experience with the Creed sends us back to Scripture with a double expectation. On the one hand we hope to find there some clues to the phenomenality of Christ which the metaphysical presuppositions of the patristic theologians caused them to miss. On the other hand we expect the language of Scripture too to be inadequate to the contemporary question of Christ, so that our use of this language too can be valid for faith only if we subject it forcibly to the present concerns of faith. Just as Heidegger aimed to understand the Greeks better than they understood themselves, in a certain sense, so we seek to understand the New Testament witness to Christ in opposition to the obsolescent frameworks of understanding in which it is emboddied. As the Johannine writings can be regarded as the most highly reflected articulation of the phenomenality of revelation in the New Testament they are the most promising source for the primordial understanding of faith to which the dogmatic, metaphysical tradition has referred us back. The violence of the following sketch will consist merely in reading John exclusively in the key of phenomenality (in opposition, for instance, to the governing descent/ascent structure insofar as it is mythical and insofar as John's own language does not at times subvert it; opposed also to the highly personalized language of Father, Son, and Spirit, again, insofar as John himself does not relativize this).

The Fourth Gospel

The fundamental teaching of John is that the phenomenality of Jesus Christ, as apprehended in faith, is one with the phenomenality of God. Only faith can make satisfying sense of the works or signs of Jesus; their significance comes into focus only in the confession which names what they reveal Jesus to be: John 1:49; 2:11; 4:53; 6:69, 9:38; 11:27; 19:35; 20:28. That significance expands throughout the series of confessions, until fully expressed in the post-resurrection "My Lord and my God." The works of the historical Jesus are apprehended from a post-Paschal perspective throughout the Gospel, although the two halves of the Gospel also mirror the two phases of the existence of Jesus Christ. Thus the works attributed to the historical Jesus are at the same time to be read as accounts of the believers' ongoing experience of the pneumatic Christ known in faith, who knows their hearts (1:48), changes old into new (2:1-11), dispels inborn blindness (9:1-7), and raises the dead (11:43). He who does these works can be understood in no lesser terms that those of 1:14: "The Logos became flesh and dwelt among us and we beheld his glory." The phenomenality of Jesus is a divine phenomenality; it cannot be named in lesser terms; these are either a lie (stemming from the world's incomprehension of the signs—6:26—or from a direct refusal of the truth—8:45-46) or a partial apprehension to be subsumed in a fuller one. Truth, spirit, love, light, eternal life—each

of these words has a phenomenal bearing, and naming dimensions of
the revelation of God in Jesus. John integrates all these themes into
a mythical structure. But a phenomenological retrieval can allow
these themes to burst this framework open. Transposing the Buddhist insight "Form is emptiness, emptiness is form" one could say
that the form of Jesus is correctly apprehended only as divine Logos
(the phenomenality of God); and this form itself subsists on the basis
of the divine emptiness with which it is coterminous; as our eyes are
opened to the form of Jesus they are at the same time being opened
to the emptiness of God. God is intrinsically unseen (1:18), yet to see
Christ in faith is to see God (8:19, 14:9). One can trace the contours
of this contemplative situation without using the language of pre-
existent hypostases which was so impressive in a mythical or even in
a metaphysical perspective but has now become a liability. The
Christ has come in the flesh (cf. I John 4:2; 2:22), that is, the
phenomenality of God is manifest in a unique fullness in and
through the figure of Jesus (cf. 1:16-17).

The language of Father and Son can be interpreted in these quasi-
phenomenological terms. God is manifest as love, of which Jesus is
the unique vehicle, incarnation and gift (3:16; I John 4:9) and when
that love is brought to its consummation the form of the risen Christ
is totally identical with the divine glory. The believers, who live
through Christ, will also share this form (I John 3:2); this is not a
matter of blind hope but is phenomenologically discernible in the
experience of love. It is when he lays down his life and takes it up
again (10:18) that the glory of God is fully revealed in Jesus (13:31)
and at the same time (*euthys* 13:32) Jesus is fully absorbed into the
divine glory, becoming the pneumatic Christ ("God will glorify him
in himself" 13:32). It is natural to speak of this as Jesus being
adopted as God's Son, or "appointed Son of God in power according
to the Spirit of holiness through the resurrection from the dead"
(Rom. 1:4). John goes further and reads the paschal manifestations
back into the life of the earthly Jesus. Furthermore, he projects the
earthly Jesus back into the realm of pre-existence; "that glory which
I had with you before the world came to be" (17:5). The phenomenological ground of this language is the realization that the earthly

Jesus has become the pneumatic Christ, one with God's phenomenality as love, light, and spirit. Since the resurrection that phenomenality is fully manifest to human beings as the Christ of faith; Jesus is henceforth inseparably identified with that Logos; the meaning of his life and death are revealed as the incarnation of the phenomenality of God as love. John images the mode of being of the risen Christ as an intimate personal communion of Father and Son, or a mutual indwelling (10:38; 14:10), in which the believers will share (17:21-23). The phenomenological ground of this language is the experience of God as love, which inevitably calls forth such representations. But one might perhaps equally legitimately use the language of the mutuality of emptiness and form—through love the humanity of Jesus (and of the believers in dependence on it) is shaped into that form which is fully transparent to the emptiness of God.

But this form of the pneumatic Christ can never be fully grasped in this life; John's Gospel teaches us again and again to discard the forms we have grasped as inadequate and instead to let the Spirit guide us into all truth (clearly a never-ending process). The Spirit might be defined as the immediacy of God, that aspect of God which vitally touches our existence. It is what lights up anew the phenomenality of Christ as the phenomenality of God; without it our memories of Christ would become idols blocking out all sense of God. John also speaks of the Spirit in personal terms, for, phenomenologically, to be touched by the Spirit is to encounter a love and a wisdom which call forth such names as "comforter" or "helper" (14:16). Spirit in its immediacy shatters all forms which fall short of the form of truth—hence the believers are to worship "in spirit and truth" (4:23); only such worship places no idolatrous blocks against the divine emptiness (hence "the Father seeks such worshippers" 4:23). The form of Jesus is similarly transcended: "If you loved me you would rejoice that I go to the Father, because the Father is greater than I" (14:28); "It is better for you that I go away. If I do not go away, the Spirit cannot come to you, but if I go, I shall send him to you" (16:7). Yet there is no gnostic disregard for the historical origins of revelations (cf. 4:22 "salvation is from the Jews") and anamnesis of past forms can mediate present insight; the entire

Gospel is an exercise in such anamnesis, refocusing the past in light of the form of the pneumatic Christ. "The Spirit blows where it wills" (3:8) constantly reforming our image of Christ (our grasp of the Christic form of all reality—cf. 1:3) so that it accords with the true emptiness of God (knowledge of which is eternal life—17:1—cf. Buddhist nirvana).

This phenomenological reduction of the Johannine language of pre-existence and of Father, Son, and Spirit is a continuation of the reductive movement of the Gospel itself, which so artfully subordinates many quasi-synoptic pieces of tradition to its own more spiritual perspectives and which frequently develops figurative modes of expression only to lead to a statement which abolishes them, as the language of the "good shepherd" culminates in the non-dualist utterances of 10:30, 38 or the images of 14:1-5 prepare the identifications of 14:6-11. A phenomenological reduction would not serve its purpose if it lost the full dimensions of what John names as Father, Son, and Spirit. Talk of the emptiness, phenomenality, and immediacy of God might lead to a colorless, modalist image of God, a danger which the biblical names ward off; but on the other hand, the repetition of these biblical names without a constant effort to realize their meaning at the level of phenomenality can be equally damaging. Two halves of Christianity have disputed for the greater part of their existence the question whether the Spirit proceeds from the Father only or from the Father and the Son; this shameful debate proceeds largely from an oblivion on both sides of the phenomenality of what is named as Father, Son, Spirit. Our makeshift terms, emptiness, phenomenality and immediacy, are only pointers intended to show the kind of questioning to which New Testament language must be subjected when its mythical terms are suspended and it can no longer be subsumed into metaphysical frameworks. Furthermore, the search for such phenomenological formulations might facilitate the dialogue with other religious traditions, whose namings of the divine might be subject to similar reductions, or whose own exercises in discerning the phenomenality of the absolute and its manifestation might reveal an unsuspected proximity to the New Testament thus demythologized. It is clear that this deconstructive reading of the New Testament aims less at a recovery of the phenomenality of revelation as the New Testament communities experienced it (for this is scarcely to be abstracted from the cultural forms which mediated it) than at a realization of the present force of revelation and a credible contemporary naming of Father, Son, and Spirit.

*   *   *

This book has attempted to sketch an answer to the question: what does fidelity to the Christian tradition entail today? The reader concerned with such fidelity will have to sift its claims critically in accord with his or her own experience. Many former bulwarks of Christian certitude have become twilight zones today, and those who focus their faith on these metaphysical aspects of the Christian tradition are bound to succumb either to corrosive skepticism or to a defensive traditionalism and fundamentalism. On the other hand the Christ of faith is becoming known in a new way as Christians become more compassionately responsive to the questions of peace, justice, and freedom which press on them so urgently, and more contemplatively aware of the unending mystery of God. As faith builds on these latter foundations it must reshape the meaning of tradition in accord with them, in a counter-metaphysical reading which frees faith from the morose, introspective provincialism characteristic of the metaphysical theology which is still dominant. It does not seem that any less radical approach can represent a faithful continuation of Christian history or effectively bring about the integral liberation of faith from its imprisonment in representations which have become idolatrous.